BECAUSE I SURVIVED

BECAUSE I SURVIVED

An Autobiography

by

Ludwig Muhlfelder

SHENGOLD

ISBN: 0-88400-210-1
Library of Congress Catalog Card Number: 00-133511

Published by Shengold
Rockville, MD

First Edition 2000

In love I dedicate these writings to:

my dear wife Bea, herself a Holocaust survivor, with whom I have shared love and life for more than 46 years, who encouraged me in this effort by her example to remember both the good as well as the tragic times;

our dear children Danny, Barry and wife Debbie, Leslie and husband Dick, as well as our grandchildren Joanna, Joshua, Jeremy, Mira, and Douglas, who give us hope for the future;

my parents, Julius and Minna, who, with my sister Ellen and me, were saved from the Holocaust; who raised me and cared for me, and who maintained the dignity of a warm Jewish home even in stressful times.

Livingston, New Jersey
September 1998

Know
Whence you camest,
And whither you are going,
And before whom you are destined
To give full account.

Pirke Avot 3:1 – Sayings of the Sages

CONTENTS

Acknowledgments x

Introduction 1

Background: History, Family, and Birthplace 5

Transitions from 1929 to 1933 19

Living under Nazi Rule (1933–1938) 28

My Last Year in Germany:
A Frightening Experience 47

The Trip to America 64

To Live Again:
A New Beginning in the United States 70

In the Service of My Country 83

Back to Europe for Uncle Sam 90

Army of Occupation 105

Home Again – Now What? 118

The Founding of a Family 125

Family, Garden, and Growth
at 15 Orchard Lane (1956–1964) 135

From Jets to Satellites:
A Transition in My Career (1957–1962) 146

In the Service of Temple Emanu-El 151

The Secular World, 1950 to 1973 157

Our Children Grow, My Parents Pass
(1964–1977) 167

We Visit Israel (Twice) 180

Professional Challenge, Success,
and Inventions (1970–1989) 187

Working for Temple and UAHC (1972–1984) 195

The Empty Nest (1978–1984) 207

Weddings, Grandchildren, and Travel (1984–1991) 219

Stepping Into Retirement 237

Return to Germany 254

Still in the Second Millennium 263

Retrospection and Reflection 270

Works Cited 304

ACKNOWLEDGMENTS

Writing an autobiography is a mental journey through one's life. Because it is not easy to look into the mirror and attempt to discern the various reflections of the passing decades, it is essential to listen to thoughtful suggestions to keep the recollections in proper focus.

First, I want to thank June Schlueter, Provost of Lafayette College in Easton, Pa. for her tremendous and unrelenting support throughout this process. Most generously, she gave of her time and intellect in the sensitive reading and skillful editing of the manuscript. She fully understood what the title of the book tries to imply: that one's negative experiences lead not necessarily to embitterment and resentment, but that it is possible to generate an appreciation of the years and events which followed survival. I was inspired by June and her husband Dr. Paul Schlueter, who displayed such a persistent interest in bringing this project to a satisfactory conclusion. I am indebted to both.

My wife Beatrice helped me in a constructive and loving way to improve my manuscript. She served as a good, though by circumstance not necessarily impartial, reviewer and I thank her so much for the important support she has lent to this effort. She certainly stood by my side with love, patience and encouragement as she has for so many wonderful years.

Many thanks go also to our daughter Leslie for her discerning and innate interest in this project. She made sure, that poignant or amusing events of the past would be properly included in the text. Her characteristic enthusiasm served as a superb catalyst towards achieving a happy conclusion.

INTRODUCTION

Having exceeded three score and ten years of my time span on this planet Earth, I embarked on this writing first because I am a Holocaust survivor, secondly for the sake of my children, grandchildren, and their contemporaries, and finally in fervent prayer for the continuity of the Jewish people and the betterment of humankind.

In 1995, I completed a book entitled *Weil ich uebriggeblieben bin* ("Because I was spared"), written in German, the language of my country of birth. That autobiographical attempt, made at the urging of our good friend Erhard Roy Wiehn, is primarily intended for today's German-speaking population, who should know about the history of their Nazi ancestors and the consequences of this dark period. By becoming acquainted with their past via a multitude of individual stories such as mine, the descendants of the Nazi generation will, I hope, be able to confront this past honestly and thus strive towards a future of human decency and justice for all peoples.

Now I am not only repeating but substantially expanding upon the story of my life in the tongue in which I am most comfortable, in the tongue of my country of refuge, in the tongue of my children and grandchildren. As generations of our future, Bea's and mine, our children should have the opportunity to learn where they came from. They should some day be able and desirous to become acquainted with the history of their family and their people, and thus emotionally and spiritually connect to those who preceded them, those human beings who are tied to them in love.

In a more global sense, future generations are entitled to have a personal link to their heritage, independent whether it was noble and precious or tragic and atrocious. Was it worthy of emulation and continuity, or did it cry out for healing and peace? The story of our lives usually contain both the sunshine and the rain, and so it has been with my own travels on this planet Earth.

After tragic and perilous times, I was privileged to experience love and growth. My life was marked by a number of antithetic events. I fled Germany as a deprived and threatened Jew, only to return there as a US combat soldier to fight the Nazi evil. In Germany I witnessed the desecration and arson of our synagogue, and three decades later I was privileged to serve as president of the synagogue in my American hometown. As a descendent of shoemakers, butchers and tailors, I participated in the pioneering effort of spacecraft design and development. In 1939 I departed from my German birthplace as a spurned, subhuman being, and in 1996 I returned there as a long lost and respected son of the town. Dear readers of today and tomorrow, you, who are the descendants of humanity, hopefully will be motivated by and learn from this story of my life, that the darkness of night can be followed by the brightness of day.

I am eager to generate this record of my experiences, values, reactions, and hopes as an attempt towards continuity. Whatever Bea and I might leave in material possessions is subject to the vagaries of time and thus somewhat transient in nature. With these lines, I am attempting to pass on something else of greater significance, something that might serve as a bridge from the todays to the tomorrows, *l'dor vador*, from generation to generation, a sacred journey.

As a Jew who survived the Shoah, our sacred texts call on me for Zachor, to remember and retell my experiences, which pale in comparison to the difficulties and tragedies of so many others, but which describe the paths I have traveled. I am a member of that ever shrinking remnant who is able to bear witness to one of the most tragic and despicable chapters in human history. As a survivor of the Holocaust, I write in gratitude for all the precious years granted to me subsequent to my lifesaving emigration from Nazi Germany. The innocent millions, and especially the younger victims, who were murdered because of who they were and not what they did, never had the privilege of life which I experienced as described in the subsequent pages. Their education was permanently interrupted or not even begun. Their eyes were never, if ever, to gaze on the wonders of our world: on snowcapped mountain peaks, verdant valleys, graceful roses and magical butterflies. Their hearts would not experience the pangs of love and the precious partnership of marriage. Their ears were not to hear the musical creations of our inspired artists. Their intellect was not to be challenged to create for and contribute to the human condition.

They were deprived of their potential progeny of children and grandchildren. All this I had the privilege to experience, all this was and still is mine, and for all these reasons I treasure it all of my days. You, dear reader, and I cannot take any of these privileges for granted. So accompany me through my days and years, and thus learn to appreciate that those who sit in darkness may yet see a great light.

And finally I put my life on paper because I am part of the "People of the Book," the Jewish people who already were subjected to so much horror in ancient Egypt, then in Canaan, the Promised Land, and later in Spain, England, Russia, and finally in German dominated Europe. Although we lost many precious human beings, the Jewish people have survived, nevertheless, and will strive to be a light to the nations of the world as they have been for over 3,000 years. During this twentieth century, a part of this people has once again reestablished roots in its own soil. Many Jews, however, do not live in Israel but rather choose to reside in other parts of this world, as I do in America. To survive as Jews, sinking roots into one's own soil is only partially but not insignificantly helpful. To survive as People *of* the Book, it is essential to live as People *with* the Book; only in this sense can we face the future with confidence.

My birthplace, Suhl, Thuringia, Germany. Farewell picture taken by me in 1938. In front of the church on the extreme left is my elementary school and synagogue.

BACKGROUND:

HISTORY, FAMILY, AND BIRTHPLACE

My place of birth was Germany, a country whose people were known for their education, culture, diligence, honesty, workmanship, and adherence to the law of the land. The religion of my parents and all my ancestors, as traced on my genealogical tree, was Judaism, a faith that believes in one invisible and indivisible God, the God of creation, the God of justice and ethical imperatives, the God who inspired the Ten Commandments. To understand, if that is even partially possible, the deeds committed by the Germans in the years of my youth, it might be helpful to take a brief look at some pertinent historical background.

The Jew of our age evolved as a direct result of the French revolution of 1791, when the Jews of France became citizens of the newly created republic. The Jews became emancipated and thus were granted the opportunity to participate in the development of the secular society. In the Middle Ages, the period of great Christian creativity, the Jews might have been granted various degrees of special legal and economic status but could not possibly become an integral part of the state or the society of their predominantly Christian neighbors. Jews were tolerated but not accepted as equal human beings. Law and order translated into special restrictions for the Jews: where to live, which livelihood not to pursue, which organization to be excluded from. If they played by the rules, Jews received a measure of protection, which was often tenuous and transient in nature.

The French revolution changed all that. It opened the door of individual equality to the Jews, and Napoleon's armies, sweeping across Europe, spread this concept to other lands. The nineteenth century witnessed both progress and regression for Jewish emancipation, but for the long-range, Jews of western and central Europe were on the road to greater freedom and opportunity. Both socially and economically, considerable progress was made in terms of Jewish participation. The so-called ghetto mentality diminished in direct response to the greater openness offered by the secular world.

The average German Jew was middle class and satisfied with his lot. Of course, there was still a deeply ingrained anti-Semitism in most of the populace. By self imposed choice as well as by Christian prejudice, social life for Jews was primarily, but not exclusively, confined to Jewish friends. There were no major pogroms in the German lands until we got to the Nazi era. But there was something much more insidious and enduring, a philosophy of anti-Semitism of the masses. The German view of good and evil more often than not depicted the Jew on the wrong side, the Satan of Goethe's *Faust*. A goodly portion of the German masses were susceptible to such a "Weltanschauung," a world view. The church-sponsored, centuries-old retention of the accusation of deicide, blaming Jews for Jesus' death, was a particularly strong catalyst in spreading and maintaining the anti-Semitic venom. Although these very brief historical comments focus primarily on Germany, the land of my birth, I must emphasize that anti-Semitism had established strong roots in other countries of diverse backgrounds: in Russia as the land of pogroms, in France as the land of Dreyfus, in Austria as the eventual cradle of Nazism, to name just a few.

As the 19th century drew to a close, the nations of Europe had divergent objectives that eventually led to World War I, but essentially all retained various degrees of anti-Semitism in their *modus operandi*. Thus, the heralded emancipation had been only a partial success, but Jews of western and central Europe looked upon the lurking prejudice and occasional excesses imbued by anti-Semitism as passing phenomena and mere episodes. The economically somewhat more comfortable Jews especially rationalized the tenor and tremor of these times into the optimistic expectation for an ever more progressive future. This also explains the unflinching and patriotic support that the various Jewish communities gave to their respective countries during the First World War. About 12,000 men of the Jewish faith made the ultimate sacrifice for their German fatherland. Among these was my uncle Louis Ludwig Frank, who, as a volunteer, and in spite of overwhelming family responsibilities, was accepted into the ranks and died in 1916 on the western front in France.

After a long and bloody struggle, Germany and its allies lost this war and surrendered in November 1918. The Treaty of Versailles was overly punitive in nature and not in concert with U.S. President Wilson's intent. It was designed to prevent the resurgence of German militarism and imposed the payment of $33 billion for the destruction visited by Germany on other European lands. The democratic Weimar Republic, founded in 1919 to govern Germany, was handicapped not only by the instability and unrest following the surrender but also by the economic results of the debilitating treaty. The country was being torn apart by the monarchists who wanted to restore the lost empire, the Communists who took their cues from the Soviet Union, and the National Socialists, the Nazis, who demanded dictatorship, rearming of Germany, and invalidating the Versailles Treaty. When my parents married in 1922, inflation was rampant and the attempt at German democracy was on tenuous grounds. In the late 1920s, the world-wide depression also settled on Europe, and high unemployment rates added to the instability and political division of the German nation. The Nazis screamed for all to hear that *International Jewry* was the root cause of Germany's misfortune. The place of my birth was Germany, my parents' religion was Jewish, the year was 1924.

Prior to emigrating from Germany in 1939, I fortunately had engaged in some genealogical research, which I also continued in later years. As a result, I possess adequate information of my direct line ancestors.

Most of my father's family originated in Thuringia, one of the smaller states, located in the central part of the country. It includes the Thuringian forest, where I was born. This is a charming region of lush forests, gentle rolling hills, verdant valleys, the "green heart" of Germany. In my paternal branch, I was able to trace the family tree back to 1768, when my great-great-grandfather Josef Muhlfelder was born in the town of Muhlfeld. Most likely, he had no surname, but instead and in accordance with Jewish practice was identified as Josef son of "his father's first name." Until recently, Judaism was a male-oriented religion, and orthodoxy follows this sex discrimination to this day. In any case, when Josef moved from Muhlfeld to nearby Bauerbach and was most likely required either to choose a last name or accept one designated by the authorities, he called himself Josef Muhlfelder, i.e., the Josef from Muhlfeld. I recall that President John F. Kennedy, when visiting West Berlin in the early 1960s, then sur-

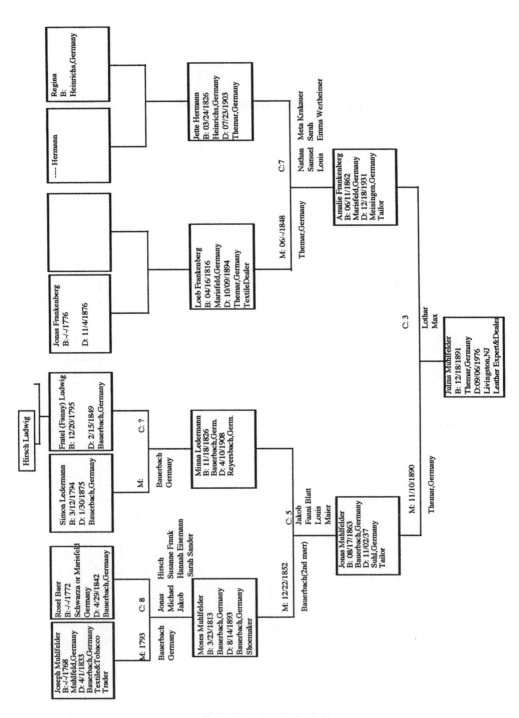

Family Tree of My Father

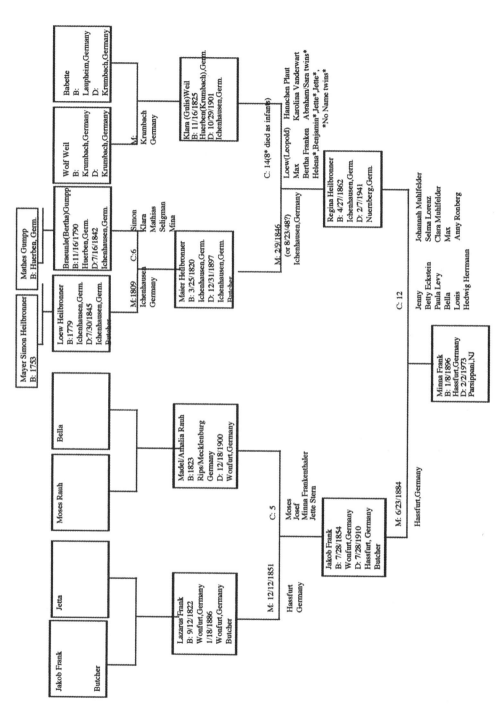

Family Tree of My Mother

rounded by Communist-dominated East Germany, in attempting politically to dramatize his identity with the city's citizens, pronounced "Ich bin ein Berliner," "I am a Berliner." My ancestor Josef used the same technique for more pragmatic reasons. He married Rosel Baer from nearby Marisfeld, and they had eight children. One of these was my great-grandfather Moses, who spent his entire lifespan of 80 years in Bauerbach. Both Josef and Moses were shoemakers, a trade apparently open to Jews. One source identifies Josef also as a tradesman of textiles and tobacco products. Maybe he had a career change at one point in his life. Moses married (second marriage) Minna Ledermann, a local young woman, who bore him five children, among them my grandfather Jonas, whom I knew well in his later years. Jonas took up the tailor trade in Themar and wisely married another tailor, my grandmother, Amalie Frankenberg from Marisfeld. This union produced three sons, of whom my father Julius was the oldest. My father's two brothers, Lothar and Max, eventually married two of my mother's sisters (Johannah and Claire, respectively), but no offspring derived from these two unions.

It is interesting and telling to observe that most of the first names up to my grandparents generation were biblical, but starting with my parents and their contemporaries, the given names were mostly of German origin. This apparently reflects a conscious attempt of Jews to adapt to the culture and practice of the land of their birth. However, each child was also given a Jewish name within eight days of birth; my father's was Josef ben Jone, Josef son of Jonas, and my mother's Mindle bas Jakob. Today, finally and fortunately, this Jewish naming gives cognizance to the obvious, that each child also has a mother.

My mother's ancestors originated primarily from Bavaria and Wuertemberg, states in the southern part of Germany. The earliest date my research penetrated on that side of the family is 1753, the year of birth of my great-great-great-grandfather, Mayer Simon Heilbronner from Ichenhausen. My maternal ancestors came from places such as Wonfurt, Krumbach, Emershausen, Laupheim, Huerben, and Ichenhausen. My mother's paternal grandfather, Lazarus Frank, was born in Wonfurt and married Amalie Rau from the vicinity of Hofheim. They had five children, including my maternal grandfather, Jakob Frank, whom I did not know. Born in 1854, he was a butcher by trade and married my grandmother, Regina Heibronner from Ichenhausen. They founded their home in

Paternal grandparents Jonas and Amalie Muhlfelder (extreme left) with Uncles Lothar (kneeling) and Max (both in sailor suits), and friends, circa 1911, in Meiningen, Germany

Hassfurt, located on the banks of the Main River to the east of Schweinfurt. Her father, Maier, was also a butcher and was married to a Klara Weil from Huerben near Krumbach. Regina was the second of 14 siblings, eight of whom died as infants. My mother's parents produced 12 children, 10 girls and two boys.

My grandfather was a particularly orthodox Jew, as was the case of many forbears in my mother's family. That might be one ex-

House of maternal grandparents Frank in Hassfurt, Bavaria, Germany, circa 1909

planation for their being so prolific. Various anecdotes related to me attest to grandfather Jakob's strict and unyielding adherence to the prescribed Jewish practices. When one of his older daughters, my aunt Paula, departed from home in 1909 to immigrate to the United States, my grandfather Jakob tried to extract a promise from her that she would continue to observe a ritually kosher diet in her new land. When Paula felt unable to make such a commitment, at least in part because of her unfamiliarity with America, my grandfather exclaimed that he did not want to see her again. His premature

My parents' wedding picture, February 1922.

death a year later sadly sealed his wish. My mother was the seventh of the even dozen offspring. This must have been a busy and complex home, with so many young women competing for attention. From these 12 offspring, nine married but only four of these (my mother, Hedwig, Anny, and Max) had children of their own (nine altogether). A fifth one, Betty, became a stepmother when she married a widower with three children from his first union.

At times, I have reflected on how many marriages and homes and caring people and quirks of fate it took in the lives of the multitude of my ancestors to make me a unique entity of this world. It is almost too overwhelming to fathom. For the answer, I need to withdraw from the pragmatic into my belief in God.

I was born on a Friday afternoon, the thirteenth day of June, 1924, just before the beginning of the Sabbath in the Thuringian town of Suhl. My parents were married in February of 1922. At that time, my father worked as a traveling salesman for a leather wholesale firm and my mother was employed as a nanny.

Suhl, which then had a population of about 17,000, is situated in the charming and inviting Thuringian forest. Vacationers who were drawn to this lovely area preferred other locations for their

The Synagogue in Suhl shortly after its construction, 1906/7.

stays because Suhl was primarily devoted to the manufacture of small arms for both military and recreational purposes. It was known as "Die Waffenstadt," the weapons town.

Its Jewish congregation consisted of about 30 families who were essentially all affiliated with the synagogue. In response to the needs of an increased Jewish presence in this area, this attractive house of worship had been built in 1906 and utilized the services of a religiously-trained Lehrer, a teacher, as its functionary to perform the duties of rabbi, cantor, and educator. Usually, such multifarious arrangements are not very satisfactory, but the limited size of the congregation did not permit a larger staff. To satisfy the diverse degrees of religious observances of the membership, the ser-

Interior of Suhl Synagogue: Bima with Holy Ark;
"Love your neighbor as yourself"; men sat downstairs,
women upstairs in the balcony.

vices followed a liberal conservative line. Women sat upstairs on either side of a U-shaped balcony, and an organ with occasional choir occupied the connecting link. A Jewish cemetery was also within the town limits. Suhl provided a rather pleasant environment for its population, including those of the Jewish faith. My parents' social life involved primarily Jewish friends, although they also had cordial contacts with some of our non-Jewish neighbors until the start of the Nazi period.

Recalling memories of one's early childhood is somewhat precarious because of the difficulty of distinguishing between the consciously-remembered impressions and the stories relayed by parents and other relatives. I used to amuse my mother with the claim that I recalled lying in a baby carriage in a small garden under the windows of my parents' apartment at Herrenstrasse 30, my place of birth. My mother laughingly rejected this claim as a virtual impossibility. I was an infant at that stage and probably based this "memory" on tales I heard in later years. The house containing my parents' rented apartment belonged to the Reich family, who were the proprietors of an adjoining lumber and furniture business. At that time, Germany was in the grips of rampant inflation. I was told that at the peak of this maddening instability, my father would receive a salary installment twice per day because of the rapid devaluation of the currency. My mother would rush out of the house to spend this cash before the rapidly rising prices would further diminish its purchasing power. In a way, I could be identified as an inflation baby.

My father was employed by the local firm of David Levy & Sohn. As a leather wholesale business, with a minor retail outlet for the local population, this firm dealt primarily with shoemakers and small shoe factories in supplying them with sole and upper leather as well as with all the accessories required to repair or produce shoeware. In 1906, when my father was 14 years old and had just completed his basic schooling, my grandparents sent him from nearby Themar to become an apprentice with David Levy & Son. As tailors with modest means and parents of three children, they could not afford to send their oldest son to Gymnasium (secondary school) to further his formal education. Thus, my father became knowledgeable in all aspects of the leather business. During the First World War, however, he had to work in a large arms factory, the Simson Werke. This substantial establishment had been developed by a Jewish family and employed several thousand workers. My father was required to seek employment there as part of the war effort after he had been rejected for military service. Although I am not sure of the reason, I speculate that his slight build and his health status at the time were the cause of this rejection. When the conflict finally came to an end after four terrible years, father returned to his former activities at David Levy. By the time he met my mother, he had been promoted to traveling salesman, covering large areas of central Germany with a chauffeur-driven car.

My mother moved to Suhl in about 1919–20 to serve as a nanny for the children of the Simson family, the owners of the large factory. She stayed in their beautiful villa, which even today is a prominent landmark overlooking the town. Subsequent to this engagement, she had a similar position with the Daniel Nussbaum family, whose head was one of the leaders of the local Jewish congregation. Mother was a popular young woman, charming, and pretty. Her numerous admirers referred to her endearingly as "Schoene Minna," beautiful Minna, a title well deserved, in my opinion, based on pictorial evidence.

When I was an infant, my paternal grandparents had already moved from Themar to Meiningen. The latter, located about 15 miles west of Suhl, was a nice town and functioned from 1680 till 1918 as the seat of an independent dukedom. This town had a substantially different appearance from Suhl, with its wide tree lined streets, an opera house, a lovely park, a theater, and the royal castle. My father's two younger brothers, Lothar and Max, still being single, also lived in my grandparents' apartment. We visited there frequently on weekends, and I always considered it a special treat. My uncles especially were a lot of fun and a positive and stimulating influence on a young boy. They had both attended the Gymnasium (equivalent to high school and the first year of college) in Meiningen and were quite worldly. Lothar worked as a traveling salesman for a wholesale paper firm, and Max was employed by a leather goods business that dealt in handbags, wallets, and briefcases.

My maternal grandmother, Regina Frank,widowed since 1910, continued to live in Hassfurt with aunt Johanna (Hannah), her eighth offspring. When I was born, only nine of the original 12 children of the Frank family were still living, but only aunt Hannah had remained with grandmother in Hassfurt. Aunts Jenny, the oldest, born in 1886, and Bella had passed away shortly after the end of World War I. Based on some of her eloquent letters and the testimonials of her siblings, Jenny was a talented, sensitive, and cultured human being. For years, she officiated as a respected teacher at the Jewish School for Home Economics in Frankfurt on the Main. Her young life (she was 35) was snuffed out as the result of a rapidly spreading flu epidemic.

Uncle Louis (Ludwig), who was then the breadwinner of the large family, had sacrificed his young life in 1916 for the fatherland while fighting at the western front during the First World War. Because his widowed mother and younger siblings were so dependent on him, Louis had difficulty being accepted into the German Kaiser's military ranks. After having been turned down a number of times, he finally succeeded with his patriotic fervor in joining a Bavarian field artillery regiment. He is buried in the German military cemetery of Marchies, east of Baupaune, France. I was named in honor of his memory.

In my childhood years, several of my mother's siblings were already residing in the U.S.A. Aunt Paula's immigration in 1909 was followed in the early twenties by Selma, Anny (the youngest, born in 1906), and uncle Max. These were the young people of that time who emigrated to the new world primarily because it was the land of opportunity. As far as I know, neither political motivation nor religious discrimination made such emigration a dire necessity at that time. Still living in Germany in addition to my mother and Hannah were aunt Hedwig Herrmann, married in Augsburg, aunt Betty Eckstein, married in Jena, and aunt Clairle (Claire), working as a nurse in the Jewish hospital of Fuerth near Nuremberg.

Late in 1927 or at the beginning of 1928, my parents moved into a spacious apartment located on the third floor at Rimbachstrasse 4. My mother engaged a live-in maid to assist with the maintenance of these larger quarters and a growing family. All living quarters and my parents' bedroom were heated with individual coal furnaces, and a bath was at our exclusive disposal at ground level. These were the days before refrigeration; therefore, a deep cellar was available to preserve perishable items such as fruit for extensive periods. It was a nice home with a good view of the Domberg, a hill that dominates the local landscape.

During this period, my mother accompanied me a number of times to the studio of Alexander Gerbig, a well known artist of the town and surrounding area. My father was kept in the dark with respect to this activity and was most pleasantly surprised when he discovered my likeness, endowed with a multitude of curls, when we visited a special Gerbig exhibition in the Realschule in December 1928. As a reward for my apparent patience during the sittings, Mr. Gerbig presented me with a lifelike wooden replica of a typically red-brown Thuringian squirrel. Both the painting and squirrel are still in my possession today.

I vaguely recall that my aunt Selma with new husband Carl Lorenz visited us from the U.S.A. while on their honeymoon trip. I became better acquainted with these two cultured people in later times. Carl had been born into the Christian faith and converted to Judaism

Maternal uncle Louis (Ludwig) Frank; 1914 WWI volunteer in Germany

Grave of uncle Louis (Ludwig); German military cemetery, Marchies, France.

at the time of the marriage. He was a gifted musician with a Ph.D. degree in that art and did some conducting for a number of years.

Shortly after moving into our new apartment, my mother suggested that I should place some sugar on the window sill so that the stork would bring me a sibling. I am glad that such methods are no longer in use today in order to prepare children for expected family additions. I recall clearly that I complied with the sugar request, and my sister Ellen was born in our home on October 25, 1928. For a few days, I was farmed out to our friends, the Sanders, presumably to protect me from all the commotion and to vacate my bedroom for alternate purposes. Contrary to modern practice, my mother was confined to her bed for a few weeks.

It seemed that all the essential components for a happy family life were in place: a father with a good position, a spacious apartment, a loving wife and mother, a boy, a girl – all in good health; the future looked promising.

Visiting paternal grandparents in Meiningen, 1930/31, with parents, sister and uncle Max (glasses).

TRANSITIONS FROM 1929 TO 1933

At the beginning of 1930, my father bought the business from Gustav Levy, the "son" of "David Levy & Sohn." Such a step required economizing at the start. Thus, my father became his own chauffeur, and, for the first time, our family possessed a car albeit primarily for business reasons. It was an Opel, the GM of Germany, and always had an odor of gasoline. This vehicle gave us the luxury of occasional excursions to visit friends, to picnic in the nearby forests, and, of course, to visit Meiningen.

Although the short automobile trip from Suhl to Meiningen was usually not compatible with my stomach's equilibrium, I always quickly recovered when my grandmother served the Thuringian specialty of roast goose and potato dumplings. When I was about five years old, uncle Lothar unveiled a modern contraption in my grandparents' living room: the first family radio, run by bulky wet batteries. Miraculously, voices and music emanated from its speaker to the delight of the assembled clan. During another weekend visit to Meiningen, most likely in 1929, there was much excitement about the arrival of an unusual means of air transportation: the new airship Graf Zeppelin. Thousands of people hiked to the top of a nearby plateau, which served as the primitive local airport. Uncle Lothar, like, no doubt, many others, was ready with his camera, and suddenly he shouted "There it is," and that funny looking flying cigar with its LZ127 marking approached. The weather was ideal, and the ground crew pulled the dangling ropes towards the designated anchor positions. Some people were even admitted to the passenger cabin, but our family and friends just walked and gazed in awe at this huge modern marvel, which must have been at least the length of two football fields. It seems the crowds and even the officials had little concern about the highly flammable hydrogen with which it was filled; I state this in retrospect based on subsequent tragic history. For a little fellow like me, it was a day to remember.

In the mid- to upper
1920s, my grandfather suffered a stroke and could no
longer continue his craft as
tailor. Instead, he became the
Schammes, the sexton of the
synagogue. I enjoyed strolling
through the well landscaped
park and castle gardens with
my grandfather utilizing a
cane for assistance, and stopping at the pond to feed the
swans. He was a kind and
warm hearted man, and I
loved going to synagogue with
him or just being in his company. It was a closely knit and
devoted family, with my
grandmother Amalie appear-
ing to have been the stronger

With passenger friend, circa 1929

and more aggressive partner of the two. Sometimes, I was able to
remain for a few days in Meiningen without my parents. Sleeping
there was an unusual experience, for my grandparents used high
goose-feather beds. Once I scaled the sides, the soft interior gave me
the feeling that I was sinking into never-never land. Getting up in
the morning was a chore. During this period, I also visited my
grandmother Regina and aunt Hannah in Hassfurt on a few occasions, but I have no clear recall of my early stays in my mother's
hometown.

My formal education began in 1930 and, as it turned out, would
not be completed until 1955. The first day is embedded clearly in my
mind. My mother marched with me to the Hoheloh Schule, and I
was carrying a large Zuckertuete, a cone filled with sweets and gifts
for the incipient scholar. I met Lehrer Hahn, who was cordial but
seemed rigid and strict, in keeping with the German custom. He
was my teacher for the entire four years of the grammar school curriculum. Throughout this time, he tried diligently to give his students, all boys, a solid basic education. It was his habit to walk on
top of the school desks when he dictated spelling exercises so that
he could quickly spot our errors. Once, when I had written a word

My first year elementary school (1930); I am in front, third from right.

incorrectly, he attempted to strike my shoulder with his ever present bamboo cane; however, I ducked and he caught my eye. My mother's complaint resulted in an apology on his part. Such corporal punishment methods, although not common, were nevertheless not unusual at that time. Generally, I had much fun and satisfaction in this school and was fairly treated in spite of being the only Jewish student in the class.

Most probably, I began with my religious school education in 1932 on a once per week basis. Meeting with his few students in the afternoon following secular school in an Oberrealschule classroom, Lehrer Levi taught us customs, Hebrew language, and Jewish history. Coming from an observant home, I was already quite familiar with Sabbath and holiday customs and practices. He was a dedicated man, but being about seventy years of age and with roots in the 19th century, he was far from a good pedagogic choice. The brightest spot of this exposure was our history book, a modern and user-friendly work written by a young Berlin rabbi named Joachim Prinz, whose path I was going to cross many years later.

On my father's 40th birthday, my grandmother Amalie suddenly died. A burst gall bladder was the cause of death; most likely, more diligent and prompt medical attention could have prevented this tragic occurrence. As a seven-year-old, I received a shocking exposure to the finality of death. Somewhat sheltered and unprepared, I had a lesson from life's harsher school. Without a woman in the house, my grandfather and his two bachelor sons were left with an apartment but only a diminished home at best. They all moved to Herrenstrasse 30 in Suhl, the apartment house in which I was born. Miss Lieben was engaged as a housekeeper to assist my grandfather and prepare the daily meals. Lothar continued to travel extensively, and Max spent his working weeks for a few years in Sonneberg, where he managed a branch store for his Meiningen firm.

My paternal grandfather Jonas sitting at his favorite spot, viewing the Lauter River flowing past the historic Malzhaus (malthouse).

Naturally, it was wonderful for me to have my grandfather and "weekend" uncles so close by. Frequently, the family gathered on Friday night in his home. This was possible because the Erev (beginning) Sabbath services prior to dinner were for men only and of short duration. At times, I also said hello to my grandfather during the week. He was proud of having served in the army under three Kaisers: in 1888, Wilhelm I, then followed in rapid succession by Frederick III and Wilhelm II. With nostalgic recall, he gave me marching commands in simulating a close order drill in his living room. I loved to please him, listen to the tales of his youth, and play board games with this kind old gentleman. Thus, we reciprocated by being good company for each other. His favorite spot was his living room window, where he looked out on a small stream, the Lauter, flowing under a bridge and then past a beautiful old Malzhaus (malt-house) that dates back to the 17th century.

Shortly after Ellen reached walking age, my parents noticed that she had difficulty controlling her legs. A specialist in Arnstadt determined that her hips were dislocated; most likely, this was a congenital condition. A year or two later, an orthopedist, Dr. Gutt-

The historical part of Suhl upon which my grandfather's eyes gazed upon. He lived at Herrnstrasse 30, the house on the extreme left, which was also where I was born.

man, with a clinic in Coburg, took over Ellen's medical care. His method consisted of resetting the hip joints and encasing the area in a plaster cast in the expectation that lengthy (several months) periods of constraining her in this position would restore the hips to normalcy. Unfortunately, this treatment was never successful in my sister's case. Today, such a failed approach, stretched over at least six years, would result in a malpractice lawsuit. Aside from the unsuccessful physical therapy, the repeated and prolonged incarcerations within the prison of the plaster cast had also a most detrimental psychological effect. My mother tried hard to center many of our activities in the house so that Ellen could participate as much as possible and be in contact with other people in addition to the immediate family. These efforts were of limited success, and Ellen's handicapped youth detrimentally affected her entire life, not only physiologically but emotionally as well.

My parents made it a practice to write birthday poetry for each other, which I then recited on the special day. I still have a small booklet in my possession with some of these writings. Once, my father had threatened in jest that he, not desiring another round of birthday gifts, would toss them out the window if my mother persisted. As a counter, with the presents attached by means of safety pins to my shirt and pants, I recited my mother's congratulatory poem, which also pleaded for my father to accept the offering and not to resort to the drastic window action. Business obligations necessitated my father's being on the road during at least 30 weeks per year, but in spite of these absences, our family life was loving and warm. Nightly, he would call our home to report and ascertain that all was well and have my mother relay business directives the following morning. With two annual exceptions, my father returned from his weekly travels on Friday afternoons, frequently with sweets or special fruit for the family. Sometimes he even brought me a book, which I particularly appreciated.

On Sabbath morning, we frequently attended the services in our synagogue. I was fond of sitting next to my father and joining him in prayer. At times, my mother would also attend with the other ladies in the upstairs balcony. Simchas Torah, the end of Succoth (the thanksgiving for the harvest), was the most joyous event of the synagogue activities for the children of the congregation. During the festive procession, led by the temple elders carrying the Torahs, the ladies would shower us with sweets from the balcony. The quickest hands and biggest bags or pockets would reap the greatest booty. It was great fun but also somewhat undignified in a house of worship. Eventually, the procedure was revised, with the ladies handing us bags of candy in the staircase leading to the balcony. Lehrer Levi was assisted in some of the services by some of the more dedicated and skilled men. Particularly on the High Holidays, it would have been impossible for him to conduct the services on his own. The brothers Daniel and Wolf Nussbaum, as well as Mr. Brylewski, chanted and read some of the prayers. For special days, the service was beautifully enhanced by a volunteer choir. Now and then, Lehrer Levi also sermonized, but that was not one of his strengths. The regular attendees could not help noticing repetition of themes and content from prior years, but some allowance had to be made for our Lehrer's advanced age.

Suhl is located in a good winter-sports region. Thus, children start at an early age to participate in this healthy fun-filled activity. One started with sleigh riding and progressed in short order to skating on the Herrenteich and skiing in the nearby mountains. I must have been six or seven when I was entrusted with my first pair of skis. Fearlessly and foolishly, I broke my skis on the very first outing. Not being sure how to stop, I gave in to the temptation to speed down a steep incline and ended up in a hedge at the bottom. My mother had the ski tip repaired with a tin bandage, and I rapidly increased my skills, not being inhibited by this badge of initiation. Cross-country trips were a special treat because of the many well-marked trails winding through a picturesque landscape similar to that of Vermont. The Thuringian forest reaches elevations up to about 3,000 feet.

My parents' friends Meta and Isidor Sander owned a nice house on the Steinweg, the main business street of the town. They not only lived there but also conducted a high quality leather goods retail business on the premises. Isidor also did some traveling as a leather wholesaler, as my father did. Thus, they were really partial competitors besides being good friends. In back of the house, there was a sizable chicken yard and beyond that a lovely garden. Meta functioned as the chief gardener and was the heart and soul of the entire establishment. She came from a farming area, I believe Bavaria. Meta was a giving and gifted human being, an intelligent and well-informed woman, a respected business person and an excellent gardener. The garden was usually at our disposal, and we spent many wonderful hours in its midst. Because of its proximity to our apartment, it was particularly convenient to bring Ellen there. Maybe this exposure was partially responsible for inspiring my later love for my horticultural avocation. During Succoth, the Sanders prepared a traditional Sukkah, a booth with branches as the ceiling and decorated with the fruits of the harvest, which we were celebrating. Often, the Jewish children were invited to help with the decorating. We were always welcome to spend special time with the Sanders and others in celebrating this holiday in their Sukkah.

On most weekends during the warmer part of the year, our family would join other Jewish friends walking to one of several available restaurants located in the neighboring woods. There, we were treated to sweet refreshments while the adults talked over coffee and cake. It was a pleasant and healthy way to spend an afternoon. During May, the children would collect the seasonal Maikaefer, which have the appearance of June bugs but are about 10 times larger. I would keep these pets for a week or two in a cigar box partially filled with leaves for nourishment and holes in the cover for ventilation.

During the 1931–32 years, I recall an ever-increasing political unrest. Unemployment was high, and the Nazi party was visible and audible. Besides the National Socialists, a number of other parties such as Nationalists, Socialists, Communists, Stahlhelm, and

Social Democrats competed in the ever more frequent elections. Propaganda leaflets filled the streets, and inciting speeches, particularly those of Adolf Hitler, filled the airwaves. Even as a young boy, I was aware of the tumult and concern. Jews, for good reasons, were particularly uneasy with the ever-increasing strength and activity of the Nazi party. Some of my parents' friends, such as Martin Rehbock, expressed their fears during repeated discussions at social meetings on Saturday evenings, some of which were in our home. One of the items that sticks in my mind was the complaint that Mr. Rehbock's frequently-voiced concerns tended to dominate and depress the evenings, which were intended to be social and relaxing. In retrospect, the captive audience should have taken his comments much more seriously.

During these waning years of the Weimar Republic, the environment of my elementary school remained stable, and as the only Jewish student in the class, I received a generally fair treatment from my teacher and my classmates. If there was anti-Semitic discrimination, I do not recall any notable occurrences.

In the summer of 1932, my parents treated me to an unusual vacation, most likely arranged by Meta Sander. For the first time, I traveled alone until I reached the city of Jena, where my aunt Betty lived with her family. There I was met at the train station and, together with another boy by the name of Friedmann, traveled further north to join a children's transport that had the North Sea island of Norderney as its destination. A small boat ferried us across the water, and I had to stay on deck to avoid becoming nauseous from the rocking motion. The few weeks I spent there in a home for Jewish children were wonderful and revealing. I discovered sunny beaches and unspoiled dunes, sea horses, and clam shells. The walk to the lighthouse was a delight. Together with a few hundred other Jewish children, I had a wonderful time in that lovely home, a place that was bright and friendly and filled to the brim with delightful activities. For that little fellow from Suhl, a whole new world opened up. These beautiful surroundings also represented an attraction to other people, who decorated their vacation bungalows or permanent residences with a forest of swastika flags. Such Nazi concentration was somewhat disconcerting, but we, as children, were not aware of any anti-Semitism during our stay. It is regrettable that I did not yet possess a camera to record some of the beauties of nature to which I was introduced at that time.

Norderney's concentration of swastika flags during the summer was matched if not exceeded by a similar display in Suhl during the following winter, when the aging President Hindenburg appointed Adolf Hitler as chancellor of Germany on January 30, 1933. The ever-escalating political unrest and the ever-increasing support of the Nazi party by the German population had finally propelled their vitriolic leader into that pivotal position. I was not aware of any disturbances on that day, just many enthusiastic people in the streets with their arms raised in the Hitler salute while brown-shirted Nazis were marching and singing. It was also an ominously momentous day for Jews, a day that escalated their concern for their German future. But during this initial part of the official Nazi rule, most Jewish people felt or hoped that this would be a passing phase on the German political scene, that the political instability would result in someone else eventually taking over the chancellorship. It was not really possible for most Jews to visualize that during the next few years the situation for Germany's Jews would deteriorate drastically and become ever more dangerous. My father's business continued as before, and I experienced no significant problems in school.

Anti-Semitism was now state-sanctioned and sponsored. Progressively, more and more Christian acquaintances avoided personal or social contact with Jews. Nevertheless, there were some non-Jews such as Mr. Rehfeld, a friend of my father, who did not participate in any Nazi activity, but such opposition was passive at best. However, one has to realize that once Hitler became chancellor, any protest or open opposition was both difficult and risky in view of the considerable power of the ascending Nazi regime. If the German people had seriously desired to relegate the Nazis to the sidelines, they could have done that at the ballot box during the numerous electoral opportunities of prior years. But most of the population either agreed with the Nazis' anti-Semitic diatribe or were willing to tolerate it in silence for the sake of the promise of economic improvements and a perceived rehabilitation of national honor. Justice and decency did not head the priority list.

LIVING UNDER NAZI RULE (1933–1938)

In the beginning, for Jews to live under the Nazi dictatorship was a degenerating experience. Each day, each month, each year, our isolation would grow, our freedoms would decline, and little by little our very being would become ever more dehumanized in the eyes of most Christian Germans. During my professional life many years later, it was a practice to pose the rhetorical question of how a program could fall behind in schedule by a whole year. "One day at a time" was the telling answer. The escalation of state sponsored anti-Semitism in Germany anticipated this answer.

April 1, 1933, was the first of many officially organized actions against German citizens of the Jewish faith. At the entrance of all Jewish business establishments, brown-shirted stormtroopers blocked and threatened and intimidated people from entering. My father's small store was also guarded by two of these supermen. When my grandfather attempted to enter the premises, the Nazis, not being aware of his identity, tried to deter him. "Can't I see my son?", the old man exclaimed as he continued up the few steps. Helmut Sander photographed his parents' store, adorned with the blocking stormtroopers. The Nazis noticed his attempt and briefly arrested him, confiscating the film. This incident is interesting, because in later years, when Germany under Nazi rule engaged in the most monstrous atrocities, it was the Nazi photographers who meticulously recorded their own criminal record.

Even under the Nazis, our family continued to function as normally as possible. During the summer, I spent several weeks with my grandmother Regina and aunt Hansel in Hassfurt. Cousin Lou (Ludwig) Herrmann was there too, working as an apprentice in a local nursery in preparation for emigrating to Palestine. Sometimes I helped him with his chores; maybe my as-yet-hidden gardening instinct showed its first signs. We had fun bathing in the Main River, picking berries, taking walks, and attending synagogue. I was now old enough to appreciate the profound depth and innate goodness of my grandmother's character. This woman, who brought 12 children into this world and became widowed early in life, impressed me deeply with her kindness and empathy. I do not believe that any of her children whom I got to know were able to attain her standards and compassion. It was a real treat to accompany her when she visited her old friend Tante Gold and listen to their conversations. I am glad I had the opportunity and the privilege for this so-special exposure.

In August of 1933, my grandfather reached the age of seventy, and his family gathered in Suhl to celebrate. Besides our immediate family, there was my grandfather's brother Louis from Unna with his granddaughter Gerda Hollaender, neither of whom I had ever met before, his sister Fanny Blatt, my deceased grandmother's sisters Meta and Sara from Themar, his housekeeper and friends. It was a beautiful day in a time when nice days became less and less frequent. My grandfather's generation was never to meet again.

Upon completing the grammar school curriculum at the Hoheloh Schule in 1934, my parents enrolled me at the Mittelschule, an intermediate school located within easy walking distance of our residence. Over a period of six years, this institution offered a wide range of interesting subjects in languages, science, and mathematics, similar to those of U.S. high school programs. Instead of having only one teacher as in grammar school, I was now exposed to a variety of educators, depending on the subject matter. Of a total student body of about 300, there were only three or four Jewish students. I am uncertain why I did not enroll for my studies at the Oberrealschule, which offered more advanced studies during additional years. Possibly, my father hoped that some day I would succeed him in his business.

Around this time, my cousin Julius (Jimmy) Herrmann paid us a farewell visit prior to emigrating to the U.S. Young Jewish men and women had begun to leave the country in which they saw no future for themselves. Most families were as yet reluctant to make such a drastic move. Thus, the congregation in Suhl was quite surprised when the Jacoby family of, I believe, six announced their decision to emigrate to Palestine. He was an attorney and married to a non-Jewish woman. This was the first family to depart from the town in response to the Nazi takeover. Instead of being surprised and viewing this as precipitous, one can state in retrospect that this family made a wise and far-sighted move that should have been a signal for all Jews of Suhl to do likewise. But hindsight is the only

My paternal grandfather's seventieth birthday, Suhl, August 17, 1933. L. to R. back row: his brother Louis, grandfather, uncle Max, my father, uncle Lothar. Front row: Housekeeper, his sister Fanni, my late grandmother's sisters Sarah and Meta, friends and extreme right: cousin Gerda Hollander.

guaranteed 20:20 vision, and most Jews as sane human beings could not visualize the horrors awaiting them just a few years hence.

In the summer of 1934, I was invited to spend a few weeks with the Herrmanns in Augsburg. They had a butcher shop in this sizable southern city, and I once again met my cousin Lou (Ludwig), with whom I shared some time during the prior summer in Hassfurt. We went to the pool to meet other acquaintances and frequently visited the store not only to observe the activities but also to taste the delectable meat products. Once, without authorization, I took a lengthy walk through the city streets to the slaughter houses. How did I ever find my way? Admittedly, I was not thrilled at seeing the butchery of the cattle, an experience that could and would transform some people into vegetarians.

Together with my uncle Hugo's family, we once made a day trip to the beautifully-situated Ammersee, the largest inland body of water I had seen up to that time. I was a somewhat finicky eater, preferring to keep the various parts of dinner carefully separated on my plate. In an attempt to teach me manners, uncle Hugo, to my dismay, once mixed everything thoroughly. This was not the preferred pedagogic method; to this day, I keep the various components of my meal

With my middle school class on Suhl's mainstreet in 1934. I am the one with the dark tie. The bald man directly behind me was my favorite teacher, Herr Boedecker.

separated on my plate. Aside from this anomaly, I recall that the Herrmanns were most hospitable and I had a nice time in Augsburg.

On uncle Hugo Herrmann's side, a substantial part of the family also lived in Augsburg; less than a decade later, most of these nice people were murdered by the Nazis. One of the lasting impressions of Augsburg was the large and elaborate synagogue, with its Bima, the elevated area in front of the Torah ark, artistically constructed of marble. While still on vacation, we heard on August 2, 1934, that President Hindenburg had died, thus removing the last, though infinitesimal, hope for the return of a democratic regime. Hitler ruled now as absolute dictator.

Life in Suhl continued without any major disturbance, although the German government continued to increase the anti-Semitic measures. Most of the Jews there had taken no action to prepare for eventual emigration. With the conclusion of my first year at the Mittelschule, I spent a few weeks of the 1935 summer in Bad Kissingen, a well-known resort with health-enhancing mineral springs. I stayed at a well-supervised home for Jewish children. During the early 1920s, aunt Betty guided this institution as director. Prior to moving to Suhl, even my mother had spent one summer there as counselor for a group of children. For me, it was enjoyable and stim-

1935 Suhl visit of aunt Anny and uncle Heinz Ronberg from the US (directly behind me). Parents to my right. At either end, Isidor and Meta Sander, very good friends of our family. Heinz urged my parents to leave Germany promptly.

ulating to be with so many other Jewish children. I could have done without the obligatory daily drink of the mineral (Rackotzi) water, the only bitter taste of these few weeks.

After I returned home, uncle Heinz and aunt Anny Ronberg from America paid us a lovely visit as part of their somewhat delayed honeymoon trip. Anny was the youngest of my mother's siblings and lived till 1998. It was fun to have such stimulating people with a great sense of humor in our midst. Together, we attended a local fair (Schuetzenfest) and roamed the Thuringian forests. In my presence, Heinz once quite seriously urged my parents to leave Germany. He anticipated that conditions there would considerably worsen for the Jewish population. My father felt that he could still make a living with his business and was thus reluctant to make a decision to emigrate at that point. Even in 1935, many Jews felt the Nazi era to be just a bad dream that would eventually disappear. But my uncle then urged that, as a minimum, my parents should, in the meantime, send me to the U.S. I am hazy about my own reaction to this proposal, but my parents' reluctance to accede no doubt had a negative influence on me at the age of 11. As a result, we remained in Germany another four years under ever more trying conditions. But I empathize with the dilemma faced by my parents at that time. Despite this hesitancy, we fortunately still managed to escape in time.

This was also the year of the Italian invasion of Ethiopia (formerly Abyssinia). Hitler's Axis ally, the fascist Italian dictator Benito Mussolini, had sent his modern army to conquer this East African state. This was to be the first of many expansionist moves of the Axis powers. The primitively-armed Ethiopians were no match for the Italian war machine. Meta Sander, who was always well informed, talked to us about the great courage of the Ethiopian soldiers, who attacked fascist tanks with homemade grenades, jumping on the vehicles barefooted. German propaganda, of course, depicted the Roman Legions as invincible. By the middle of 1936, Ethiopia fell and was absorbed into Italian East Africa. The rest of the world stood by and took no action.

The few non-Jewish playmates I had became ever more reluctant to associate with me. Essentially all belonged to the Nazi youth organizations (Jungvolk and Hitlerjugend) and were thus under pressure to avoid Jewish contacts. There were a few Jewish kids of my age with whom I could spend some of my leisure hours. One of these, Karl-Heinz Friedmann, was related to part-owners of a horse trading establishment. Thus, they had a large enclosed paddock for exercising and showing their handsome animals in addition to many stables and barns. This was a great place to play and to watch a multitude of activities. Karl-Heinz's father was married to a non-Jewish woman, thus making my friend a "Mischling" (half-breed) in the Nazis' racial ideology and placing him in the never-never land between those persecuted and the persecutors. My father, being aware of the growing isolation of the Jewish youth, made an area in his large leather storage room available for setting up a ping pong table. Thus, the few young people of our congregation had a place to meet and play in a somewhat protected environment.

I also spent time listening to the radio, especially to music and sports. The German boxer Max Schmeling was then at the peak of his career, and I recall listening with my father to his two fights with the U.S. great Joe Louis. Because of the time difference, these broadcasts took place in the middle of the night, which added an extra aura of excitement to the occasion. Besides that, I did a lot of reading and thus my days were filled with a multitude of activities.

On a few occasions, my father gave me the special treat of letting me accompany him on one of his business trips when school vacations

*Together with sister Ellen, mother and uncle Lothar in beautiful Sanders'
garden, circa 1936.*

made this possible. Generally, father departed on his journeys on
Mondays and returned prior to the Sabbath on Fridays. To travel
with him was naturally a real thrill for a young boy. I loved to discuss
the expectations with which he approached his shoemaker customers
and his assessment of the sales results after each visit. At the end of
the day he would phone my mother and we would stop for the night
at an inn or a small hotel. Cherishing every part of this special experience, I loved my father with hero worship. Usually, he traveled
alone, trying to see each one of his customers twice per year. Until
about 1937, the Nazi decrees and anti-Semitic activities had no significant detrimental impact on his business. I recall his relating to us
around 1937 that when entering the Franconian town of Weiden as
part of his customary tour, he was greeted by a banner spanning the
road which proclaimed in form of a rhyme: "Die Christen in Weiden
können die Juden nicht leiden; Drum bleibt uns fern und habt uns
gern" ("The Christians of Weiden dislike the Jews; therefore stay far
away from us and get lost"). The message was crude and clear.

The anti-Semitic Nuremberg laws enacted in September 1935
had a direct effect on our household. These Nazi directives prohibit-
ed intermarriages between Jews and non-Jews and forbade the employment of female domestic help below the age of 45 in Jewish

homes. These "race-laws" were enacted "to protect the German blood and the German honor." Our talented and pleasant Fraeulein Mia had to leave our employ, and my parents hired another helper who was above the specified age threshold. This woman, who had never married, had spent her entire life in a small village and was somewhat naive, but there was no alternative. She did enjoy listening on the radio to the beautiful musical renditions of the German tenor Richard Tauber. After we informed her that he was of the Jewish faith, she praised him with enthusiasm as "Der Yiddische Mann." This particular restriction of female domestics reflected the mania of the Nazi press, particularly the virulent national organ "Der Stuermer," published by the fanatic Julius Streicher, which constantly depicted Jewish men as rapists of young Aryan (Caucasian gentile) women.

The streets of Suhl contained a number of "Stuermerkasten," display cases exhibiting in full spread the most recent issue of this most virulent Nazi paper. The government-sponsored bombardment of hate disseminated by the press, radio, and literature, which depicted Jews in the most vile manner, paved the way for Germans to tolerate, condone, and commit within the next decade the atrocities known as the Holocaust. At that time, Jews were deprived of their German citizenship, and the names of the Jewish soldiers, who died while fighting for Germany in World War I, were removed from the war memorial by the Nazi authorities. These monuments, which dotted the German landscape, were usually inscribed with the theme: "The gratitude of the fatherland is surely yours". I thought of my uncle Louis and the 12,000 German Jewish soldiers who died for the "fatherland"and whose memory was being erased and desecrated by the Berlin government. The revulsion which marks this action is epitomized by a post World War II inscription on a gravestone located in the Jewish cemetery of Ichenhausen, the birthplace of my maternal grandmother Regina. On the tombstone of a family Gertle one reads:

Here rests Nathan
whose wife Sophie was gassed in Auschwitz
whose son Gustav was deported and murdered
whose son Isak died fighting for Germany in World War I

For generations on end, my ancestors had lived in Germany as law-abiding and upright citizens, but from then on all rights associated with such a status were withdrawn for those defined by the Nazis as Jews.

Mainstreet (Steinweg) of Suhl, 1934/5. Hitler Youth is marching. Note Swastika bedecked buildings and enthusiastic crowd on sidelines. Scene is very close to our home.

My parents' social contacts were from then on exclusively confined to Jews. My father enjoyed playing skat with some of the other men while the ladies were engaged in conversation. Skat is a German card game that has some similarity to bridge and is played with three persons at a time. Uncle Lothar was a sophisticated and lucky player and relished being primarily on the winning side. His loud chuckle of triumph still resonates in my mind's ear to this day. In 1935, more than ever before, Martin Rehbock was less interested in the card game and preferred to voice his heightened concerns about the ominous future for German Jews. How did I hear all these interesting interplays of the adults during the Saturday evening socials? I listened from behind the closed door, not polite but very enlightening. On the street, former non-Jewish acquaintances would ignore us; in fact, my mother would try to cross the street when spotting such a person to avoid face-to-face difficulties or embarrassment.

From our apartment, we had a good view of the Steinweg, the main business street of the town. Whenever there was a parade of the brown- and black-shirted Nazis, interspersed with units of the uniformed girls and women of the movement as well as drum and bugle corps and bands, with swastika flags flying in profusion, I had a birdseye view of the tumult. The rest of the population stood on the sidewalks and cheered, raising their right arms in the Hitler salute. They sang not only the German national anthem "Deutschland ueber Alles" ("Germany above all, above all in the world") but also others such as the Nazi "Horst Wessel" song "Die Fahne hoch" ("The Flag On High") and "Wir werden weiter marschieren" ("We will continue to march, even if all falls into smithereens, for today Germany is ours, and tomorrow the entire world"). Most revolting of all, however, was the chilling "Wenn das Judenblut vom Messer spritzt" ("When Jewish blood spurts from the knife"). Like millions of others, I also learned in my lifetime that words of hate do not simply disperse in the wind but lead to violence, untold suffering, and mass murder. In one of the back-court rooms of the apartment house where we resided, a group of the Hitler Youth (uniformed teenagers) met regularly. They committed no deliberate disturbances within the residence, but their proximity to our living quarters was frightening to me and probably to my parents and sister. We lived more and more in a poisoned atmosphere.

For the time being, grandmother moved in with aunt Betty in Jena. After all these years in Hassfurt and having raised 12 children, she now became the proverbial "fifth wheel on the wagon." Betty was not a particularly sensitive person, to say the least. Having married a widower with three children somewhat late in life following an executive career gave her a certain domineering and abrasive characteristic. My grandmother was not too happy in Jena and opted to visit us in Suhl whenever possible. I guess that she could not make our home her permanent residence because of space problems and my mother's preoccupation with Ellen. During these visits, grandmother Frank and grandfather Muhlfelder frequently provided good company for each other.

Now and then, our synagogue was the forum of interesting lectures supplemented with slides on Zionism and Palestine. Younger single adults were particularly attracted to the Zionist adventure and the challenge faced by these idealistic Jewish pioneers. During such programs and also the regular Sabbath services, a Gestapo agent would sometimes sit in the rear and observe our activities but, except for his presence, would not cause any disturbance. Now and then, Nazi vandals would toss rocks through the synagogue's stained glass windows when the building was not in use, but we had no recourse, no one to complain to.

A good part of the 1936 summer I spent home listening to the radio. Following the winter Olympics at Garmisch-Partenkirchen,

Germany pulled out all stops to put on a grandiose show as host for the Berlin summer Olympics. My interest was certainly not in the degree of success of the Nazi propaganda but rather in the multitude of sports events. Although newspapers reported all the results, I preferred to keep my own scores as reported by radio eyewitnesses. There were many outstanding achievements, but none greater than Jesse Owens' four gold medals in track. Years later, I found out that Hitler refused to shake hands with this outstanding athlete because he was not of the Aryan race. I still have an album in my possession that depicts these great games in words and pictures. In spite of the blatant Nazi propaganda stamp and the self-serving and transparent efforts of film director Leni Riefenstahl, the beauty of the sport prevailed.

In the fall of 1936, uncle Lothar was arrested after returning from a brief trip to Czechoslovakia, where he allegedly had made unfavorable remarks about the Nazi regime. Years later, I discussed this matter with Lothar, and he denied emphatically ever having made such statements. He pointed out that it would have been insane for him to take such a risk, knowing that within days he would return to Nazi Germany. In any case, he was imprisoned for several months in the Suhl jail while the case was being prepared for trial. My father had engaged an attorney for the defense of his brother, but the case was either dropped by the Nazi authorities or dismissed by the court.

As Lothar was released from prison, two Gestapo agents took him into custody at the gate and transported him to the Dachau concentration camp. My father ascertained that Lothar's release from there was conditional on his immediate emigration from Germany. Naturally, speed was of the essence for someone incarcerated in such an infamous place. Strenuous efforts finally resulted in the reluctant British authorities granting Lothar an entry permit to Palestine, which was then a mandate of Great Britain. This certificate of entry was conditioned on the financial and living quarter guarantees of a very distant relative who had a farm in Naharia. Even then, the doors of the world were not wide open to admit refugees who were being persecuted for ethnic or religious reasons. My uncle, looking haggard and emaciated after six months in Dachau, with his head shaven like a convict, was permitted to spend three days with us before my father accompanied him to Germany's southern border. During that brief period, we stayed at his side as

Uncle Lothar after returning to Suhl in summer 1937 after six months incarceration in Dachau concentration camp. My sister Ellen and I are sitting with him on Friends Bridge

he embarked on a buying spree for personal items that were believed useful in his country of refuge. When he bade his old father farewell in that summer of 1937, both men must have realized within their hearts that they would never meet again. A week or two later, we received confirmation of Lothar's safe arrival in his new home. All of us breathed a sigh of relief and gratitude.

Early in 1937, my parents requested affidavits from our U.S. relatives to enable eventual immigration. Most German Jews, including my parents, had by this time obtained more than enough evidence that life for them under the Nazi regime would be untenable. Uncle Max Frank, who worked as an engineer for Colgate-Palmolive, and Carl Reuning, the brother-in-law of aunt Selma's husband, Carl Lorenz, furnished the required guarantees to the U.S. immigration authorities. After these submittals, we were put on a waiting list of the Berlin U.S. consulate; the established quota restrictions for German immigrants were about 27,000 per year, while over half a million were seeking to emigrate. Together with a few other Jewish youths, I started to take private English lessons with Carl Plaut, a cousin of my mother. For this, we traveled by train to nearby Meiningen about once a week. Carl, who was blind and master of seven languages, permitted no German conversation during class after the first lesson and effectively utilized records to assure proper pronunciation. As a result, I initially spoke English with a British accent. Carl Plaut, accompanied by his wife Melitta, also came to the Suhl synagogue once a week to teach English to the adults.

In May of that year, while uncle Lothar was still imprisoned in Dachau, I observed my Bar Mitzvah. Even in the midst of these trying living conditions, it was a great day. Lehrer Levi had prepared me with great diligence during the prior months, and I recall with some nostalgia how Mrs. Levi would sit quietly in the corner of their living room to listen to my progress. My Parsha (reading portion from the Torah) was entitled "Naso" from the book of Numbers. Our good Lehrer also handed me the speeches I was to make as part of the service and at the dinner for family and friends in our large dining room on Saturday evening. The service was very beautiful; for the special occasion, our choir with organ enhanced the ritual, and old Mr. Daniel Meyer, a synagogue founder, sang with his stirring bass: "Baruh Haba B'Sheim Adonai," blessed be the one who comes in the name of God. My grandfather and other male members of our family, were called to the Torah, and my mother was beaming from the upstairs balcony. Many congregants stopped by in the afternoon to congratulate and bring me gifts. From my family I received my first bicycle and a wrist watch. The evening dinner was elegant and enjoyable, although my aunt Betty could not resist taking this occasion to teach me how to eat while maintaining my elbows at my side. With minor modifications, I had recited Lehrer Levi's script as my speech during the morning service, but for the evening I took the liberty of using my own words and thoughts. Hopefully, he did not

My religious school teacher and Bar Mirzvah tutor Abraham Levi, flanked by his wife and daughter, both of whom were deported and perished in the Shoah. A. Levi, who also presided at our services, died a natural death. On extreme left is Flora Sander, in whose apartment we lived during the first half of 1939.

mind. At the conclusion of the festivities, my grandfather told us that he would have been sorry even a day after his death if he could not have been present at this event.

Shortly after my Bar Mitzvah, aunt Hedwig and uncle Hugo Herrmann emigrated to the U.S. Grandmother left Jena to move into the Jewish senior citizens' home in Nuremberg, a convenient arrangement because aunt Claire was working as a registered nurse in the nearby Jewish hospital of Fuerth. With family being scattered to the various corners of the world, it was fortuitous that at that time the "Israeli Family Paper," a weekly publication for German Jewry, announced a competition to stimulate genealogical research. Jews always placed great emphasis on the family unit both in terms of our heritage and with an eye towards the future. My paternal grandfather and maternal grandmother were particularly helpful in supplying the desired information about my ancestors. My submittal to the paper was worthy of a book as consolation prize, but the most valuable reward turned out to be the formulation of the family tree itself, a project I continued to pursue for our children and grandchildren. It was the beginning of a most worthwhile endeavor.

In my youth, I was always interested in sports both as participant and spectator. In the company of friends or my father, I would
occasionally walk to the Aue fields to watch the Sunday soccer
games. When approaching the entry gate in 1937, I was confronted
by a new sign: "Forbidden to dogs and Jews." Restaurants, movie
theaters, and public pools also prevented Jews from entering the
premises.

My middle school situation was still tolerable. In fact, one of my
teachers, Mr. Boedecker, took unusual risks in the classroom to register his distaste for the Nazi ideology. We were required at times
to write short compositions on current events or imaginary happenings. One such occasion was the parade of the first of May, a day
which, though originally dedicated to the workers, the Nazis had
transformed into a fascist holiday. I put in extra effort to excel in my
description of the festivities and parade, and my uncles would at
times stimulate me with helpful suggestions. They were avid readers and had a good command of the German language. When Mr.
Boedecker returned the graded compositions, he admitted his supposed embarrassment that the single Jew in the class had received
the only "1" (equivalent to an "A"). I got the message and appreciated his veiled compliment.

On another occasion, when teaching the obligatory race science
course, he called on various students to rise and illustrate the Aryan race features so admired by the Nazis. After calling on a few of
my classmates to point out the typical blond hair, tall build, and
blue eyes, he surprisingly asked me to rise, the only Jew in the class
and the very antithesis of the so-called Aryan race. Pointing to the
elongated shape of my head, he identified another feature of the
Aryan race.

During another lesson, Mr. Boedecker utilized a vocabulary exercise for his own agenda. The word under discussion was "Undankbarkeit," ingratitude. To convey the concept to the class, he chose a
personal experience as example. He reminded us that his family
used to live in the Lueneburger Heide, a forlorn large moor in northern Germany. His son suddenly took seriously ill with diphtheria
and the boys breathing became dangerously difficult and irregular.
It was night time and no doctor lived in the vicinity. Finally, a Jewish
doctor risked driving a considerable distance over dark and unpaved
roads to reach and save the young patient. "You know of my son," Mr.
Boedecker continued, "he is now a prominent Nationalsozialist (Na-

zi), who despises the Jews although a Jewish doctor once saved his life. That is 'Undankbarkeit.'" But such implications of simultaneous disapproval and empathy were rare and courageous exceptions.

In May of 1937, the German dirigible Hindenburg, after crossing the Atlantic, tragically crashed and fiercely burned while attempting to land in Lakehurst, New Jersey. This news was conveyed to us while we were eating our lunch in the schoolyard by Studienassessor Keitel, but with one additional explanation: the American Jews were responsible for this terrible accident. Suddenly, my fellow students stared at me and the few other Jews of the school. On the way home, a few Nazi ruffians gave me a beating, an event that happened only rarely. When I returned to my mother, with my clothing disheveled and soiled, I did not give her a truthful explanation, claiming instead that I had fallen.

On another occasion, also while spending some time in the schoolyard, I was manhandled by a somewhat older boy named Loesch, who had previously taunted me because of my religion. In this instance, I threw caution to the side and challenged him to a boxing match, although he was somewhat taller and certainly stronger than I. Before I knew it, we were encircled by a dozen or more excited and interested classmates, who formed a ring of spectators, i.e., they did not interfere on his behalf. After some preliminary sparring, I surprised myself by landing a blow on my adversary's nose, which immediately gushed some blood. Loesch walked away from me and I, the small Jewish boy, became the undeclared winner. Boxing was a sport included in our gym activities, in that case with padded gloves, and I was invariably matched up by our Nazi teacher with boys who were much bigger than I. Without exception, I came out on the short end of these timed encounters. And without exception, I never complained about such deliberate harassment of the only Jewish boy in the class.

On the retirement of Lehrer Levi, the congregation engaged a young teacher, Lehrer Faerber, to conduct services and run the religious school. His youth enabled him to relate more effectively to the students of our small group. On Friday afternoons, the Jewish children (about eight) met in our home for singing and Oneg Shabbat under Lehrer Faerber's guidance. In this way, my sister Ellen could also participate.

Through all these years, Ellen's condition of dislocated hips prevented her from going to school. Instead, she received private lessons at home, even when incapacitated by the plaster cast, which encased her hips for months at a time. Where possible, she would accompany us on shorter walks while being pushed in a carriage. She did have one non-Jewish friend, Hildegard, who came at times to play with her in our apartment. In late 1937, the Gestapo summoned her, together with her mother, to the police headquarters for questioning, including whether she had received compensation for playing now and then with my sister. Fortunately, there never was any payment involved, and she confirmed this fact to the interrogating Gestapo official. Had she done otherwise, i.e., distorted the facts, this matter could have turned out terribly for our family because of the Nuremberg racial laws. Thereafter, Hildegard never visited my sister again.

A few months after uncle Lothar was released from Dachau and was able to settle in Palestine, my grandfather's health declined markedly. Similar to the fateful coincidence of his wife's passing on one of her children's (my father's) birthday in 1931, he took his final raspy breaths on my uncle Max's birthday on November 2, 1937. I sat in the room next door and heard the last moments of this good man, with whom I had spent many lovely hours. He could afford to enter the eternal sleep now, having had the privilege of attending earlier in the year his grandson's Bar Mitzvah and the release of his son Lothar from Dachau. He was buried next to my grandmother in Meiningen, but I was not able to attend his funeral because conservative Jewish tradition of that time still precluded my entering the cemetery while both of my parents were living. This was an odd twist, which liberal Judaism has fortunately corrected.

At the end of the 1937–38 school year, I left the Mittelschule to spend more time studying written and conversational English with Carl Plaut. Together with one or two other Jewish children, I commuted by train to Meiningen a few times a week for this purpose. Principal Sparkuhle, an active Nazi, interviewed me to ascertain my reason for this decision. I told him that my family intended to emigrate to the U.S.A. "Oh, so far away," he exclaimed, and then he wished me well. For the subsequent few months, I also took some business courses in a trade school.

In the summer of 1938, my father's youngest brother Max, who had worked in recent years in my father's business, and my mother's sister Claire, who was a nurse in the Jewish hospital in Fuerth near Nuremberg, announced their engagement and imminent wedding date. When this news reached Lothar and Hannah in Palestine (my father's brother and my mother's sister, respectively), they as the "older" siblings took the prerogative to announce their wedding date for a week prior to the Nuremberg wedding. Thus, our family had the unique distinction of three brothers marrying three sisters. For a while I thought, half in jest, that this speaks of a lack of imagination in deciding on a spouse. But upon reflection, it appeared that the very difficult and trying times most likely played a role in these cupid decisions. In any case, all three marriages turned out to be successful unions, although circumstances prevented the two younger couples from producing offsprings. That could have led to some interesting comparisons and potential similarities between double cousins. At that point in time, Max and Claire also initiated efforts towards emigration from Nazi Germany.

After Hitler was able to remilitarize the German Rhineland in early 1936 in complete violation of the treaty of Versailles and without opposition from the international community, he felt free to flex his ever-growing muscles. In that same year, which saw Nazi Germany as host country of the Olympic games, the Nazis also concluded alliance treaties with Italy and Japan. In March of 1938, German troops entered Austria and were received with unbridled enthusiasm by most of the population. This annexation brought an additional 180,000 Jews under Nazi control. After Germany was defeated about a decade later, Austria was falsely identified as the first victim of Nazi aggression, whereas in fact it was the very cradle of Nazism. Most of the Austrian population loved the so-called unification, were an integral part of it, and openly expressed their support for "Greater Germany's" aims and actions, including the immediately instituted abusive treatment of Jews. The pictures of that period speak even louder than the words.

Encouraged by success, Hitler's Germany continued its expansionist efforts, utilizing the three million ethnic Sudeten Germans living in Czechoslovakia as a pretense. Threatening invasion of that country was the impetuous for the infamous Munich conference of the leaders of France, Great Britain, and Italy with the German dictator. For the sake of Chamberlain's delusory "peace in our time" declaration, England and France agreed on September 30, 1938, in spite of being treaty allies of the Czechs, to surrender the strategic border area called Sudetenland. A mere six months later, Germany occupied all of Czechoslovakia. Peace at any price leads to war.

While appeasement was practiced by the two major democratic powers of western Europe and while Germany worked feverishly to escalate its military capabilities, more and more of the German and now also Austrian Jewish population attempted to emigrate to escape the ever-escalating anti-Semitic measures of the Nazi regime. Unfortunately, as the numbers seeking refuge increased, the entry doors of the world stayed barely ajar. Immigration restrictions, instead of being relaxed to respond to the urgent need, were sometimes even escalated in severity. Where were the Jews going to go? In response to this question, a conference on the refugee question, called by President Roosevelt, took place in Evian, France, in July of 1938. For more than a week, the delegates from some thirty countries primarily offered excuses why little or no relief could be implemented to solve the plight of the refugees. Although in part this lack of response may have been based on economic conditions, more often than not there was a reluctance at that time to admit a significant number of Jews in many countries of the world, including the U.S.A. This message was not lost on Germany.

MY LAST YEAR IN GERMANY:
A FRIGHTENING EXPERIENCE

In late summer or early fall of 1938, our family received an invitation from the U.S. consulate to appear in Berlin in December for a visa examination. Sister Ellen was living at the Jewish Children's Home of Bad Duerrheim to provide her with a more sheltered environment during those uncertain times. My father took steps to close out and possibly sell his business. Mother decided which furniture, household goods, and clothing to take along. The massive black oak dining room set had to remain behind, but much of the rest was selected to make the trip across the Atlantic Ocean. We visited Nuremberg to bid farewell to grandmother Regina Frank and aunt Claire. The parting was bittersweet, because it was unlikely that we would ever again see my grandmother, who was 76 years old at that time. In a positive and somewhat optimistic vain, we assumed that our emigration shortly after year's end to be a nearly foregone conclusion. Although we were anxious to leave, we were not panicked by the process.

A new German government regulation effective January 1, 1939, forced all Jews to insert the middle name "Israel" for males and "Sara" for females. Shortly thereafter, passports for Jews required the additional identification of a large rubber-stamped "J." During the 1990s, it came to my attention that the "J" identification was instituted at the request of Swiss authorities, who thus wanted to facilitate the return of Jews attempting to enter Switzerland illegally in order to escape from the Nazis. Here is another instance that demonstrates that until 1940/41 the problem for German and Austrian Jews was not how to get out but where to get in. Although a relatively small number of German Jews received permission to immigrate to Switzerland, Swiss authorities were not sympathetic, to say the least, about admitting many more desperate Jews who were knocking at their entry gates for sanctuary.

*My parents and I bidding a somewhat premature farewell to my maternal
grandmother, Regina Frank, in Nuremberg in the summer of 1938. Next to
grandmother is aunt Claire, and behind her two other nurses from the Jewish
Nurses' Residence*

In early November of 1938, a German consular official in Paris
was killed in a senseless act of desperation by a 17-year-old Jewish
youth named Herschel Grynszpan, whose parents were deported by
Germany with 17,000 others because of their Polish origin, but
whose homeland Poland would not readmit them because of their
religion, thus relegating these unfortunate people to the no-man's
land at the border. We, as Jews living in Nazi Germany, were nervous about the potential consequences of Grynszpan's act.

Our fears were justified, for the event that took place in the
night of November 9–10, 1938 exceeded our wildest and most pessimistic premonitions. "Kristallnacht," as it subsequently became
known because of the Nazi shattering of the windows in Jewish
homes and business establishments, was the end of the beginning
and the beginning of the end of the destruction of German and, as
it developed, European Jewry by the Nazi machine. From 1933 until this point, the German government had instituted policies and
laws to make the country "judenrein" (cleansed of Jews). Although
individual acts of intimidation, arrests, and even murders had tak-
en place, the primary thrust of the German anti-Semitic action dur-

Kristallnacht, November 9/10, 1938. The synagogue of Suhl in flames one year after I became bar mitzvah there. The picture was taken by a non-Jewish resident of Suhl.

ing the first five Nazi years rested on vile propaganda, escalating discrimination, and eliminationist directives. With the advent of Kristallnacht, this initial phase reached its conclusion and we saw the beginning of government-initiated, organized, and implemented terror, the beginning of the end.

Neither my father nor my sister was in Suhl during those early November days. Ellen was spending her time in a home for Jewish

Skeleton remains of the synagogue of Suhl, November 1938

children in south-western Germany, and my father was on a final close-out business trip. Because of the ominous situation, my mother permitted me to sleep in father's bed. The fire sirens started to wail during the night, an unusual event for our small town. When I looked out of the window, someone in the street shouted: "The Jewish church is burning." Turning my head in the direction of the synagogue, which was about a half a mile from our home, I saw the dark sky lit by the reflection of the flames of hate, a Teutonic pyre of our house of worship. This glowing sky appeared as an evil illumination not only of the darkness of this night but of the darkness of the time.

Shortly thereafter, we discerned loud knocking and the alarm-like ringing of our doorbell. Three or four brown- or black-shirted stormtroopers invaded our home in search of my father. I sat up on the bed as my mother explained that he is out of town for business reasons. With that, one of these uniformed Germans asked me, "How old are you?" "Fourteen," I replied as calmly as I could. "We will get you the next time," the Nazi commented before leaving. Little did I comprehend at that intense moment the full implication of the stormtrooper's remark. Within a few years, the Nazis would kill about one-and-one-half million Jewish children as part of Germany's Holocaust activities. The stormtrooper meant what he said!

Quiet returned, an eerie quiet. The flames that consumed our synagogue must have died down, for the night sky became dark again. But neither quiet nor darkness enabled sleep; we had been violated beyond belief. In retrospect, mother and I were still fortunate, for the Nazis had not laid hands on us or on the contents of our apartment. Subsequent reports indicated that numerous other German and Austrian Jews did not fare "this well." Glass was shattered in many places. People were beaten; furnishings, and even sometimes human beings, were tossed out of windows.

Slowly, daylight returned with the dawn of November 10. We heard that all Jewish boys and men between the ages of 16 and 70, including uncle Max, had been arrested by SA and SS troops during the night and transported to Buchenwald concentration camp. Of course, in this emotional upheaval our thoughts and concerns focused immediately on my father. "Where is he? Was he arrested while traveling? Did the Nazis harm him? Is he still alive?" We did not have the slightest idea on that day. My mother was courageous and resolute. I accompanied her to inspect father's business establishment, where nothing had been touched. Then she walked alone to the police station and inquired in the Gestapo offices about my father's whereabouts and fate. They could not or would not give her any information. Mother returned home very upset, and began to sit at a living room window next to our antique desk. She deluded herself in the belief that by sitting there and viewing the street father would somehow appear and return to our midst. And so she sat there in the night of November 10–11, 1938, and I kept her company during these long dark hours. I realized that this effort, though understandable, was useless, but I did not express that thought to her. The next day and the day after, she repeated her Gestapo inquiries and finally was informed that father had indeed been arrested on his journey and transported to Buchenwald. Later, father told us that he was apprehended in his hotel room during the Kristallnacht action. The Nazi stormtroopers checked every room in their search for Jews. When they knocked on his door with the standard question, he replied: "Yes, I am a Jew." They drove him in his own car to nearby Buchenwald. As he stepped out, dressed as a businessman in hat and coat, he was struck on the head with a fist or a blunt instrument with the shouted admonition that he should remove his hat when stepping on "holy ground." Since that time, my father's hearing was impaired.

It appears incongruous that this infamous concentration camp, was located so close to Weimar. This city of culture had been associated in prior times with such famous names of literature, music, art, and philosophy as Johann Sebastian Bach, Johann Wolfgang von Goethe, Johann C. Friedrich von Schiller, Franz Liszt, Walter Gropius, and Martin Luther. Now its vicinity has become a symbol of man's inhumanity to man.

We were relieved to know about father's whereabouts, although it was no great comfort to learn that he was in Buchenwald. At least, and not insignificantly, he was alive and there was hope to eventually see him again.

My thoughts now returned to the synagogue. We found out that most of the synagogues of Germany and Austria had been destroyed by the Nazi authorities. The German government and press tried to depict this as a spontaneous reaction of the population in response to the assassination in Paris. But the simultaneous arson and desecration of most synagogues, the arrest of about 35,000 Jewish men and boys, and the vandalizing of many Jewish homes and business establishments was obviously conducted under the central authority of the German government in Berlin. I could not convince myself to view our destroyed synagogue. At that time, Jews were still permitted to leave their homes during the day in order to shop and visit each other. But I was not able to overcome the emotional obstacle to walk the short distance and cast my eyes on the destroyed house of God where I had celebrated my Bar Mitzvah during the previous year, where now all the Torah scrolls had been burned, my Tallit (prayer shawl) and Tefila (prayer book) likewise. This house, which was dedicated only 32 years prior to this horrible event, where our small congregation met to pray, to learn, to observe life-cycle events, was now all rubble. I strongly believed that Adonai, our God, had been violated there, that the two Tablets of the Law, which Moses had brought down from Mount Sinai, had once again been broken. Everything that stood for human decency seemed to have been desecrated.

We learned from the authorities that concentration camp inmates, for whom proof of impending emigration could be furnished, would receive release priority. Others, whose departure arrangements were still more distant and tenuous, would be detained in the Buchenwald, Dachau, and Oranienburg camps for longer periods.

Rollcall at Buchenwald concentration camp immediately after Kristallnacht. My father Julius is tenth from the right in the first complete row. Photograph taken by Nazi photographer.

My mother provided the Gestapo with a copy of the American consulate's invitation for our family to report for immigration purposes in December, 1938. Thus, after what seemed to be three long weeks, my father was one of the first Kristallnacht prisoners to return to Suhl from Buchenwald. He looked haggard and unkempt, reminding me of uncle Lothar's appearance after he was released from Dachau. His head was shaven like that of a convict and his face was covered by a stubbly beard, quite a contrast to his usually meticulous appearance. But he was alive, our father and husband, and we were infinitely thankful that he was once again in our midst. Uncle Max was released from camp a few weeks later. To the best of my knowledge, all the Jewish boys and men of Suhl arrested during Kristallnacht were eventually discharged from Buchenwald, although some were incarcerated there for as long as three to four months.

About father's experiences in Buchenwald we learned only much later. Prior to his release, he was forced to sign a statement, obligating him not to convey to the outside world any description of the conditions and happenings within the camp. He naturally did not want to take any chance of creating additional dangers for our family, including his possible rearrest by the Nazi authorities. After

Enlarged section of preceding photograph showing my father.

we were safely in the U.S. a year later, we learned some specifics
about the conditions that father endured in Buchenwald, such as
the by now well-known overcrowded barracks, with their unheated
multi-layered bunks, the endless standing at roll calls and the fear
of collapsing, with its dire consequences; the slop served as soup
and the resulting diarrhea; the large open latrines, where loss of
balance on the crossing beams meant almost certain death; and the
thirst that could only be quenched by catching rain water off the
roof. Once, my father nearly fainted because of diarrhea and started
to shout irrationally. Fortunately, my uncle Max was near him, covered his mouth, and somehow brought him back to his senses. Otherwise, father's life would have been in grave danger.

Immediately after Kristallnacht, all Jewish business establishments (about a dozen in Suhl) were ordered to be closed or disposed
of (Aryanized) by January 1, 1939. Jewish children were no longer
permitted to attend public school. Furthermore, a directive was issued making the entire Jewish community responsible for all material damage incurred during the Kristallnacht action. Jews were
precluded from collecting compensation for the private property
losses sustained by individual families or by business establishments. About 7,000 commercial Jewish establishments were de-

stroyed and looted. The rubble of hundreds of destroyed German and Austrian synagogues and prayer halls had to be cleared at the expense of the Jewish community; a fine of one billion Reichsmark (about $400 million) was imposed collectively on the Jewish community by the German Nazi government. The effect of these measures was not pragmatically significant for my family. My father's business had to close or be sold anyhow in view of the planned emigration, I already had left public school to focus primarily on English language skills, and the monetary requisitions of the German government were academic for emigrants, who were, in any case, permitted to leave with only $10.

Prior to our scheduled appearance at the American consulate, Ellen returned in the company of a family member from Bad Duerrheim. In expectation of receiving our U.S. visas, my parents prepared to ship our belongings, such as furniture, household goods, china, kitchen equipment, photo albums, books, ritual objects, part of our clothing, and even my bicycle in a huge wooden container called a "lift" (the size of a medium-sized truck). The packing was accomplished by specialists under the scrutiny of customs personnel. Currency and jewelry were not permitted to be exported.

Finally, the big day arrived when the four of us reported at the American consulate in Berlin. The affidavits had been on file for well over a year, the necessary applications and passports were all in order, and we were confident that we would pass the final formalities. The American consul entered the room in which we were waiting, looked us over, and said after a brief period while pointing to my sister: "Das ist doch ein Krueppel" in absolutely perfect German ("That is, after all, a cripple"). My sister could walk but was handicapped with a noticeable limp because of the dislocated hips. After my sister and I left the room at the consul's request, he informed my parents that we as a family would not receive permission to enter the United States because of my sister's physical condition. Merely a month after the infamous Kristallnacht and only two weeks after my father's release from the Buchenwald concentration camp, this State Department official then proceeded to propose two alternatives to my shocked parents: either the whole family would have to remain in Germany or my father could receive the necessary entry visa while leaving his wife and his two children behind in Nazi land. A classical Hobson's choice indeed, to take that which is offered or nothing at all.

My parents had to decide almost immediately, and they made a judicious choice while under considerable duress and pressure. My father was to leave for the land of freedom and opportunity, leaving his family behind in the land of fanaticism and oppression. At least one life could thus be secured. Furthermore, the possibility existed that father, with his substantial leather expertise, just might find a small job that could serve as basis for the most effective of all affidavits, that of the husband and the father of the potential immigrants. Maybe via this scenario, which was not arrived at with 20:20 hindsight, we still hoped some day, somehow to escape from the Nazi onslaught and be reunited as a family in the safety of the U.S.A.

The American State Department at that time was not enamored with the immigration of substantial numbers of Jewish refugees. In the first place, in the aftermath of the serious depression that began with the 1929 stock market collapse, any immigration was viewed as undesirable because of the prevailing high unemployment rate. Secondly, and possibly even of greater weight, was the anti-Semitic attitude of a not insignificant number of State Department officials.

That was already most noticeable at the previously referred to conference on refugees in Evian in July 1938. There, all eyes were on the American example; the U.S.A. was the original sponsor of the conference. What should be done about the German and Austrian Jewish refugees? The State Department representative announced that the yearly German immigration quota would be raised from about 27,000 to 28,000, a pitiful 3.7% adjustment while hundreds of thousands of Jews desperately tried to escape from the Nazi tyranny. Many years later, I learned that in late 1938, the time of our visit to Berlin, about 220,000 applications for visas to America were on file at the U.S. consulates in Germany, and even at that, only two-thirds of the quota was filled during that year!

It is of utmost importance to emphasize here that, until 1941, most Jews had no problem receiving emigration authorization from the German Nazi government. The overwhelming difficulty faced by these refugees consisted of receiving an entry permit from one of the countries of the world outside the Nazi sphere. The Germans were desirous of eliminating the Jewish presence within their borders and thus encouraged emigration by ever-escalating anti-Semitic measures. In most cases, the German exit doors were open to the Jews, but the entry doors of the world to receive them were more often than not barely ajar.

Many years later, I read a book by David S. Wyman with the title *The Abandonment of the Jews*, which details the insensitivity, obstinacy, and outright prejudice of our State Department during that trying time. So as not to be misunderstood, I consider myself a most fortunate individual, who still found refuge on these blessed shores in spite of the policies and practices described in Professor Wyman's book and which I experienced first hand. I will be forever grateful to my adopted country, my homeland of the U.S.A., for rescuing me from almost certain annihilation by the country of my birth.

After returning from Berlin, we dissolved our apartment, Ellen returned to Bad Duerrheim, and my parents and I found living quarters with local friends, Lilly Goldmann, son Werner, and her mother Flora Sander. Husband Siegfried Goldmann was able to obtain British immigration permission and departed early in 1939. These good people were most accommodating and hospitable, especially in view of the fact that I was stricken with scarlet fever shortly after moving in. We were permitted to stay with them while my mother played nursemaid. Towards the end of January 1939, my father departed (with his personal belongings and the allowable $10 cash) via the Hamburg-America Line for the U.S. Parting must have been difficult, but I cannot recall this emotional moment. My greatest pleasure during these six weeks of confinement was the receipt of mail from father. He diligently shared his travel experiences and first impressions of New York with us. In our correspondence, we had carefully refrained from making any comments that could possibly be interpreted as critical of the German Nazi regime; all mail from and to foreign countries was regularly opened and censored.

Shortly after his arrival on February 7, father was able to find a job with a wholesale leather firm in Manhattan. He had to sort and grade all kinds of leather as received from the tannery and then prepare it for shipment to the customers of Loewengart & Co. This business had been founded a few years previously by German Jewish refugees. Earning $15 per week, father took immediate steps to secure an affidavit for his family and submit it to the immigration authorities within three weeks of his arrival. This was good news for us, but we had no idea how long it would require for the State Department to process this additional guarantee. To preclude possible future problems, father arranged for our lift, stored at the port of Hamburg, to be shipped to New York; he had to borrow the money to pay for the U.S. storage charges.

Father wrote to us about the fascinating New York skyline, the hustle and bustle of the city and harbor, the rumbling and crowded subways, his contacts with friends and relatives, and even his dining experiences in the Automat. The latter, not in use any more, provided in a cafeteria setting various kinds of food from small locked compartments, whose glass doors could be opened upon insertion of a specified amount of change. He observed that "native" Americans could generally be identified by the habit of generously salting their food without first tasting it.

During my lengthy illness, I did considerable reading including the book *Vom Winde verweht*, the translation of *Gone with the Wind*. After six weeks, I was permitted to leave my sickbed for brief periods of time and found that the walking skill had to be relearned. Sandwiched between two persons, I remember practicing in the Goldmanns' living room. In the meantime, our U.S. relatives had made additional efforts to obtain supplementary affidavits for us, their stranded relatives in Germany. Thus, we were informed that a Carl Laemmle, a cousin of my maternal grandmother and the director of Hollywood's Universal Studios, had deposited in escrow a sum of $1 million with a Swiss bank to serve as security for affidavits, which he had rendered for me and a few other German Jewish relatives and acquaintances.

By the end of March, Jews were forced to "sell" to the Nazi authorities all objects made of gold, silver, precious stones, and pearls. The sale was, of course, a sham and represented a requisition. My mother, sister, and I had, by that time, no such articles in our possession, but we were the exception with respect to all the Jews then still residing in Suhl. During the spring and summer of 1939, the Jews of Suhl lived in isolation and fear; our possession and use of radios was no longer permitted. We did not leave the house unless really necessary, such as shopping between the permitted time of 9 and 10 am at two designated stores.

In May, I received an invitation from the U.S. consulate in Berlin to appear there in June for another visa examination, a response to the submitted Laemmle affidavit. I traveled there alone by train and was once again denied the visa, this time ostensibly because father's affidavit had not been processed as yet.

Many years later, I became aware that Carl Laemmle, who was the producer of "All quiet on the Western Front", had committed himself to hundreds of affidavits for German Jews during this period. Although well known and of considerable means, he ran into great difficulty with our State Department to receive the essential US visa authorization for these people. In his efforts to extract these threatened Jews from the Nazi's clutches, Laemmle corresponded not only with the American Consul General in Stuttgart, Germany, but also with our then Secretary of State Cordell Hull. Quoting from an April 1938 letter(National Archives) in answer to objections about his age and the many affidavits he had issued:

"The Consul General takes the position that I am past 71 years of age and I might not live much longer. But I, on the other hand, claim that if my guarantee is legal, it should be good as far as my heirs are concerned and if it isn't, then my affidavits should be drawn in such form that it make it binding on my heirs. I know that my children are very willing to assume these obligations.

It is true that I have given a great number of affidavits to people who are related to me; also to life-long friends and in a few instances, to strangers. I feel it is the solemn duty of every Jew in America who can afford it, to go to the very limit for these poor unfortunates in Germany. My heart goes out to them and I have never in all my life been so sympathetic to any cause as I am to these poor innocent people who are suffering untold agony without having done any wrong whatsoever.

It seems to me, Secretary Hull, that my efforts should be appreciated even by your Consul General because, after all, he is a human being just as you and I and he is so close to the situation on the other side that he must know what is going on and he should cooperate in every possible way and give a man like myself the benefit of the doubt if it is compatible with his position.

I don't have to tell you of my standing in the United States. I'm quite sure you know my record and you can be equally sure that when I sign an affidavit, I mean to live up to every word in the affidavit as expressed by me."

Although Laemmle was apparently pleading on his knees for understanding and cooperation of the American authorities, his efforts often came to naught due to the deliberate obstinacy of the US State Department, as was true in my case.

My reaction to this turndown was quite ambivalent. In view of the deteriorating circumstances for Jews in Germany, immediate emigration would have been welcome. But the thought of leaving my mother and sister behind was most disturbing and distressing. Fortunately, I was not confronted with this decision and, in a way, was relieved to be able to share my mother's and my sister's fate instead.

In August, the three of us received the hoped-for notice to report to the consulate on September 12. In preparation, uncle Max picked up Ellen from Duerrheim, and things seemed to be falling in place towards our exit for the U.S.A.

Although the German government was forever stirring the pot of aggressive intentions towards its neighboring countries, we were nevertheless shocked to wake up to hear about the invasion of Poland on September 1, 1939. As the consequence of treaty obligations for common defense, Great Britain and France entered the hostilities on Poland's side and World War II officially began. Appeasement of the aggressive Nazi machine had proven to be an abject failure and a monumental disservice to the human family. Our first reaction to these momentous events was one of utter dejection and the belief that emigration to the U.S. is no longer possible, that we were doomed to remain in Nazi Germany. From our perspective, the future looked bleak indeed.

On or about September 6, we were thus surprised and encouraged by the arrival of a telegram from the Berlin U.S. consulate, confirming that we should appear as scheduled on September 12. This made more sense than our initial reaction, because the U.S. was still "neutral" at that time and continued to maintain diplomatic relations with Germany. Consequently, on my third attempt and my mother's and sister's second, we were granted our U.S. entry visas. Miraculously, my father, with his $15 a week New York job, had been able to achieve what well to do friends and concerned family members were not: to satisfy the American immigration authorities. My Quota Visa No. 5574 was a most precious possession, even more than I realized at the time, it was my passport to life.

The war precluded our travel out of Hamburg on a German ship as father had done, and we thus could not pay for the passage with German currency. Our family had no U.S. funds at its disposal and was precluded by the German authorities from transferring any funds abroad. My father borrowed the money for the tickets from friends or relatives and succeeded in booking passage on the SS Statendam of the Holland-America Line, scheduled to depart from Rotterdam during the last week of November.

Shortly after our return from Berlin, Jews were ordered to consolidate into a few residences called Jew-houses. The three of us were assigned a small room in the Brylewski house; it was a large villa with a garden. For many years, the Brylewskis had run a high quality knit-clothing store until Jews were forbidden to operate business establishments; the store was requisitioned by the township authorities. Aron Brylewski had been a prominent member of the synagogue board of trustees and had ably assisted in conducting the High Holiday services. Uncle Max and a Mannheimer family (two brothers with wives) were also assigned to live in that building.

In addition, the Brylewskis' married daughter, Friedel Spangenthal, with family, including two young boys, from Eisenach were staying there too; they hoped to emigrate to Canada. In total, 13 Jews were sheltered in this home. My photo album of the thirties contains two pictures of Ernst-Jochem, the younger one of those two grandchildren, pictures that I have viewed over and over again for many years. "Maybe that precious reddish blond four year old survived the Shoah," I thought, as I repeatedly stared at his picture. This dream came to an end. Based on the 1946 archival records of Suhl, referred to in the 1995 book *Juden in Suhl* by Nothnagel and Daehn, Friedel Spangenthal and her two children were deported in 1942 to the Belzec extermination camp; the husband and father of this little family was murdered in a concentration camp.

The onset of the war brought with it strictly enforced blackout regulations and more severe food rationing. For Jews, it was particularly important to guard against any ray of light emanating from our house at night, for this could be interpreted as an attempt of sabotage and lead to dire consequences. Except for the few Jewish hospitals located in distant larger cities, Jews had no further access to such a facility. Our radios and telephones had to be surrendered to the Nazi authorities. Food rations for Jews were especially meager; it must be remembered that Jews had lost their German citizenship in 1935. For us Jews, many normal food staples such as meat and eggs were hardly ever part of our menu; we were frequently hungry but not starving; somehow, however, we managed. I recall a Christian man who at night climbed the backyard fences several times to bring us food. I never knew his name, but I will always remember and appreciate his human decency and great courage.

During the night of November 9–10, the doorbell of the villa rang with great urgency. My mother answered and was confronted by four or five Nazi stormtroopers who demanded that Mr. Brylewski step outside. This man, who was in his sixties, complied and was

My sister Ellen and Ernst-Jochem Spangenthal, age four, a grandson of the Brylewskis in whose "Jew-house" the three Muhlfelders lived in 1939 during the last months before emigrating from Nazi Germany. In 1942, the little boy and his older brother became part of the 1.5 million Jewish chidren murdered by Germany. His parents and maternal grandparents also perished.

immediately beaten unmercifully. My mother called through the open door: "Leave the man alone." In answer, a rock smashed through a glass side panel as the troopers approached, and mother slammed the door shut. For at least the next half hour, but to us it seemed much longer, we listened to the pitiful, desperate, and agonizing cries of pain and terror while Mr. Brylewski was being brutally beaten by the Nazis in the adjoining garden. He sounded like a wounded animal in excruciating pain. I will never forget it. Those piercing sounds must also have entered the ears of our Christian neighbors, but they remained silent bystanders. Eventually, quiet returned. Mr. Brylewski could not be located on the grounds; my uncle Max was also missing. Next morning, we were informed that both were in jail at the local police station. While hearing the attack on Mr. Brylewski, uncle Max thought that he might be the next victim and fled over the backyard fence. In the process he was caught and also attacked, but not as severely. Both men were released during that day and returned to the house. Mr. Brylewski had been mercilessly beaten into a pulp and was seriously injured. The Nazis had celebrated their first anniversary of Kristallnacht. Except for my own family, all the occupants of the Brylewski house were exterminated by the Germans within less than three years of this event.

A few days later, all Jewish males over a wide age span (I was only 15 then) were ordered to register to work as slave laborers in road gangs. With trepidation, we reported to the local employment office at the market square, furnishing the requested information to the German authorities. "A few more days," I thought, "and then I will be gone"; however, I did not share this thought with the Nazi officials. Shortly after our departure from Suhl, the Jewish men and boys, including my uncle Max, were called on to perform heavy physical labor in the repair or construction of local roads under harsh winter conditions.

THE TRIP TO AMERICA

November 21, 1939, the day of departure for our trip to the United States, had arrived. Our few suitcases with personal belongings had been packed and may have already been transported to the train station the day prior. Mother was permitted to take along the official $10 allowance; all other funds had to remain in Germany and were transferred to my grandmother in Nuremberg. Eventually, these resources ended up with the German Nazi authorities. We bade farewell to each of the residents of the Brylewskis' house; those were difficult and emotional moments. I recall being ushered into Mr. Brylewski's room where I saw what appeared to be a heavily bandaged mummy. I shook a hand extended to me and heard his voice saying weakly: "Ich wuensche Dir alles Gute" ("I wish you all the best"). Upon exiting the room, I was fortunately distracted by other matters of our departing from the villa and its occupants. Uncle Max accompanied us on the walk to the train station. The shortest path led past the ruins of the synagogue, the first and last time that I viewed this sad and terrible sight. I had to steel myself to do so, for I felt that it was improper to look at these remains. I believed I had committed a sin. Without incident, we boarded the train, waved goodbye to uncle Max, and, miraculously, we were on our way. Although we harbored great concern for the Jews we left behind, little did we know or even imagine in our wildest nightmares that most of those would be murdered by the German Nazis less than three years hence.

Quoting in translation from the first page of my diary: "We just departed from Suhl. We had to leave behind dear, good uncle Max, in Nuremberg the dear grandmother and aunt Claire, and the many, many other good people. Although we are glad to be going to America, our hearts are aching that we are not able to take along all these good people. Hopefully, they will soon be able to begin their own journey, which we have now begun, especially dear uncle Max, aunt Claire and grandmother."

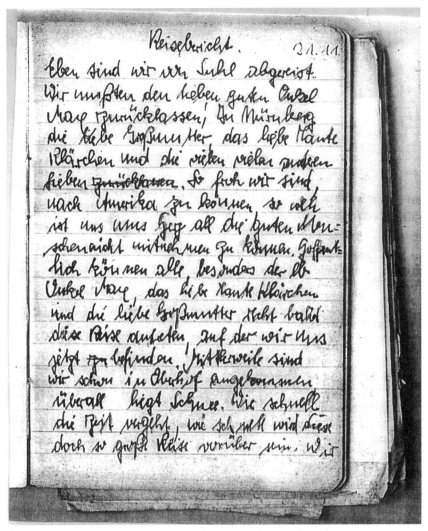

First page of my diary of the trip to the United States (Nov. 21, 1939).

At the time of our departure, about fifty Jews were still remaining in Suhl and its immediate vicinity. Except for 1) my uncle Max and possibly one or two others who were still able to emigrate subsequently, 2) Lehrer Levi and Daniel Meyer, who died of natural causes prior to the first deportation in May 1942, 3) one man (Isaac Nussbaum) who, according to the Gestapo records, committed suicide just before being deported, 4) one man (Hugo Rehbock) whose wife was not Jewish and thus miraculously was spared, and 5) one

ID page of my passport. The picture shows me as a fourteen year old.

woman (Selma Friedmann) who survived the concentration camp, the remaining 43 men, women, and children between the ages of 6 and 76 years were deported to extermination camps, most to Belzec near Lublin in Poland and the rest to Theresienstadt (Terezin), Czechoslovakia, the way-station to Auschwitz. There they became part of the Six Million who were murdered during the Holocaust because they had been born as Jews (Nothnagel and Daehn).

We stopped over in Erfurt (the first large city north of Suhl) for a few hours with friends and departed from there early on the 22nd for Duisburg and then the Dutch border. At 2:45 pm on that day, we entered Holland from Emmrich to Zevennar and reached Rotterdam at about 5 pm. The border crossing may have been tense in our minds but uneventful in actuality. After detraining with our luggage for what seemed like a perfunctory check, we boarded a Dutch train and were pleased to see Dutch train personnel. We just could not yet grasp that we were already in Holland; mother warned us to be careful, for she suspected Gestapo agents to be on board the Dutch train.

While in Rotterdam, we were hosted with great care and generosity by the local Jewish refugee-relief organization. I have often reflected what might have happened to all these fine people who assisted us with such dedication and kindness. Post-Holocaust statistics show that more than three quarters of the Netherlands' Jewish population was exterminated by the German Nazis.

During our first meal (sausage and potato salad) in back of Salomon's butcher shop, we met Family Meinhardt from Nuremberg, who were good acquaintances of my aunt Claire. Little did their son Al and I know that this meeting would lead to a life-long friendship between us (his name was Albrecht, later changed to Albert). Al and I performed an errand at the train station on the 23rd and felt we were in the middle of a great adventure – and we were indeed. After repeated gastronomic pleasures at the butcher shop (I guess I was a bit starved), we took a street car to the pier and boarded the brightly lit Statendam of the Holland-America Line at 7 pm. My diary indicates, that the "cabin is little, but that is not important."

At 5 am on the 24th, the ship lifted anchor, and we were on our way to cross the Atlantic. Mother, Ellen, and I shared our tiny cabin, with little heat and access to a community washroom. During the first night, we

First page of my passport. The middle name Israel was mandatory for Jewish males (Sara for females). "J" was added at the request of the Swiss authorities to identify Jews and and prevent them from fleeing across the border.

opted to sleep in our clothing. But all that did not matter; we were out of Germany and on our way to America. Based on my diary, I was overwhelmed by the quality and quantity of the meals – quite a contrast to the rations in Suhl. Very, very slowly we crossed the heavily mined English channel; our safe path was marked either by buoys or by small, anchored ships. We had to wear our lifebelt at all times and were drilled on how to reach our lifeboat station in case of disaster. In the afternoon, we reached the British coast, where we anchored in the vicinity of many other ships. After almost two days, we left this area on the morning of November 26. Mother rented two deck chairs at $1 each, thus reducing our cash reserves to $8. When the ocean was well behaved, I had fun eating, exploring the boat with other young people including Al, playing ping pong, and even getting kicked out of the first-class area. But such fun was frequently not the case for me. A good part of the trip, particularly during

Passport to life: Lu's US immigration visa

My passport to life: the United States immigration visa for which I had waited well over two years.

the Atlantic crossing, I was seasick and spent my time stretched out in misery on one of the deck chairs.

In the afternoon of November 26, we reached the harbor of Southampton, after passing through the submarine gate, a series of chains used as protection against German submarine intrusions. While the ship lay at anchor, about 300 additional people came on board, increasing the total number (passengers and crew) to about 1,500. In the afternoon of the next day, we departed English waters. According to my diary: "The pilot was picked up by a small motorboat. He waved to us once more, and then it was goodbye Europe, which we do not want to see again." The crossing of the Atlantic was uneventful; I was indisposed more often than I care to remember. On December 2, the Sabbath before our U.S. arrival, I attended an overcrowded service in the tourist lounge. We even had a Torah scroll at our disposal. Dr. Kober, a rabbi from Cologne, urged us in his sermon to thank God for having rescued us and, once settled in our new homeland, to do our utmost for the liberation of those left behind.

Word had it that we were supposed to be able to see the coast of America at about 5 am on December 5. I was on deck at that time and saw a series of lights: Long Island. An hour later, we were in the midst of a multitude of other passenger ships, freighters, coast guard boats, tow boats, and fireboats. Suddenly, someone shouted, "Da sind die Wolkenkratzer!" ("There are the skyscrapers!"). As I noted in my diary:

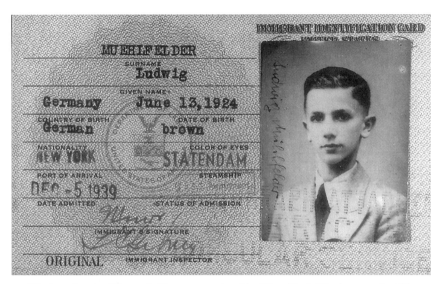

My immigrant ID card. Note we arrived in New York Harbor on the SS Statendam on December 5, 1939.

"And really, through the fog we could recognize the tall fellows of Manhattan, and, shortly after, on the left side, the Statue of Liberty: "Yes, to be free, that's what we want to be. . . On the deck, many people gathered, and several waved small American flags; all were in a mood of happiness and deliverance."

We docked in Hoboken and disembarked, setting foot on U.S. soil for the first time. After an initial search on a huge pier, where mother and I walked in opposite directions to locate our reception committee while we left Ellen with the luggage, "Then, quite suddenly, our dear father stood in front of us. This reunion I am not able to describe. Whoever reads this report should be able to imagine our mood. Like a gift, we regained our father and our freedom. This day I shall never forget as long as I live." Besides father, there were a number of relatives and friends to greet us: aunt Hedwig, uncle Lew Levi, Curt Sander (from Suhl), and uncle Ignaz Eckstein. Via the Pulaski skyway, uncle Lew drove us in his step-down Hudson, very impressive for a fifteen-year-old boy, to Newark and aunt Paula (1054 Hunterdon Street, Weequahic section). "We are glad, that God protected us during this dangerous journey and led us into this free America and to our dear father. We pray that grandmother, uncle Max, and aunt Claire and all the others will still be able to come real soon. This is our greatest worry, otherwise we are very happy."

TO LIVE AGAIN:

A NEW BEGINNING IN THE UNITED STATES

Aunt Paula's rented home was located on a rather quiet residential street of one- and two-family homes. This most southern part of Newark, New Jersey, was known as the Weequahic section in recognition of an Indian tribe of yester-years. With its little gardens, tree-lined streets, and well-maintained homes, it displayed a suburban characteristic and had a substantial Jewish population. One short block from our new residence, the main street of the section, Bergen Street, was the site of a multitude of small owner-operated business establishments. Immediately after my arrival, I demonstrated with some youthful pride my command of the English language. Consequently, Paula sent me to a nearby delicatessen store, Tabatchnick's, to purchase a few items. As I gave the clerk my order, a few other customers, elderly ladies from my perspective, overheard the transaction and inquired with a somewhat Yiddish inflection whether I was an English refugee. Apparently, the British pronunciation I had acquired during my studies with Carl Plaut masked my German language origin. After I corrected their misconception, one of the women asked how long I have been in the country. "I arrived today," was my quick reply. With that, the ladies gasped in utter amazement and touched me to confirm that this was reality. It was a confidence-building experience and contributed to my rapid American acclimatization.

On the morning of December 6, 1939, I woke up in aunt Paula's attic and had to rub my eyes a few times to make sure that all this was real: we were out of the Nazis' clutches and now lived in the U.S.A., where no stormtroopers were knocking on our door during the night, no swastika flags decorated streets, houses, and public buildings, no restrictions existed when we could leave the house during the day and where we were allowed to purchase our staples, no signs were on the doors of restaurants, stores, and sports facilities forbidding Jews to enter, and where nothing prevented me from attending public schools although I was Jewish. Absolutely amazing to a 15-year-old, who had experienced Germany's first Kristallnacht anniversary barely one month before.

The attic was my voluntary abode because of crowded conditions on the floor below. I loved the privacy that it offered and, with some help from Paula and mother turned it into comfortable quarters within a few days.

Paula was engaged in a home based knitting business. She sold the wool to her customers and then guided them through the intricacies and obstacles of the knitting process. She enjoyed this activity, which represented the amalgamation of a social setting and a business venture. Years before, Paula and Lew had lived in considerable comfort if not luxury. But Lew's connection with the movie distribution business deteriorated while the acquired upper class living style did not. Thus, earning a living became a necessity for Paula, particularly since Lew's presence and support dwindled to little more than unfulfilled hopes and promises. At this time, they still maintained a semblance of a personal relationship, but it was obviously on a slippery downward slope, heading for separate and divergent life paths.

My parents helped cover the expenses of the combined household. During these first few months after our arrival, Paula was very helpful in assisting us in adjusting to our new environment. Nevertheless, all of us, and particularly mother yearned to have our own home once again. Father happily announced that Loewengart granted him a raise in his weekly salary from $15 to $18, and mother supplemented this by $3 to $4 by working part-time as a domestic helper, a cleaning lady. That represented quite a switch for this woman, who for many years had enjoyed the assistance of a live-in maid. For that matter, my father's status had also changed drastically from an employer to that of a modestly compensated employee. After having lived in New York City for the first 10 months subsequent to his immigration, he now had to commute to his workplace on Gold Street in downtown Manhattan for about an hour, starting by bus to the train station, then by Hudson tubes, and finally by foot. All this, however, was of minor importance when compared to the freedom and security that we enjoyed in our new homeland.

Now and then, Al Meinhardt visited us. At first, his family lived in New York City, but after a month or two his father was able to obtain a job as orderly in Newark's Beth Israel hospital, which was located a short walk from Paula's residence. I had not as yet established any contacts with people of my age, and so it was especially good to see my friend with whom I had shared a most historic voyage. In mid 1940, the Meinhardts also moved to Newark, a decision welcomed by both Al and me.

Within just a few days after stepping on U.S. soil, Ellen and I applied to be enrolled at the nearby Maple Avenue school, a kindergarten to eighth grade institution. Ellen was accepted and I was instructed to attend the Weequahic High Annex (ninth grade) on Hawthorne Avenue, where I started my U.S. education as a freshman in mid-December. We occupied the top floor of a grammar school building. My English was adequate, and I had an easy time in subjects such as algebra and science. For some reason, I had also opted to register for a course in ancient (Greek) history, where the language tended to be more complex and convoluted. Not only was the subject matter of little interest, but my ability to keep pace with the lessons was fading rapidly. The only saving grace was the very attractive teacher, a young lady who had just recently completed her pedagogic training. I consoled myself with the thought that the semester would conclude at the end of January and in the meantime enjoyed the view of the pretty teacher. I failed this course but did very well in all other subjects. During the subsequent spring semester, I became better acquainted with some of my classmates and made satisfactory progress in all of my studies. Al Meinhardt suggested that I should arrange for some placement examinations prior to the fall semester in order to skip some grades. After all, quite a few of the subjects taught during the first two high school years were similar in content to my prior German Middle school education.

The students were all pleasant and inclusive in their approach. When they invited me to watch and later participate in a game of football on the school grounds, I was at first under the misapprehension that they were referring to soccer, "Fussball" in German. Being "very observant," I quickly realized that they were referring to a different game as soon as I saw the egg-shaped ball. It was a friendly touch football encounter to minimize the chance of injury. Eventually, I joined in my first huddle and was selected, as an element of surprise, to be the prime receiver on the next play. I speedily ran in the direction of the fence, somehow managed to catch the ball and continued onward. I noticed a few big fellows touching me but in ignorance paid no heed. By the rules, I should, of course, have stopped my forward advance. Suddenly, I was thrown to the ground and ended up under a pile of crushing humanity. I feared that every bone of my fragile anatomy might be broken, but I was OK. However, I never engaged in this sport again.

Once, while I was walking to school on Hawthorne Avenue, a particularly densely Jewish populated area, a man addressed me while standing in front of a store on the sidewalk. I indicated that I had difficulty understanding his comment, which was neither in English nor in German, whereupon he asked: "Tust a reden Yiddish?" ("Do you speak Yiddish?"). My denial of that ability was promptly followed by another question; "Bist du a Yid?" ("Are you a Jew?"). I was utterly stunned; here I was, a refugee from Nazi Germany, only two months after escaping from that hell, and this man questions my Jewishness! I understood his problem, for Eastern European Jews across the board were fluent in the Yiddish language, whereas in Germany and Western Europe that was usually not the case.

Now and then, I attended services at the nearby Young Israel Synagogue, which occupied a second floor above a drug store. Services were conducted in accordance with the Orthodox ritual. Although it was somewhat different in nature than the liberal conservative approach with which I grew up in Suhl, I felt comfortable there. Most of the congregants were Eastern European Jews or their first generation descendants. These were warm and welcoming human beings, and I was glad that I had the opportunity to become acquainted with them and to pray in their midst. On Sabbath, between the usual Mincha (afternoon) and Maariv (evening) service, refreshments were served. That is where and when I became fond of the delightful and delicious combination of schnapps and herring. I attended religiously and was duly rewarded. To this day, I miss this custom in my own synagogue in Livingston and would gladly trade it for the tea and cookies at the Oneg after Friday evening services. No such luck!

Nearby, we had the lovely Weequahic Park at our disposal. It was a large and easily accessible natural resource for the residents of the area, particularly appreciated by people of limited means such as us. It offered considerable variety of recreation; in addition to inviting walking paths and expansive play areas, there were sports facilities, a lake for row boating, and even a trotter race track. At times, our relatives visited us and, when Lew was home on weekends (not always the case), we rode in his Hudson to see the Ronbergs in Connecticut and the Max Franks in Leonia, New Jersey. Via bus, train, and subway, we also dropped in on the Herrmanns, who lived near the George Washington Bridge on Manhattan's west side. That section contained so many German Jewish refugees that it was dubbed "Vierte Reich" ("Fourth Reich") in distinction to Nazi Germany's so called "Third Reich." Uncle Max Frank, my mother's brother and guarantor of our first immigration affidavit, worked as an engineer for Colgate-Palmolive and in my mind was an occupational inspiration, a professional example possibly to be emulated. He had immigrated to the U.S. in the twenties and, while working during the day, had attended night college for eight years to attain his B.S. degree.

In the spring of 1940, we rented our first U.S. apartment on the second floor of a three-story house at 119 Custer Avenue, a few blocks from Paula's residence. Nearly one and a half years after packing our lift in Suhl, we were reunited with our earthly possessions. It was a special day when we finally saw again all these familiar and sentimental things: furniture, household goods, books, ritual objects, photo albums, pictures, my bicycle, and so much more. It was a happy feeling, and we again realized how privileged we were. For the $30 monthly rent, we occupied a living and dining room, kitchen, two bedrooms, and an alcove. We even had a small veranda. Except for the living room, all rooms were relatively small. I slept on the couch in the living room, and Ellen slept in the alcove. The second bedroom was sublet to a bachelor, also a refugee from Germany, thus generating a little income to pay part of the rent. My parents were still working off the loan for our passage from Holland. Particularly on Shabbat and holidays, we were especially conscious of our good fortune to be able to live in this land of the free, to be once again united in our own home, and to celebrate these special days with love for each other and with gratitude to God. In our thoughts and discussions, we were frequently occupied with those still left behind in Germany, especially our close relatives. My parents and other members of the family tried diligently and urgently to speed up their emigration.

On April 9, 1940, Germany attacked neutral Denmark and Norway and quickly occupied both countries. Only a month later, on May 10, the German aggression machine overran neutral Holland, Belgium, and Luxembourg. By June 22, France capitulated to Germany, and thus more and more of the European continent, and with it its Jews, fell under Nazi Germany's oppressive occupation. In the early autumn of 1940, Germany concluded a three-power agreement with its Axis partner Italy and the Japanese Empire. By November, Romania, Slovakia, and Hungary joined this alliance as well.

With the beginning of the outdoor season and my 16th year, I obtained my first job — in a refreshment stand at the periphery of Weequahic Park. The owners, named Greenebaum, were also German Jewish refugees. They were a hard-working young couple who were expecting their first child. We primarily dispensed hot dogs, soda, and ice cream. Earning five cents per hour, I became an expert in preparing hot dogs with the works, i.e., sauerkraut, mustard, pickle and anything else that might come to mind. When I was asked to serve the order to customers who were waiting in their car in the adjoining parking lot, I would receive a five-cent tip on lucky days. I recall that on Labor Day I was still working at two o'clock in the morning when my father appeared, being quite worried about my whereabouts and well-being. It was a bit embarrassing, but I fully understood and simultaneously empathized with this parental concern.

During the summer, I prepared for a number of placement exams in English, German, algebra, and geometry in order to catch up with the students of my age group. Everything went well, and I qualified to skip the sophomore and enter the junior year in the fall of 1940. I was puzzled and amused that my exam for German rated a "B" while that for English earned an "A." Maybe my extra effort to become proficient in English paid off, whereas my innate native acquisition of the German language did not fully measure up to American foreign language expectations. The main high school building was a new and modern structure, only a few years old at that time. The teaching staff was excellent and the courses were interesting and challenging. I was thrilled to be there and enrolled in courses such as history, literature, social studies, trigonometry, biology, physics, and chemistry. Frequently, I used my Bar Mitzvah bicycle to commute to school and sometimes had my friend Al as passenger. After completing his first academic year in New York, Al Meinhardt had also enrolled at Weequahic High. Once, one of my female classmates asked me in a hallway of the school if I could do her a favor. Upon inquiring what I could possibly do, she replied: "Never lose your accent." "Don't vorrrrry!" I exclaimed in amusement, rolling my German "r" with particular emphasis. Immigrants who are 15 years or older such as I was when entering the U.S. have a difficult time shedding the accent associated with their mother tongue.

So it was easy to comply with this request for the rest of my life. I found my classmates and people in general most accommodating to my newcomer status, also known by the greenhorn designation. The U.S.A. is a country of immigrants and their descendants and therefore does not generally harbor an ingrained xenophobic prejudice.

With the end of the warmer outdoor season arrived the termination of my hot dog job. During the 1941–42 years, I worked during after-school hours in a variety of business establishments in order to supplement our family's very limited income. There was Green's 5&10 store on Bergen Street, where I functioned as a stock clerk to replenish the counters at ten cents per hour. Later, I became a soda jerk at a nearby sweet shop, which my friend Al would occasionally frequent. His ice cream cone was always a particularly generous one. Al had acquired a newspaper delivery route, a very early morning preschool activity. Twice he was rewarded with a short trip for his diligent and effective efforts, and I substituted as delivery boy in his absence. During one of these early morning excursions, I was requested to join briefly as the tenth man in the services of a small synagogue along my route, 10 attendees being the "quorum" requirement for reciting the Kaddish for the dead. For about half a year, I was employed on Saturdays at Larkey's downtown clothing store, where I tagged the purchased suits for alterations and brought them to the tailors in the back rooms. One way bus fare cost five cents, so that I not infrequently chose to walk to the store for almost an hour. "Time is money," I had learned, and apparently I had more of the former. During summer and winter school vacations, I accompanied my father to New York and helped in the leather business, earning as much as a few dollars per week. Each one of these jobs of my high school years was of not insignificant benefit. Aside from the monetary compensation, the various experiences helped in my maturing process and taught me to appreciate and respect throughout my lifetime the labors of other people, no matter how menial the task.

Friday evenings were always reserved for the Sabbath. Our apartment had a festive atmosphere, and the table in the dining room, covered with a white tablecloth, was set to welcome that special day with mother lighting the candles and father chanting the Kiddush over the wine. After the Mozi blessing with mother's home baked Berches (special crusty white bread), we usually had chicken noodle soup before the main course. Ellen and I were always blessed by each of our parents before we sat down for dinner. The meal concluded with father reciting the Benschen, the thankful grace for our food. Each Friday night, this was a magic and beautiful hour. If father did not return from his New York job too late, we at times managed to attend services at B'nai Abraham, a large and beautiful synagogue within about 20 minutes' walking distance from our home. With the famous rabbi Stephen S. Wise serving as intermediary, this congregation had engaged the young and extremely talented Berlin Rabbi Joachim Prinz in 1938 or 1939. This man had already established a fine reputation in the German Jewish community. I had had the privilege of studying the history of the Jewish people from his textbook in the years leading up to my Bar Mitzvah. His knowledge extended far beyond the Jewish world, and he was able to convey his great intellect as a fascinating speaker and teacher. I learned so much from this dynamic and passionate man about Judaism, history, politics, art, literature and Zionism. As if this would not have been enough, Rabbi Prinz was complemented by the gifted cantor Abraham Shapiro, who was renowned in his own profession and added much to the beauty and reverence of these memorable services.

The social life for new immigrants often revolves around organizations founded by their predecessors, and the German Jewish refugees adhered to this pattern as well. The Jewish Unity Club of Newark was led by Dr. Curt Silbermann, an attorney and a charming and talented individual, and consisted of German and Austrian immigrants. In a rented space within walking distance from our home, it offered to the arrivals of recent years the comfort of sharing experiences and fellowship during regular Thursday evening meetings. Young and old were equally welcome and comfortable there. Simple refreshments, card games, ping pong, spontaneous singing while gathered around the piano, and animated conversations constituted the usual fare. At times, formal entertainment and lectures were offered. In addition, the club sponsored a soccer team that competed in the Eastern District Soccer League. Their home games took place in Weequahic Park, where I had a chance to cheer and watch my future brother-in-law Bert Bravmann as a star performer. During the summer, the young and old would travel primarily by bus to nearby lakes for picnics and associated outdoor fun.

In February of 1941, we received word that my grandmother Regina Frank had passed away. She was in her seventy-eighth year and had the privilege of meeting her end quietly and with dignity. I had loved and respected this woman, the mother of 12 children, and mourned her death in gratitude to have known her. The admiration and love of her progeny was well deserved; she certainly was a woman of valor. It seemed to me that of those of her children whom I got to know, none attained her level of compassion, insight and unselfish love. Fortunately, God spared her from becoming a victim of the Holocaust.

In the month following grandmother's passing, uncle Max and aunt Claire finally received their visas from the U.S. consulate just before the gates literally closed. While deportations such as those of southwest German Jews to the Gurs concentration camp had already taken place, Max and Claire were able to travel via occupied France and Spain to Portugal and to board a ship headed for the U.S.A. With their arrival on these shores, we experienced the great relief and joy that all of our close relatives were out of the German grasp and in safety. As later events would so tragically demonstrate, we were very fortunate because most of those who survived the Nazi terror lost at least one if not more members of their immediate family.

During our first few years in Newark, my sister underwent one or two operations to correct or at least improve her dislocated hip condition. Unfortunately, the success was limited because the earlier years of medical mismanagement had taken its toll. Nevertheless, her walking ability improved somewhat and she was mobile enough to move and even travel by herself with only minor difficulty.

We were, of course, in regular correspondence with uncle Lothar and aunt Hannah in Palestine, where there was much unrest and danger because of Arab terrorists. One could never be certain how our relatives could be affected by these disturbances. Many years later, they related to me how they had to duck bullets and take circuitous routes on their way to work to stay out of harms way. However, the Jews of Palestine could at least defend themselves, an ability that was not applicable to the Jews of Nazi Germany-occupied Europe. For a while, Lothar worked as a gardener. Eventually, my uncle and aunt opened a butcher shop, an activity in which Hannah had some homegrown experience. They lived in a tiny house in Kiryat Bialik, just north of Haifa.

In the first half of 1941, after Bulgaria became an ally of Germany, the Nazi aggressors swallowed up Yugoslavia and Greece and invaded the Soviet Union. The latter was a fateful and monumental decision of Adolf Hitler and the German leadership. It resulted in monstrous deeds, millions of deaths, untold suffering, vast destruction, and, in the end after four long years, the defeat of Nazi Germany. On August 14, 1941, the announcement of the Atlantic Charter signaled the active support to our embattled friends, particularly Great Britain, that was the only European country besides the Soviet Union which still fought the Nazis. The Charter was not a commitment to war, but it was a step closer towards our involvement.

On a Sunday afternoon in December of that year, on the seventh of the month, Al and I went to a movie at the Park Theater on Bergen Street. As we exited after the show, someone told us that the Japanese had attacked Pearl Harbor. I was then 17 years old and Al was 16, and we realized that our country, now at war, would soon involve us directly in this struggle. Four days later, both Germany and Italy declared war on the United States. We wondered whether our rearming effort could be accomplished with sufficient speed to maintain the military integrity of our primary allies, Great Britain and the Soviet Union, and eventually lead to the liberation of Europe and with it that of its incarcerated and threatened Jewish people.

In order to prepare myself for the post-high school period, I enrolled in the spring of 1942 in a course on machine tool operation at the Essex County Vocational School in Newark and also applied for fall admission to the night school of Newark College of Engineering. In the vocational course, I became acquainted with the basic operation of the lathe, the shaper, and the drill press. The class took place in late afternoons and thus did not interfere with my high school attendance. Such an acquired skill would most likely lead to my employment in the rapidly expanding war industry. I had no illusions that I could attend college during the day; our family simply did not have the funds for such a luxury. I hoped to help my family financially by working during the day (my mother was still cleaning people's homes) and helping myself by attending college at night.

In June, I graduated from Weequahic, having satisfactorily completed the so-called College Prep curriculum. Time limitations had precluded my participation in the social aspects of school life, and the graduation ceremony, preceded by yearbook inscriptions, constituted the only activities to mark this milestone of my life. Al had already graduated in January of that year and was employed as a paper distribution manager by the Newark *Star Ledger*.

I promptly applied for employment to a number of plants involved in the war industry but had difficulty obtaining a position in spite of many available openings, because I was not yet a U.S. citizen and was actually classified as an "enemy alien." But I persisted and finally obtained a job as machine operator in a small shop that subcontracted for a larger firm. Working five and a half days per week, I simultaneously attended Newark College of Engineering at night from Monday to Thursday to study electrical engineering. Friday evenings, I always reserved for Shabbat with the family. It was a busy and full schedule, because most of the weekends were required for study. Without potential interruption because of the war, I expected to keep up with this type of arrangement until graduating eight years later.

After a few months of machine shop employment, I succeeded in locating a similar job with better compensation at the H.A. Wilson Company near downtown Newark. The production work was highly repetitive and therefore boring. To make the time go by and keep my sanity, I decided to ration my thinking process during working hours. I would permit myself, for example, to review an opera I had heard or a book I had read or a trip I had made for an entire morning or afternoon, without letting my background thoughts deviate to other subject matter. Of course, I had to pay attention to my work, but that did not involve too much mental capacity.

College was a pleasure. I took four courses per semester and submerged myself with intensity in technical subjects such as physics and mathematics. Even so, the course that remains most vividly in my memory involved English language and English literature. During this time, I once saw a poem in *Life* magazine by Edna St. Vincent Millay and decided to recite it to my class. She described therein the terrible German act of revenge perpetrated on the population of the little Czech town of Lidice, which was located about 10 miles outside of Prague. Reinhard Heydrich, a ruthless man who had functioned as deputy chief of the Gestapo and Reichsprotektor of Czechoslovakia, had just succumbed from injuries sustained in a grenade attack by two parachutists sent from London by the Czech government in exile. In June of 1942, the Nazis, in a gruesome and repulsive action, murdered all of Lidice's men and some of its women and abducted all remaining women and children, of whom only a few survived. Here are excerpts from "The Murder of Lidice":

> It was all of six hundred years ago,
> It was seven and if a day,
> That a village was built which you may know
> By the name of "Lidice" . . .

Now how did the year turn-how did it run
In the year of nineteen forty-one?
In the village of Lidice?

First came Spring, with planting and sowing;
Then came Summer, with haying and hoeing;

Then came Heydrich the Hangman, the Hun . . .
The women and children out to the square
They marched, that there they could plainly see
How mighty a state is Germany! –
That can drag from his bed unawake, unaware,
Unarmed, a man, to be murdered, where
His wife and his children must watch and see;
Then carted them off in truck and cart
Into Germany, into Germany, –

The whole world holds in its arms today
The murdered village of Lidice,
Like the murdered body of a little child,
Innocent, happy, surprised at play, –
The murdered body, stained and defiled,
Tortured and mangled, of a helpless child!
From the throat of a whole world, reach his ear –
The maniac killer who still runs wild –
Careless America, crooning a tune:
Catch him! Catch him and stop him soon!
Never let him come here!
Think a moment: are *we* immune? . . .
Catch him! Catch him! Do not wait!
Or will you wait, and share the fate
Of the village of Lidice?
Or will you wait, and let him destroy
The village of Lidice, Illinois? . . .

This poem and its message made a deep impression not only on me but on my fellow students and professor as well. The tentacles of Nazi atrocities had reached the press and the classrooms of the United States.

In the fall of 1942, English troops under General Montgomery beat back the German Africa Corps commanded by General Rom-

mel. This was one of the first Allied victories and constituted the beginning of Germany's defeat in North Africa. The Germans had
aimed to drive further eastward to Palestine and, with the help of
the Nazi-sympathetic Mufti of Jerusalem, eliminate the Jews from
that area. In September, the German steamroller had reached Stalingrad, yet by November the Soviet armies, in one of the pivotal bat-
tles of the war, had not only stopped the German aggressors but had
partially caused them to withdraw from the vicinity of this key city.
Meanwhile, Allied forces had landed in North Africa and opened up
a new front to fight Nazi Germany. Much fighting and sacrifice still
lay ahead, but the tide seemed to be slowly turning.

We became more and more aware of the desperate situation for
European Jewry and the ever increasing Nazi atrocities but had no
knowledge of the large scale exterminations that were in full swing
in eastern death camps at that time. These facts, although known
by the Allied governments including the Roosevelt administration,
were either suppressed or received only scant public acknowledg-
ment. Indisputable evidence showed after the war (Wyman) that a
telegram sent through confidential channels by Dr. Gerhart Riegn-
er, World Jewish Congress representative in Bern, Switzerland, informed the U.S. State Department and Rabbi Stephen S. Wise,
president of the American Jewish Congress, of a top German decision (1941 Wannsee conference) to exterminate all Jews in German
controlled lands after concentrating them, i.e., about four million
human beings, in eastern Europe. Actually, by that time, Nazi mass
exterminations were already being carried out. The State Department not only withheld this telegram from Rabbi Wise, who eventually received briefings from alternate sources, but furthermore
took steps to prevent such news from being transmitted and reaching the general public. For at least another year, little or no action
was taken by our government to address the urgent problem of possibly rescuing part of European Jewry or at least slowing down the
murderous activities of the Nazi genocide machine. Basically, our
government officials in the executive department knew what was
transpiring but tried to conceal the evidence and failed to take the
appropriate humane action. Subsequent justifications of this policy
were based on doing nothing to distract from our ultimate objective:
the utter defeat of Nazi Germany, a defeat that would also hypo-
thetically, as a by-product, rescue Europe's Jews.

IN THE SERVICE OF MY COUNTRY

In April of 1943, I received a draft notice from the Selective Service. As a non-citizen, I had first to give permission to be drafted into the armed forces, to which I consented immediately. There was no question that I wanted to serve my country, which had given me and my family refuge from Nazi tyranny and thus saved our lives. Without condition, I had to help this country fight and defeat the evil that had almost devoured me. In order to complete my academic year, I pleaded for and received a one-month delay. On May 14, I reported at the local armory for my physical examination. At first, the doctors were hesitant to accept me because they noticed a noisy heart murmur with their stethoscope. This problem I was aware of; it originated from the time I was ill with scarlet fever. I explained that, in spite of the leaky valve, I had led a physically active and unencumbered life. They asked me to step aside and I was upset by the thought of possibly being rejected. But fate was kind, and after some wait I was given the green light and sworn in to serve my country.

A week later, I kissed my mother and sister goodbye, and father walked me around the corner to Pershine Avenue school from where I left with a group for Fort Dix, New Jersey, the transient processing center. We were greeted by First Sergeant Lighting, who, according to *Life* magazine, was reputed to be the toughest man of his rank in the United States Army. I was proud of my new uniform and tried to adjust to the necessity of military discipline. During the second night and without prior notice, we were ordered out of our barracks at 2 am and marched to the mess hall for an Intelligence Quotient (IQ) test. The result would be important to qualify for possible admittance to the Army Specialized Training Program (ASTP) following the completion of three months of basic training. I was groggy, particularly because of a number of 3% beers that I had imbibed the previous evening. As luck would have it, I scored 115, the absolute minimum to qualify for ASTP. Although I never entered this army sponsored college program, this episode still represented an important fork in the road for me as later events would prove.

After one week, I was shipped by train to Fort Bragg, near Fayetteville, North Carolina, for basic artillery training. This was a huge military base where artillery and airborne (parachute) units received their military knowhow. It was a hot summer, with what appeared to be endless training exercises, 15-mile forced marches, bed bugs, poison ivy, kitchen (police) duty (KP), barracks inspections, close order drills, and food not cooked to order, but I gained 20 pounds because of much more sleep than at home and lots of healthy outdoor exercise. Many of the fellows complained about "lights out" at 9:30 pm, but I considered this rule as a treasured luxury after my prior civilian schedule of daytime work and nighttime study. We trained on 155mm howitzers; there were seven men assigned to each crew. I, just by chance, was selected to be number seven. Although of slight build, I had the job of lifting the by then armed 95-pound projectile from the ground to the cradle, from where it was subsequently inserted into the barrel of the howitzer. If I would have ever dropped it, truly perish the thought, then the whole gun-crew would have disintegrated and I could not write this auto-biography. Henry Nathan, another member of my gun crew, was also a refugee from Germany but with an accent twice as thick as mine. With the projectile on a cradle, it was his job to ram it with the help of another man past the breech block. To this day I can still hear him shout: "quadrrrent thrrree hundrrred, rrrready rrrrrram." In our crew, a British fellow was the gunner, whose function it was to align the howitzer properly by optical means. Subsequent to one target practice, which because of the concussions were always very loud, he called out: "I caaan't hear on one ear." He was sent to the dispensary, and I never saw him again. Consequently, I was promoted to take his place and be the gunner, a much better position than lifting that heavy projectile. But now, the gunner had a German instead of a British accent! During one of the exercises on the range, the soldier assigned to insert the powder charge in back of the projectile of our piece selected, as a prank, a double dose. He no doubt thought it to be a big joke, but the startled forest rangers near the impact zone were not amused.

Saturday afternoons and early evenings, I frequently visited nearby Fayetteville together with a few of my buddies. Our highlight was to consume adequate quantities of beer and steak, and sing at the top of our voices "Begin the beguine, the steak was so tender." This town was then packed with soldiers who tried to concentrate their recreation of the week into a few short hours and compensate somewhat for the prior week's tough training, sometimes with explosive results. It was not unusual to witness unruly GIs being expelled like projectiles through bar room doors. Once, I made a short voice recording at the local USO (United Service Organization) to send this greeting

The new soldier after induction at Fort Dix, NJ in May 1943

to my family. To my utter amazement, I heard on replay an overpowering accent, something one cannot discern while speaking. For recreation on the post, we occasionally played soccer on the battery street. I used to tend the goal and threw myself with enthusiasm on the hard ground to prevent the opponents from scoring. Walter Jaffe from the Newark Jewish Unity Club happened to be in the same battery and was one of my soccer playmates. During weekdays after chow (supper), we frequented the Post Exchange (PX) for beer and social relaxation.

Once, while on a local weekend pass (Saturday noon to Sunday evening), I decided to make a surprise and unauthorized visit to my family in Newark. Expecting to return well after bed check on Sunday night, I had put a dummy consisting of towels and a broom in my bunk to assure that my planned tardiness would not be detected. I arrived at home about 2 am on Sunday and waited a few hours before waking the family. The surprise and joy were great, and mother immediately embarked to prepare a delicious dinner. By noon, I already had to start my return trip. Unfortunately, the train broke down because of an axle failure. One of the two non-commissioned officers (noncoms) of my barracks discovered me while people were being shifted to other cars. He was, fortunately, sympathetic with my predicament. After we arrived in Fayetteville just before daybreak, Sergeant Green saved the day. He managed to squeeze into the first taxi and reached the battery street in time for roll call. "Here," he answered when my name was called, thus avoiding my being found absent without leave (AWOL). When I finally reached my barrack and that incriminating dummy in my bed, I learned that KP duty was my lot for the day. Being the last to report to the mess sergeant, I ended up being garbage man, the least desirable job, but I was a happy trooper that my transgression remained officially undiscovered.

By February of 1943, heroic Soviet resistance and a bitter cold winter had not only halted the Nazi advance on the Eastern front but resulted in the surrender of the Sixth German army at Stalingrad. In July 1943, Allied forces landed in Sicily and went on to invade Italy in September. Two months later, Soviet forces advanced in heavy fighting to recapture Kiev, the capitol of Ukraine.

After basic training was completed, i.e., in early September, ASTP qualifiers such as I were shipped to Fort Riley, Kansas, to form a new outfit: the 288th Field Artillery Observation Battalion (FAOB). Almost all others were shipped almost immediately overseas for combat duty. Some lost their lives a short time later on the precarious Anzio beachhead in Italy. If I would have scored one point less during that IQ test in Fort Dix, my destination might well have been Anzio instead of Kansas. Life can play "funny" tricks at times, and not always so funny, and I was most fortunate at some fateful forks in the road, including this one.

I arrived in Fort Riley, Kansas, on September 12, 1943.The camp specialized in the training of Field Artillery and Cavalry units. The cadre for my outfit was furnished by another FAOB. Our task was to determine the accurate location of enemy artillery by means of Sound and Flash ranging. After a survey of the locations of four or more observation stations, which were spaced at one half to one mile intervals and consisted of wire-connected microphones for sound ranging and of manned optical instruments for flash ranging, the location of the enemy artillery piece could be determined within 100 to 150 yards accuracy. The sound base equipment was activated by a forward observer, who was located in infantry territory. This was most interesting work, and my limited college training, especially trigonometry, came in handy.

I was assigned to the survey section of Battery A; the battalion consisted of three batteries: Headquarters, A, and B. I taught some mathematics applicable to our task. Within nine months, I advanced to PFC (Private First Class), Corporal, and finally Tech Sergeant. Our team developed into a cohesive organization and consisted of a great bunch of guys, a home away from home. Lieutenant Bert Grunden and Staff Sergeant Rex (Redass) Wilson, our officer and noncom, respectively, were honorable and capable human beings who earned our confidence and respect. Rex earned his nickname in his previous outfit by falling asleep, dressed in his birthday suit, while lying on his stomach in the hot desert sun. My buddies came from all parts of the country, not just from the East coast, with which I already had some familiarity. It was a great experience, and I learned a lot about the U.S.A., from sea to shining sea, truly a league of nations, a wonderful variety of people with a multiplicity of backgrounds, ethnicities, religions. Vern Eastman from Thermopolis, Wyoming, became my best friend. Although he was about 12 years older than I and came from a different background, we shared many interests and values. I hold him in fond memory. Throughout our training, travels, and the combat to follow, our survey section worked together as a well-oiled team. A number of them were not only my comrades, they were my friends. I never went to the ASTP while in service, but this unique exposure was a special educational course that left a lifelong most positive impression on me. One extra curricular activity that caught my fancy was gambling with dice. I was an amateur in comparison to many of my barracks mates. I enjoyed the excitement and mathematical probabilities of the game but avoided the higher stake encounters. Thus, it was all in good fun and a nice diversion.

Fort Riley is located between Junction City and Manhattan, the latter the site of Kansas State Teachers College. Junction City was a soldiers' town similar to Fayetteville, whereas Manhattan, because of the academic environment, was more refined and attractive. Now and then, I visited both places on weekend passes, but I preferred Manhattan not only because of its more peaceful atmosphere but also because of its wartime-induced very one-sided female enrollment at the college. General (later U.S. President) Eisenhower's brother Milton was its president during my Kansas residency.

The mainline east-west railroad track passed within a few hundred yards of our barracks. On Saturday, if one passed the noon barracks inspection and had arranged for a pass, the eastbound would stop on the open track to accommodate eager soldiers. My most memorable weekend excursions were visits to Kansas City and St. Louis. Aunt Selma (one of mother's sisters) and uncle Karl Lorenz lived in the latter city and hosted me for two lovely days. I even took a Mississippi riverboat ride with their secretary. Kansas was a dry state at the time and the nearest city where alcoholic beverages were legally available was Kansas City, Missouri. This sudden freedom at times proved to be our downfall, such as when I discovered one of my buddies resting peacefully in full dress uniform in the partially filled bathtub of our hotel room. In this instance, too many sloe gins put a damper on our planned activities.

Our training was intense and the technology we had to master both interesting and demanding. At times, we practiced our surveying even at night. One of our azimuth direction references was the north star Polaris; we referred to this as shooting Polaris. The transits, which were utilized to measure angles, had small battery-powered illumination for the scales. Measuring with metal tapes and plumb bobs in line of sight with a dimly-lit rod was quite difficult because of the rough terrain. I utilized seven-place log tables, a clipboard with prepared forms, and a flashlight to perform the trigonometric calculations, with an intended precision of one in 5,000. No one questioned how this eventually would work out in combat.

The huge campfire which we built when we finally rested on the range during one of these exercises was certainly not combat-compatible. I was dozing while lying on the ground in the bitterly cold Kansas winter when I was roused by screams of pain from a soldier jumping and gesticulating wildly while silhouetted against the flames. It was Jerry Schwarz, who must have rolled in his sleep a little too close to the pyre and had a good case of the proverbial hot foot.

In the late winter of 1944, we spent three miserable weeks on Tennessee maneuvers. The area was located near the Cumberland River, but that was not the only water in our vicinity. It poured for almost the entire duration of our extensive exercises. The churning of trucks and other heavy equipment turned the landscape into a sea of mud. Once, while wading through that knee-high brown stuff towards the chow truck, I met Jerry Schwarz who was balancing his loaded mess kit. Suddenly, he slipped and disappeared in the muck and was subsequently unrecognizable. Some fun, but at least maneuvers are not conducted with live ammunition, a not insignificant consolation. Finally, we encamped next to a railroad siding for our trip back to Kansas. Vern and I shared a pup tent, each supplying half of this modest abode. The rain had stopped and we were attempting to dry out. In the middle of our final Tennessee night, we awoke with rain pouring once again from the heavens and with no pup tent to shield us because the wind had pulled it up from the soft ground. There I stood in my underwear with frustration and amusement conflicting with each other. No more maneuvers.

The little town of Junction City became a significant part of my history when on June 23 I was sworn in to become a United States citizen at the county court house. The process of naturalization was accelerated by the army to assure legal protection before I was shipped overseas to a theater of war. Many years later, I became aware that Bea, then

Last furlough before shipping overseas (June 1944)

still a minor, derived her citizenship from her parents on this very same day, the 23rd of June, 1944. Call it serendipity, call it fate! It is an amazing coincidence and for me certainly of symbolic significance. Two refugees from Nazi Germany, who as Jews were deprived of their German citizenship in 1935 and who had no notion of each other's existence in 1944, attained U.S. citizenship so coincident in time but still so far apart in distance and relationship, yet who were eventually to be united in matrimony.

During the summer of 1944, I was granted a furlough to spend about one week with the family; it was a blessing but also a message of things to come. The Allies had landed on June 6 in Normandy in a successful and miraculous invasion and had broken out of these coastal confines before the end of July. On June 13, the first V-I rockets fell on London. By the end of August, other Allied troops had established a foothold in southern France. The 288 FAOB was ready for action, our training had been completed, and we departed from Fort Riley on September 12, 1944, one year to the day that I arrived there.

BACK TO EUROPE FOR UNCLE SAM

After arriving in Camp Shanks, New York, our staging area, I had two opportunities to visit with my parents and sister. Of course, I was precluded from divulging anything about my outfit's activities and plans. There was no need for this in any case, my family sensed the score. On the second of my visits, each one lasting but a few hours, I was accompanied by Vern Eastman. It was reassuring for my parents that I had acquired such a fine man as my friend. Mother, always concerned about her "little boy," asked him whether I took up playing poker. Without hesitation, he could assure her that I did not engage in this gambling game. During the crossing to Europe, I became acquainted with this entertainment, but not because of my mother's inquiry. Vern was appalled by the concentration of humanity and the resulting congestion of the greater New York City area. He could not understand how anyone would choose to live there, and I could appreciate the feeling of this man from Thermopolis, Wyoming.

In the evening of September 28, 1944, we boarded our ship in New York harbor. The Red Cross personnel was serving coffee and doughnuts on the pier before we climbed up a steep gangplank to the deck of our British transport, His Majesty's Ship Arrowa, carrying a heavy duffel bag slung over the shoulder. I declined the food, for this was Yom Kippur, the most solemn of all Jewish Holidays and reserved for introspection and fasting from sundown to sundown. I had a lot to think about and pray for, although the environment for this was rather unusual. The Arrowa was a converted refrigerator ship that at one time carried meat from Australia to England. Now it transported live cargo from America to the same destination.

We departed from the harbor the following morning and joined a huge convoy for the Atlantic crossing. Our ship was in the midst of an armada of troop transports and freighters, all heavily guarded against possible German U-boat attacks by destroyer escorts and

90

other warships. The troops on our ship were packed like sardines, no doubt quite typical. We were assigned to the lowest "passenger" deck (E), one level above the hold that carried supplies. Sleeping accommodations were available on the floor, on large tables, and in hammocks. Recognizing that fresh air would be in short supply, I quickly staked out my claim for a hammock with one end hooked near an air vent. Each morning, everyone was most eager to climb up to deck-side. Only a small detail of men was left behind for clean-up purposes; this was not a desirable assignment, but, unfortunately, I was put in charge of this task for the duration of the crossing. In spite of my previously demonstrated tendency for sea sickness, I was never once even slightly nauseous during this entire trip. Meals were usually served deck-side. Some of my buddies noticed that the large containers utilized for the hot food looked suspiciously similar to the buckets used by the ship's crew while mopping the decks and alley ways. At first, those assertions were met with disbelief; however, a further check confirmed this disgusting fact and led to a thriving black market in crackers, cheese, and other alternative food items. Crews, one of the somewhat "older" members of our battery and already the father of two children, acted as a non-compensated go-between after having established a convenient contact for such supplies.

In darkness near midnight, we landed on October 10 in Glasgow, Scotland and immediately boarded a ship side train for southern England, a wartime trip that took about a day and a half. We were quartered in the dormitories of a school for boys called Canford in the small rural town of Wimbourne. Except for equipment maintenance, there was little further training. Thus we had time to watch rugby games on the school grounds and wiled the time away by reading or playing cards and dice.

A couple of times, I visited nearby Bournemouth, an attractive seaside resort during more peaceful times. Once, I joined a few friends to venture into London while on a one-day pass. Like elsewhere in this part of the world, everything was blacked out because of the frequent and at times devastating German air raids. During our brief stay, there were no disturbances. We even relished the luxury of a good steak dinner but realized a little too late that we apparently were being served a former "Epson Downs" resident. The taste of horse meat was somewhat on the sweet side, but the whole experience was, nevertheless, a most enjoyable one.

With friend Vern Eastman just before embarkation at Weymouth, England, for Channel crossing to France, December 6, 1944.

The time had come to prepare for the crossing of the English Channel. Now fully dressed in our combat uniforms, including steel helmets, we left Canford on December 3 and traveled in jeeps, weapons carriers, and two-and-a-half-ton GMC trucks to the port of Weymouth on the southern English coast. After three days of readiness and delays due to storms, we boarded an LST (Landing Ship Transport) on December 6. Finally, after some more waiting, we crossed the channel on the 10th of December. The sea was a bit rough and I took a few motion sickness pills as a precaution. Together with a few members of my surveying team, I participated in a spirited dice game in the back of our weapons carrier, which was chained securely to the deck. One by one, the participants fell by the wayside because of sea sickness until there were only two of us remaining. Eventually, fatigue and medication must have overtaken me. The next sensation I remember was finding myself and a pair of dice rolling in unison on the floor of the weapons carrier with the gentle rocking of the ship. We had dropped anchor within sight of the port of Le Havre, which was almost completely destroyed during the June D-Day invasion.

While traveling in convoy towards the front lines, which were by then in eastern France and Belgium, our weapons carrier developed engine trouble and the supposed last vehicle designated for pickup and aid in such circumstances either bypassed us or took an alternate route. In any case, we were stuck somewhere in northern France. The local people of Cany-Barville, south of Dieppe, were marvelous in their assistance and hospitality. For two nights, we were given food and shelter by a very nice French family, and I even slept in a most comfortable bed. By December 13, our truck had been repaired by the local auto shop, and we rejoined our unit in Fry; from there, we traveled onward to a muddy campground in Rambucourt near Nancy and St. Mihiel. Our battalion had been assigned to the Third army under the command of General George Patton of "tank breakthrough" fame.

Under the cover of heavy fog and inclement weather, the Germans launched a major counter-offensive on December 16 in the Ardennes forest located substantially north of our position, an area that was assigned to the U.S. First and Ninth army. Personally planned by Hitler and executed under the overall command of General Von Runstedt, a 38-division force struck in a surprise action along a 50-mile front to split the Allied armies in half. The initial success of this attack resulted in a deep westward bulge of the German front lines and gave this great struggle its name: "Battle of the Bulge." The entire Third army was to proceed northward at top speed, with headlights on, as in our case, in order to save time. This "caution to the wind" approach was typical of General Patton's tactics and invited German strafing attacks, but our losses were minimal and speed was of the essence.

Patton was a great general and the skilled tactician of rapid and deep thrusts of his armored columns into enemy territory. Warfare represented his professional peak; it was under these circumstances that he could best satisfy his tremendous ego. He was the right man for the task on hand. As a human being, he had many shortcomings; his lack of compassion was repeatedly demonstrated, and he appeared to be proud of it. In fact, according to his biographer, Martin Blumenson (*The Patton Papers*), he made no secret of his anti-Semitic sentiments as commander of the occupation forces in Bavaria and Austria after the war. The remnants of European Jewry, generally identified as displaced persons, were forced under Patton's directives back into camps where living conditions were only marginally better than those experienced in German concentration camps. The October 1, 1945, issue of the U.S. Army weekly *Stars & Stripes* carried as its lead front-page article an official report by President Truman, noting that the American Military Government in Europe "appears to be treating Jews as the Nazis treated them except that they do not exterminate them." The President ordered Eisenhower to "clean up" conditions for Jews in Germany and Austria. Eventually, Patton was dismissed for insubordination by General Eisenhower. But here, in the December 1944 upheaval of the Bulge, he was the man of the hour. His human frailties and defects should not, in retrospect, detract from his most noteworthy military accomplishments in the defeat of Nazi Germany.

The whole situation was confusing and very fluid. In quick succession, i.e., within a four day period, my outfit moved from Dohlem, Luxembourg, to Villers La Roue and then Arlon, Belgium, and Platen, Luxembourg. We were located in an area south of Bastogne, where General McAuliff of the surrounded 101st U.S. Airborne Division told the Germans "Nuts" when asked to surrender. Third army armored units were able to pierce the German vice and relieve the heroic and beleaguered troops of Bastogne. There were reports of German troops in American uniforms operating behind our lines, a most disconcerting input. The weather was atrocious during those days, heavy snow slowing our ability to respond to the German spearhead and dense fog precluding our air force from aiding the embattled troops on the ground.There were many casualties on both sides. I was struck by the youthful appearance of some of the German dead.

On Christmas day, the weather finally and fortunately cleared. In brilliant sunshine, I remember gazing in awe at the sky and the huge armada of Allied planes, mainly bombers, heading north. Never in my life had I witnessed so many planes within a couple of hours, and never in my life could such a sight have been more welcome. Much fighting and many sacrifices still lay ahead, but there was hope that this was to be Nazi Germany's final chapter.

A day later, we advanced to Eschdorf on the south side of the Sauer River, where we established our first observation bases. A partially damaged old farmhouse served as our sleeping quarters. Its thick stone walls gave us a sense of security and some protection from the biting cold. In place of the missing door, we utilized army blankets. During one critical period, we carried on without any sleep for 36 hours. Eschdorf served as our base from December 26 until January 13, a considerable period of time when compared to the instability of prior weeks. Surveying at night proved to be impossible. The small lights, which were essential to provide minimum illumination for our work, were not only give-away targets for our enemy but also intolerable for our own troops, in particular the hard pressed infantry units. The slightest suspicion, sound or light would provoke combat soldiers to shoot first and ask questions later, a most understandable reaction. I had discarded my gas mask and used the pouch for carrying the bulky seven place log tables required for the surveying calculations. Maybe that was somewhat careless, but to the best of my knowledge the Germans fortunately did not use poison gas for military operations in World War II.

Vern and I usually teamed up to take our turn for the nightly guard duty near our farmhouse. Once, in the darkness supplemented by heavy snow fall, we detected a suspicious noise. A "Halt, who goes there?", I called out per SOP (Standard Operating Procedure). The expected reaction from friendly troops would involve an exchange of sign and countersign, such as "Abe" and "Lincoln," a code that was changed at least once a day. In this instance, we heard only silence. At Vern's suggestion, I repeated my request, but without success. Nervously, we fingered out carbines and hand-grenades. When Vern finally tried the challenge, we were relieved to receive the proper sign, answered with the corresponding countersign, and two shaken GIs came forward out of the darkness and whirling snow. Only then did we find out that these two poor souls had feared to have run into the German lines when they heard my German-accented challenge. The two men were the only survivors of an infantry patrol that had infiltrated enemy-held territory near the Sauer River. The countryside was strewn with enemy dead, who were frozen at times in grotesque positions of their final moments – upsetting at first but accepted in time as the terrible cost of fighting the Nazi evil. We also saw American casualties in the woods and fields of Luxembourg. These were fewer in number because our burial details gave priority to the American dead before removing those of the enemy. Several times, especially while on guard duty, I witnessed convoys of large trucks, filled to the top, traveling towards the rear with the saddest cargo of them all: young Americans who had made the ultimate sacrifice.

While still using the partially-damaged Eschdorf farmhouse as our night quarters, we carelessly created a near tragic situation during one evening. With several GI blankets substituting for the missing door, we were able to provide some indoor light with a kerosene lamp. Supplies were low, and, because of the precarious military situation, first priority had to be given to our reinforcements as well as to weapons, ammunition, and medical requirements. Thus, we ran out of our kerosene. Someone had the idea of siphoning some gasoline into a steel helmet from the tank of our truck and using it as a substitute fuel. Attempting to pour this highly flammable liquid into the lamp resulted in an immediate conflagration in our farm quarters. Probably, the mantle of the lamp had still retained a tiny glow. Impulsively, we all dashed outside to escape the danger, and immediately realized the foolishness of our response. Returning to the smoke-filled room, we beat out the fire with blankets, clothing and anything else at our disposal. The day was saved, and so was our equipment.

While surveying near a secondary road on a hilly ridge, we discovered the corpses of about a dozen white-clad German paratroops. They were apparently on a special mission when they ran into our infantry. Their unusual uniforms made sense, but this camouflage did not protect them after all. Returning to our assigned mission, I noticed one of our P-47 fighter planes flying high overhead. Not giving it another thought, I sat on the side of the road performing some calculations. Suddenly, this plane, with machine guns blazing, flew parallel to the road and I dove into the side ditch, which offered me no cover whatsoever. Momentarily, 50-caliber bullets were dancing all around us and then quiet returned. When I got up, it seemed I had returned from the dead. Miraculously, our section sustained not a single casualty from this unexpected attack. We suspected that this American fighter aircraft had possibly been captured during the breakthrough and now had a German pilot. In retrospect, it could also have been a "friendly fire" mistake. Within a day or two of that incident, we received word that Crews had become the first fatality of our A Battery. He was hit by a German shell while functioning as

At Kaundorf, Luxembourg (south-east of Bastogne) during the Battle of the Bulge in January 1945,

a flash observer in a church steeple. We did not require a reminder that we were engaged in a life or death struggle and deeply mourned his death while thinking of his wife and two young children.

On the 14th of January, we crossed the Sauer River and operated out of Kaundorf for the next 10 days. This location was about a mile and a half behind the infantry lines. Frequently, we had to survey within mortar range of the enemy, i.e., close to our infantry units. Thus, we received reminders how fortunate we were to be part of an Artillery Observation outfit. Yes, we were exposed to frequent danger, but the difficulty and risk of our task paled when compared to that of the courageous GIs in the infantry and tank units. During heavy German mortar fire, a piece of shrapnel dented Hank Hamlin's helmet. To relieve the tension, he exclaimed: "I quit" while walking away from his transit. We laughed and continued surveying. A short time later, I was sitting by myself on the side of the road performing some survey calculations with the aid of my log book and a clipboard. Suddenly, a voice interrupted the more common sounds of mortar and artillery fire and "screaming meemies." "Bert, Bert – Bert, Bert," someone called as he crawled up in the ditch. To my surprise, it was our battalion commander, Lieutenant

Sound Survey Section, Battery A, 288 Field Artillery Observation Battalion during the Battle of the Bulge in Luxembourg, January 1945. I am at the extreme left, rear. Staff Sergeant Wilson, front, left; Lieutenant Gruden next to him, front, right.

Colonel Edward Melton. I was amazed that he ventured so far forward into dangerous territory. For some reason, he was looking for Lieutenant Bert Grunden. "Further forward, Sir," I replied to his inquiry. A short time later, he returned on his way to a safer environment and asked me to relay the message, that he "had been here." Not very inspiring! The above mentioned "screaming meemies" were German missiles or shells operating at low altitude, which emanated a screeching sound while on the way. The danger began only when this sound stopped and impact was imminent. Every time we became aware that the screeching had ceased, we silently and fatalistically awaited the telegraphed explosion. Fortunately, we always were spared from the immediate proximity of impact.

Frequently, the miles of wire that connected our flash and sound observation stations were cut by enemy fire or infiltration and also by our own tanks and trucks inadvertently running over them. Our wire crews were busy not only installing the original bases but also keeping these repaired and functional. Both surveying activities and wire installation were also at risk because of minefields; this was on our mind but we had to accept it as part of the territory.

Shirley, one of the tape men in my survey section, became irrational and refused to leave the basement of our Kaundorf abode. He insisted that the Bible's admonishment "Thou shalt not kill" precluded him from further participation in our mission. Unable to be convinced otherwise, he was sent to the rear and never returned. It was also in Kaundorf where we foolishly decided during a lull in our activities to take some pictures of our auspicious group. I carried a camera with me throughout the war and thus am fortunate to have a whole album of pictures of that unusual period of my life. Within a fraction of an hour after our photographic session, a German 88mm shell landed in that immediate vicinity and damaged our weapons carrier as the only "casualty." That night, Jerry Schwarz was slightly injured by a piece of shrapnel that hit the roof of our two-story house. Thus, he became the first purple heart recipient of our section. Fortunately, we were quartered on the first floor; someone who was staying upstairs, without authority and with female company, was not that lucky.

By word of mouth, we found out that a tragedy had occurred with a sister outfit of ours, the 285 FAOB attached to the First army. During the initial days of the German breakthrough, its B battery was surrounded by enemy troops of SS Kampfgruppe Peiper and taken prisoner. Defenseless, they were herded into an opening of the woods near Malmedy, Belgium and, under the overall command of SS Hauptsturmfuhrer Wilhelm Mohnke, at least 86 GIs were mowed down in cold blood with machine guns and pistol fire. Such blatant violations of the Geneva convention with respect to prisoners of war on the part of the Nazi Germans were not at all unusual on the eastern (Soviet) front and, as later reports indicated, occurred on a much larger scale. However, this atrocity on Germany's western front hit close to home and was therefore particularly shocking for us. By December 20, 1944, the Malmedy massacre was not the only atrocity committed by Colonel Peiper and his troops of the first SS Panzer Division. By then, they had murdered about 350 American POWs at twelve different locations. (Years later, I was appalled when President Reagan chose to meet German Chancellor Kohl and honor SS war-dead in the Bitburg cemetery.)

The food supplies during the first few weeks of the Bulge were erratic; preference had to be given to ammunition and equipment. We primarily lived on "K" rations (crackers and cheese, peanut butter, etc.) and "C" rations (cans to be heated, which contained vegetables and meat products). Later on, our kitchen truck was able to obtain more desirable supplies and resume the cooking of some meals. In any case, our digestive systems were somewhat out of kilter, not so much because of the quality of the food but because of the intensity of the fighting. Diarrhea was the order of the day. While I was once in agony at our toilet facility, known as a slit trench, an enemy shell exploded within a few hundred yards, to be followed by a second and third ever closer. I had decided to dive into this trench if I would hear another one approaching, but fortunately the German gun crew decided to stop. After six weeks, we were treated to our first shower. That was an event. Special facilities had been set up in back of the combat lines. The showers themselves were mounted on raised platforms,while the pre- and post-processing took place in large tents. We retained only our helmets (steel and liner), boots, identifying dog tags, and the personal effects carried in pockets. All clothing was deposited in designated bins and was replaced by a clean set after the shower. It is safe to say that we felt tremendously rejuvenated.

On January 25, we moved on to Clervaux, Luxembourg, operating from there for an entire month. The Battle of the Bulge was over and won, but at a high price. It was a difficult battle, by far the most trying in which I participated. The U.S. forces sustained about 16,000 fatalities and 60,000 wounded or captured; German losses including prisoners were approximately triple of these numbers. Thankfully, my 288th FAOB sustained relatively light casualties.

Just before the end of February, we crossed the vaunted Siegfried Line near Binscheid, Germany, and moved north-eastward, parallel to the Mosel River, towards the Rhine. On March 13, as we were driving through Brohl, one of those "fairy tale meetings in the midst of a war" took place. While I was sitting next to our driver Roberts, with the rest of the crew in the back of the weapons carrier, I heard someone shouting "Ludwig, Ludwig." We pulled aside, and I fell into the arms of my good friend Al Meinhardt. Because of his familiarity with the German language, he had joined a military government unit, which had been stationed in the southern anchor town of Echternach during the Battle of the Bulge. While standing at the roadside, he had spotted the designation of my outfit on the passing vehicles. We had only a minute to embrace and I promised to see him that night if I would return to Brohl from our forward mission of this day. This serendipity culminated in a night of talking and very little sleep. When we parted the next morning to go our separate ways, we were grateful and hopeful young fellows.

The Mosel area is a world famous wine region, and we quickly became acquainted with this local delicacy. Somehow we even procured a small barrel of this liquid and carried it along in our truck. Egbert Ash, the youngest member of the section, overdid a good thing and became socially unacceptable. As a temporary measure, we strapped him in his intoxicated state in front of the windshield across the hood of our weapons carrier.

Now and then, I refer in my army tales to humorous occasions that involved a degree of camaraderie and also included the intake of alcoholic beverages. This might give the misleading impression that our military effort was overshadowed by a nearly continuous drunken brawl. This, of course, was not at all the case. To be away from home for an extended period generated certain stresses, which were exacerbated and intensified by the discomfort and danger of overseas combat duty. The relaxation provided by an occasional alcoholic interlude represented a welcome though only temporary relaxation in our unnatural existence. It was nothing more and nothing less.

After crossing the Mosel River southwest of Koblenz, we rapidly advanced towards the Rhine. The front now moved too fast to permit the surveying and operation of sound and flash ranging bases. In fact, there remained little need for such sophistication at this stage of the war. Just before crossing the Rhine on March 27 under a smokescreen via a pontoon bridge, we noticed an extremely fast moving German fighter plane, the first jet that ever crossed my eyes.

My knowledge of the German language came in handy to arrange quarters for the members of my outfit. There was no reason why we should sleep in pup tents and lie on the ground while the German population had the comfort of houses. Where- and whenever possible, I requested that some of the local people move in with their neighbors so that we could briefly use their houses for shelter. I always suggested that they take their valuables along; we desired only their quarters and not any of their possessions. Some members of my outfit objected to this latter caution and tried to convince me to omit same in the future. I rejected this outright and ceased to serve as interpreter for this purpose; such a function was not my official duty in any case. I had neither the patience nor the intent to deviate from ethical and honest behavior incumbent on a U.S. soldier. It would be fundamentally wrong and morally corrupt to utilize the temporary requisition of houses as shelter in order to plunder jewelry, art, or any other possessions of the home's usual occupants. Although such a transgression would pale in comparison to the criminal acts committed by our enemies, I was adamantly opposed to lowering our standards even one iota towards those of the evil forces we were attempting to defeat. Deeds speak louder than words.

The ability with my mother tongue permitted me to speak with and interrogate numerous German prisoners of war. Repeatedly, I asked: "Are you or were you ever a Nazi?" Not a single positive answer resulted. But I remember very clearly, when leaving Germany in 1939, that there were almost no Germans who were not Nazis either in an active or at least in a most sympathetic passive sense. To oppose the Nazi regime took courage, of course, and such an action, even in a modest form, represented a rare exception indeed. I wonder what happened to all these Germans of the 1939 vintage? By April 1945, I could not locate a single Nazi during my many contacts with the German population.

In a small village, Zell, near Fulda, buddy Roberts "arranged" with a German woman whose house we were temporarily using as quarters to prepare a roast goose for our surveying team. After she had disclaimed ownership of the flock of geese roaming in her front yard, he had caught one by the neck and twirled it with several rotations through the air. Just before the meal, which we shared with the German family, a big moan emanated from upstairs in house. A member of my unit had thrown himself on an inviting bed, which instead of a mattress contained several cases of apricot brandy hidden under the sheet. The celebration that followed affects me to this very day: I have a permanent aversion to apricot brandy!

Not all of our experiences during this last phase of the war, however, were on the amusing side. While in the small village of Schleid in early April, I was called to a farmhouse during the evening hours to act as interpreter. A girl in her teens, seeking to reach the outhouse, had violated the curfew, which was strictly enforced because we were still close to the front lines. One of our men on guard duty detected this unexplained movement, called for a halt and identification, and subsequently only heard fleeing steps in reply. He fired into the dark and tragically scored a fatal shot. In sadness and frustration, I looked at this young and wasted life, one of the products of the Nazi madness. There was little to interpret between our troops and her grieving family; I just located the priest so that he could give last rites.

We reached Themar in Thuringia, my father's birthplace, on April 8. I had only vague recollections of the town. Being close to my birthplace of Suhl, I tried to obtain permission to travel there together with three of my comrades. This request was denied and for good reason; engaging in unnecessary excursions in time of war may have tragic consequences.

In the meantime, on the eastern front the Soviet forces had also made substantial progress, having entered Warsaw on January 27, Budapest on February 13, Vienna on April 13, and Berlin on April 22. As the climax of our western and their eastern drive, the American and Soviet forces met in an historical moment at Torgau on the Elbe River on April 25. My outfit kept on advancing easterly as far as Markschorgast, located north of Bayreuth.

On the 12th of April, we received the sad news that President Franklin Delano Roosevelt, our Commander in Chief, had suddenly died. Although he met his end in Warm Springs, Georgia, I felt he gave his life just like so many soldiers at the front. In spite of significant health problems, he consented to making himself available for this taxing position for an unprecedented fourth term. He wanted with his heart and soul to complete the destruction of the Axis powers, of the fascistic and nationalistic evil, as well as to rebuild this world to attain a better, a just, a peaceful future. Like Moses in ancient days, he was not destined to enter the "promised land," dying barely one month before the end of the European war. But like Moses, he recognized the land and the potential for a better future. As a great visionary, he was far ahead of his time, and he is most deserving of the gratitude of the U.S.A. and that of the entire world. On the 15th, I joined some of my comrades on a small hill near Marktschorgast, where we bid farewell to this dedicated and great man with a 21-volley salute.

From Markschorgast, we advanced south as far as Wimpassing, north of Munich. About a week later, on May 8, Nazi Germany unconditionally surrendered. VE (Victory in Europe) day had finally arrived. All of us were relieved that the European war was over, but everyone was simultaneously aware that the Pacific war was still going on. We engaged in some deer hunting for a venison dinner which was washed down with alcohol in a brief celebration. Then we moved north to Kirchrottenbach near Nuremberg to clean ourselves, our vehicles and our equipment.

During the last weeks of the war, we received scattered reports of gruesome discoveries made by Allied troops (Russian, British, American) during the liberation of German concentration and extermination camps, which dotted the map of Europe. During prior years, we had concerns about the fate of minorities under the Nazi yoke, and particularly about those of the Jewish faith. Refugees such as I, of course, had more reason to fear for the safety of the Jewish population trapped on the Nazi-occupied European continent. Sometimes I heard reports of such terrible nature that it was hard to believe that even our enemies would be capable of such actions. With the discovery and liberation of the concentration and extermination camps, we gradually received confirmation that the Germans and their willing accomplices committed crimes against humanity which, in both cruelty and magnitude, far exceeded the very worst a normal human being could possibly imagine. Millions were tormented and murdered because they were born as Jews. Utterly defenseless men, women, and children were sent to their deaths by the uniformed representatives of Nazi Germany.

I was very, very grateful to be still among the living at the end of the European war. Beyond that, I was thankful for having had the opportunity to contribute in a tiny way to the Allied effort and particularly help my country of refuge, the United States of America, in a cause that freed Europe and managed to save a small remainder of its Jewry. I found myself in full agreement with General Eisenhower when he made the following statement in Frankfurt, Germany, one month after the cessation of the European combat: "More than any other war in history, this has been an array of forces of evil against those of righteousness. It had to have its leaders and it had to be won – but no matter what the sacrifice, no matter what the suffering of populations, no matter what the cost, the war had to be won."

ARMY OF OCCUPATION

Beginning with the 22nd of May, my battery spent one month in Maiach, a small northern suburb of Nuremberg. We were quartered in a former restaurant and assigned, as the army of occupation, to patrol the streets of Nuremberg in our vehicles. The steel helmets were no longer required and the light plastic helmet liners carried the "SP" (Special Police) identification. It felt very strange that it happened to be particularly the city of Nuremberg where I was assigned to perform occupation duty, the city of the infamous Nuremberg laws, the city of the yearly Nazi Party Congress attended by tens of thousands of uniformed Germans, and the city of the arch anti-Semite Julius Streicher and his virulent Stuermer newspaper with which he spread the most vile propaganda. Most of this city of Nazi pomp and excesses was now in ruins as the result of repeated Allied air raids.

One day, I was instructed to inspect a local hospital that was no longer being used by the Germans and required by the American military authorities. The place was in shambles, but the building, except for minor damage, was intact. The only resident was a custodian who lived with his family in a basement apartment. I informed him of the imminent takeover by the U.S. military and advised him of the need to vacate the place by June 6. When I returned by jeep with my driver on that date, the custodian with family were still living there, a fact that I pointed out to him with some displeasure. "It's only the 5th today," he replied. When I asked my driver to verify the date, he waved him off with a condescending gesture: "Amerikaner." Seeing a case of champagne sitting in the corner of his room, I offered to bet a carton of cigarettes (valuable black market goods) against these nine desirable bottles. He accepted, and the matter was quickly settled when I hailed a passing German pedestrian for confirmation of the date. The stunned man looked on, as I lifted the champagne onto the jeep and admonished him to move out this very

Meeting my best friend Al Meinhardt in Nuremberg, Germany, after the end of World War II in Europe. Al worked for the military government.

day. A week later, I celebrated my 21st birthday in Maiach. A few of my buddies toasted me endlessly until all the champagne was gone and so was I as well. I recall that I required assistance to reach my bunk. Sleeping soundly, I was awakened by someone shaking me and exclaiming: "Happy birthday, Ludwig." My visitor was Al Meinhardt, who had traveled all the way from Fuerth, a sister city south of Nuremberg, to surprise me and wish me well. I was in no shape to rise and receive him, and he was disappointed not only by my condition but also that he was too late to partake in the champagne. I visited Al once or twice in Fuerth, where he was working for the military government. His detachment lived in a rather nice villa that had belonged to a former Nazi.

While I was stationed in this area, I visited the grave of my maternal grandmother Regina, who died there in 1941. The cemetery was in good order, and I arranged for continued maintenance of her grave. Mercifully, this good woman was blessed to die a natural death and thus escaped the murderous Nazi fate that otherwise would have awaited her only one year later.

I also took a brief look at the reviewing stands and huge parade grounds that were the site of the annual Nazi Party Congress. It was strange standing in the spot which Hitler used to occupy and from which he returned the "Heil Hitler" salute to the multitude of his uniformed admirers. There was no joy for me in viewing the almost completely ruined and formerly beautiful ancient inner city of Nuremberg. Looking at such destruction, however, I remembered, importantly, that Germany, after occupying Czechoslovakia, had started this conflagration by invading Poland, Denmark, Norway, Luxembourg, Belgium, Holland, and the Soviet Union, as well as other countries, without provocation and was thus the initiator of untold suffering and destruction throughout Europe. One has to recall how London and other British cities were indiscriminately decimated by day and night bombardments of German planes and German rockets. The subsequent destruction suffered by Germany was not simply a matter of revenge but basically one of dire consequences due to unbridled Nazi aggression and atrocities.

During the last third of June, my outfit was assigned to guard four to five hundred SS troops in "Camp Congress," which was located near the Nazi party meeting grounds. The complex was surrounded by barbed wire fencing and watch towers with mounted machine guns and floodlights. From the perimeter, the view of the center of the encampment was blocked by rows of barracks arranged in rectangular fashion.

My captain, the commander of our battery, requested that I serve as his interpreter during this assignment. I recall particularly vividly the first of the daily roll calls, for which I accompanied him into the compound. The two of us left our weapons with the guards at the entry gate and proceeded to walk towards the center square. Suddenly, I heard a piercing shout of an SS officer: "Bataillion stillgestanden" ("Battalion attention") and the subsequent precision click of hundreds of Teutonic heels. It was a peculiar feeling; I was not pleased but conscious of the irony of the moment. Here I stood, the refugee, the Jewish refugee from Germany, together with my captain facing the unbelievable sight of hundreds of SS troops in their black uniforms standing at attention. This so-called elite had been in the forefront of the worst atrocities perpetrated by the Nazis against my Jewish people and others as well. Each one of these men was not necessarily a murderer, but each one had chosen to join an organization which was dedicated to the violent eradication of all Jews. It was a symbolic moment in my life. My captain insisted that the rigid military stance be relaxed and the prisoners stand at ease during the count. He teamed with the commanding SS officer while I did the same with their leading noncom in performing the subsequent inventory. It took two tries before we could agree on the exact number of prisoners. I was glad that during our watch at this place nothing untoward happened. No one attempted to escape, nobody was hurt, and everything was in order when we were relieved on June 29 by another U.S. detachment.

From there, we moved to the large formerly German military reservation of Grafenwoehr near the Czech border. My outfit remained there until being dissolved in the following year. At the time, we were expecting to be moved to the Pacific theater operation. Having reached the "mature" age of 21, I decided to apply for admission to Officers' Candidate School (OCS). To initiate this process, I was required to take another IQ test, which was administered in Regensburg, a city located south of us on the Danube River. Within a month or two, we expected to learn about the results of this exercise. Accompanied by about 10 other GIs with similar ambitions, we celebrated after the exam in a beer garden serving delicious 12% brew. The ride back to Grafenwoehr in the back of a truck was marked by a lot of hilarity, to say the least.

Our expectations of the future changed drastically on August 6, 1945, when the U.S. destroyed Hiroshima with a single atomic bomb, followed by another bomb dropped three days later on Nagasaki, with the same devastating results. Not surprisingly, the Japanese surrendered on August 14, and the war came to an end on the 2nd of September. Most likely, the use of the monstrous atomic weapon shortened the war, thus saving many lives, primarily American.

But the beginning of the atomic age introduced a most terrifying chapter to humankind. All options seemed to be open in the violent interactions between nations and between people. No method, no action, no atrocity, no weapon seemed to be excluded from possible human conduct. I hope that such mayhem and suffering will never happen again, because the consequences for humanity and the planet Earth would be intolerable. It may just be that our technological ingenuity has produced "swords and spears" of such monstrous and unimaginable consequences that their future use by rational leaders of nations will be recognized as counterproductive and suicidal. The Cold War between East and West, which dominated the four decades following World War II, is possibly an encouraging example of such restraint.

Finally, World War II had come to an end. About 15 million military people had been killed; total casualties were about 45 million. In addition, the Germans and their cohorts murdered about six million Jews and five million non-Jews. There is no such thing as a "good" war, but, contrary to most other conflicts, the war against Nazi Germany was a struggle of survival for most of humankind, a struggle for decency over evil, for humanism over despotism, for human rights over human suffering, for compassion over depravity. A diverse world community had prevailed over megalomaniac national and racial delusions that had led to untold suffering.

Subsequent to the cessation of hostilities, I was informed that I had been accepted for OCS. Although I was pleased with the score of 151, I respectfully declined to accept, which caused my captain to be very unhappy. My participation in the U.S. military was really no longer required; the conflict had come to an end with the unconditional defeat of the Axis powers. The time had come to prepare myself for the life ahead.

A short time later, I visited Berchtesgaden for a few days. It was the site of Hitler's large villa, the Berghof, which was partially destroyed, and his Eagle's Nest. This area, a part of the Alps, is blessed with much natural beauty, spectacular mountain peaks, peaceful meadows, romantic lakes. It is so utterly incongruous that such evil plans were hatched in the midst of such a surrounding where God was particularly lavish in decorating our earthly landscape.

Although the war was over, the phase-out of military personnel would take considerable time. There were millions of troops deployed in various parts of the world who were eager to return home. The U.S. military devised a point system for the priority of such redeployment. I had a score of 54, based on one point per month for service in the U.S. and two per month while overseas plus five points for participating in various campaigns such as the Battle of the Bulge. It appeared that I might return to U.S. shores during the first half of 1946. Therefore, I applied to attend one of the two experimental American universities, one in England and the other in France, which had quickly been organized by the U.S. government to assist in the transition of its troops.

I succeeded in being accepted in Biarritz, the fabulous French resort also known as the playground of the royalty of Europe and located just north of the Pyrenees mountains. Our semester lasted from the beginning of October till the end of December. After being

unable to participate in an over-
subscribed art course featuring
female models, I signed up for
two hours of electrical engineering and one hour of calculus per
day. The courses were interesting and the academic load quite
light, thus leaving adequate leisure time for alternate activities. It was fascinating to view
all the beauty of this lovely
place on the Gulf of Biscay, the
tree-lined avenues, the wide
beaches with arch-shaped rock
formations extending into the
ocean, the huge luxury hotels
and casino (not open), and the
night clubs. I was quartered in
the small Hotel Britannia and
took my meals in the dining
room of one of the large hotels,
where French chefs performed
culinary miracles with our

*The French touch in Biarritz, October
1945. I attended the experimental
American University for one semester.*

American rations. I used every trick in the book to maximize this
gastronomic pleasure, such as tips in the form of a few cigarettes for
the waitress for seconds or returning for an entire second sitting after removing my cap and disheveling my hair to avoid recognition.
Biarritz was an expensive environment ($2 for one alcoholic bever-
age), and it took special effort to pay for my limited social activities.
My pay as sergeant amounted to $100 per month, half of which I
sent home to my parents. There was enough inducement to give up
smoking, thank goodness, and I sold my allotted carton per week for
$20 on the black market. One of my first purchases was a beret, cus-
tomary attire for this area. I almost looked like a Frenchman, but
unfortunately could not speak like one. Sometimes I attended Shabbat services in the synagogue, where I could understand only portions of the sermon. It was strange to hear the familiar Hebrew
prayers delivered with a French accent.

Once, I joined a few buddies for a weekend trip to the Pyrenees.
This wild and rugged terrain stood in stark contrast to the seaside

picture of Biarritz. We were impressed by a number of small but in-genious hydraulic power stations, which utilize turbine driven gen-erators connected to mountain lakes from much higher elevations. We even stopped at the Roman Catholic shrine of Lourdes, where, according to legend, the Virgin Mary appeared to a peasant girl named Bernadette. Crutches left behind at its shrine over the years by handicapped pilgrims serve as evidence of their miraculous cure.

But all good things must come to an end, and at the end of De-cember, with somewhat increased knowledge and a bundle of pleas-ant memories, I departed with a large contingent of army of occupation troops on a special train headed back to Germany. On our way back to Munich, the train stopped on the open track in the vi-cinity of Paris. With four of my comrades, I had previously discussed the possibility of briefly visiting the famous French capital, and to do so even without authorization. Taking advantage of the opportu-nity during a brief stop on the open track, we jumped off the train with our duffel bags and walked a short distance to a small station.

A local train took us to Paris, where we brazenly inquired upon arrival about accommodations for the night at the U.S. military counter. When we complied with the request for identification, our AWOL status was recognized and the personnel called for Military Po-lice. Naturally, we departed in haste, piled into a waiting taxi and told the driver "Tout de suite," get going at once! We managed to rent a couple of rooms in a little hotel, and one of my buddies and I decided to forgo the normal Paris night life and do some sightseeing instead. I remember moving as if in a trance as we walked along the Champs-Elysees, the Place de la Concorde, past the Arc de Triomphe, under the Eiffel Tower; we were like little boys enjoying our lollipops.

After a few hours of sleep, the five of us took a guided bus tour of that fabulous city and then boarded a military train at the Gare de l'Est for Munich. On that 31st of December, 1945, it was tempt-ing to stay one more night and greet the new year in glamorous Pa-ree, but good sense prevailed. We had no difficulty, in spite of our AWOL status, being admitted on the train, where no ticket was re-quired for U.S. military personnel. Who in his right mind would leave this city a few hours before the beginning of a new year? We shared our compartment with an UNRWA (United Nations Relief and Works Agency) employee, who supplied the alcoholic necessi-ties for a new year celebration. He became somewhat socially unac-ceptable from this intake, and we strapped him into the overhead

Just before boarding a train in Germany for repatriation, February 1, 1946. Such cattle cars were used by Nazi Germany from 1941 until 1945 to transport the Jewish millions to be slaughtered.

baggage compartment to sleep it off. Because of the holiday, we were served, track side, a delicious turkey dinner during a stop in Strasbourg, to be followed by a second such dinner in Augsburg, Germany. When we reached Munich, we found our group still there waiting for trucks to pick them up for the trip to Grafenwoehr. So our AWOL was never officially noticed.

During my last few weeks in Grafenwoehr, there were many partings from people with whom I had shared a difficult, dangerous, yet uplifting time of my life. Although contacts were lost a long time ago, I still value their decency and comradeship. For some reason I cannot explain, I spent time in Grafenwoehr writing a technical manual on surveying techniques for field artillery observation. I still possess this booklet as a souvenir of these waning days of my military life. On February 1, my turn for repatriation arrived; together with a few other members of my outfit, I departed by train for Cherbourg.

We traveled in a freight car with a pot-belly stove in its center to provide the essential warmth for the approximately dozen passengers. Years later, after I learned more details of the Holocaust, it dawned on me that such means of transportation was also used for the horrible extermination purpose, only the so-called cattle cars were heading east instead of west, had no source of heat in the cold winter weather, contained a hundred or more terrified men, women, and children in each car, who had no access to food and toilet facilities, and traveled with the doors locked from the outside. I wrote on the outside of our car "Joisey (Jersey) bound Hurry so long Heinie." One more time, we witnessed the marks of war: destroyed bridges, the rubble of towns and cities, hungry people.

In Cherbourg, we lived in a tent city close to the harbor, waiting patiently for a boat to take us home. The shipping schedule was posted daily on a centrally located board. While I learned to play bridge, I participated in one last poker game, which had a modest call limit. I recall a seven-card draw option, where one eventually may choose the five best cards. The first two and the last cards are dealt face down and the other four are exposed for each player In any case, it became apparent after the fifth card had been dealt that each of two men had a full house, a powerful holding. All the others dropped out at this point except for over-optimistic me, who had a measly pair of fours. With the sixth and seventh card, against all odds, I received two additional fours and won the whole pot of over forty dollars, a lot of money in those days for a cash-poor GI. After a three-week wait, I finally boarded a U.S. Navy ship and left Cherbourg on February 24, reaching New York harbor on March 5 after much seasickness. This clean and stable ship did not prevent the recurrence of the ailment experienced during my first crossing in 1939.

Seeing the Statue of Liberty a second time was a most emotional welcome for me. Ever since then, I have included in my daily prayer a thought of gratitude for having reached the safe haven of these shores twice in my life after having been exposed to great danger.

We tied up at a Hoboken pier near the place of my first arrival. The public address called out my name together with those of a few other fellows, to be marched down the gangplank onto the pier. I was leery that we would end up with one last lousy detail (job). At the end of the pier, we received a "fall out" command near a small

After almost three years of military service: "Make me a civilian!"

group of civilians, and then I spotted my mother who was there to greet me. We were so excited by this reunion that our embrace temporarily trapped a small child between us. Somehow, mother had found out where and when my ship would arrive. She brought me a banana, the first one in a year and a half.

From there, we were promptly shipped to Fort Dix, New Jersey, for discharge processing. During the second night, utilizing a convenient hole in the camp fence and a waiting cab on the other side, I made a brief visit to 119 Custer Avenue to see my parents and sister. Being conscious of all that had occurred since our last meeting in 1944, this reunion was a most emotional event for all of us. There were so many soldiers who would never come back.

The 11th of March was discharge day for me. Because of the favorable weather, the proceedings took place outdoors. As I was progressing from table to table to take care of the formalities, a noncom tried to convince me to join the military reserve units. After I politely declined, he continued to persist that in this way I could preserve my sergeant's rank. My patience came to an end and I pounded on his table, exclaiming: "There is only one thing I want, I want to get out of here!" "Next man," he said in submission while I moved on toward the exit. Soon thereafter, I was home again, being greeted by the family and a large sign over the front door "Welcome Home Ludwig." I was proud to have been able to serve my country and thankful that I did not incur any bodily harm in the process. Here I was, with my three battle stars for the Ardennes (Bulge), Rhineland, and Central Europe, and with the medals for American Service, European African Middle Eastern Service, Good Conduct, and World War II Victory. The Section Chief, Technical Sergeant fourth grade, had been promoted to be a civilian with a separation pay of $220.15.

As I settled in at home with my parents and sister, in the midst of my friends and relatives, the realization of the enormity of the Holocaust tragedy began slowly to sink in, particularly with the discovery and description of the camps and of the atrocities that had taken place. I knew relatively little about the unimaginable scope and the utter cruelty of the extermination of our people until the spring of 1945. It was so unbelievable that one needed time to comprehend, if ever, this darkest chapter of human history.

Who could have imagined that Nazi Germany would murder six million Jews? We are aware that the German military authorities, the SS and the Gestapo, had some willing cohorts in the various occupied countries while carrying out these criminal deeds. This was particularly but not exclusively so in Austria (the cradle of Nazism), the Baltic states of Lithuania and Latvia, as well as Vichy France, Poland, Romania, and Croatia. However, the entire initiative, leadership, organization, and implementation of the murder of six million Jews as well as other "racially undesirable" minorities such as Gypsies emanated from Germany and was primarily carried out by Germans. Here was a so-called civilized nation, the enlightened and cultured country of Beethoven and Goethe, that followed its leaders into an abyss in which it ceased to be human.

There were exceptions. The Danish population showed their humanity, decency and courage as a people when they successfully resisted the German attempt to deport Denmark's 8,000 Jews and thus almost miraculously saved the lives of most Danes of the Jewish faith. After the fact, we became aware of many individual rescuers in other occupied areas such as France, Italy, Holland, and in the East, who at great risk to themselves hid and aided Jews to save

Army discharge at Fort Dix, NJ, March 11, 1946

their lives. Those are the "Righteous among the Nations," who are now honored in the Israeli Holocaust Museum "Yad Vashem" as well as in other memorials such as the U.S. Holocaust Memorial Museum in Washington.

There were even some brave Germans who surreptitiously opposed the Nazi regime and aided Jews, but they were far too few to make a significant difference. These heroes, who preserved their own humanity by saving threatened human beings, deserve recognition not only from Jews but from all members of the human family who stand for decency, justice, and morality.

What we experienced until my own family's emigration from Germany pales in comparison to that which followed: the criminality sponsored and organized and carried out with Teutonic determination and fanatical thoroughness by the German regime and its compliant people. The memory of this tragedy will remain within every fiber of my heart and soul for the rest of my days.

My mother and sister Ellen welcoming me at 119 Custer Avenue, Newark, NJ, March 11, 1946.

HOME AGAIN – NOW WHAT?

Three years had passed since I had entered the army just before my 19th birthday. My military chapter had come to its conclusion, and I faced my return to civilian status with hope and with confidence.

I had no doubt about returning to college. The strong desire to remain home after the lengthy absence motivated me to apply for readmission at NCE for daytime studies under the GI Bill of Rights. My military service credits, which were identical to the point system used for determining repatriation priorities, were more than sufficient to cover the tuition and to provide for a modest living expense allowance for an entire four-year undergraduate program. Immediately upon my return, I visited the college and requested to join a special "veterans spring semester" that had begun a week or two before. I hoped that this study, in combination with my credits accumulated during the one year of night school prior to my military service, would suffice to qualify me for the sophomore year in the fall of 1946. Dean Hazell met my request with a double denial. Not only did he refuse to grant me the academic credits earned at night between 1942 and 1943, but he also declined to enroll me for the spring semester that had just begun. Condescendingly, he suggested that I take an entrance examination to compete with a thousand applicants for one of the 400 places in the freshman class scheduled for the fall of the year. This high official of the school appeared to be most insensitive if not hostile towards accommodating a returning veteran who simply asked to be credited with his prior academic record at NCE. Without reasonable options, I took the exam and was accepted for fall admission as an electrical engineering major.

During the very first week of my return, I attended a Saturday night dance at Temple B'nai Jeshurun, a large Reform synagogue in Newark. Maybe because I went stag and might still have been in uniform, I met or got reacquainted with a good number of people. While standing on the sidelines, I spotted a very vivacious and at-

118

tractive young woman who was on a date with Peter Hirschmann, also originally a refugee from Germany and more recently repatriated from a German POW camp. I immediately became very interested in Beatrice Bravmann and thought, possibly in jealousy, that Peter was not the suitable escort for her. Subsequently, I saw Bea now and then in the Jewish Unity Club young people's group, at picnics, and soccer games. She was a popular and charming young woman, so I did not have the courage to ask her for a date till the end of the year.

While waiting for the fall semester, I filled in the interim period with a temporary job at the New Jersey State Highway Department. There I joined up with one of their crews and assisted in surveying for the Garden State Parkway near Cranford and Union. If the grade or the curvature of this well-known road is questionable, I will have to take part of the blame. My military experience came in handy. My co-workers were most pleasant and even were instrumental in preparing me for my driver's license test. On Saturdays, I assisted a private surveyor in establishing small developments around West Orange. To acquire and maintain a car was out of the question; I had no money and did all my commuting by bus. Part of my earnings were used to defray household expenses, and I was relieved and pleased that my mother, now 50 years old, had finally stopped working as a domestic cleaning woman.

Shortly after my reacquisition of civilian status, Al Meinhardt also returned and accepted a position as circulation manager with the Newark *Star Ledger*. His father had founded a leather goods business, and his mother was a dedicated partner in the development of this jobber activity. I sometimes played chess with Al or my father until the late hours of the night; while waiting for the opponent's move, we occasionally dozed off and had to be roused for our turn.

For a brief period, I was a member of the Jewish War Veterans because I believed this to be an appropriate affiliation. However, a short exposure led to utter disillusionment. It turned out to be a self-serving organization, that in concert with other veterans' groups was pushing for the government to declare a veterans bonus. I had no patience for people who clamored for monetary rewards after helping our country fight a pivotal struggle for the survival of humankind. I considered this to have been our duty as good citizens. Their meetings centered on trivialities and their pleasures involved, among other activities, joy riding with their girlfriends in the post ambulance. I resigned in short order and have never participated in veterans organizations since.

September brought the resumption of my studies, now a full-time activity. The student body at NCE consisted of a mix of recent high school graduates and returning veterans. The curriculum was demanding and usually consisted of six majors. Because of the so-called lost time and family responsibilities, the veterans took themselves particularly seriously and studied with ferocious determination. This resulted in a possibly unfair environment for the recent high school graduates. I customarily studied till late hours during most nights and also on weekends. I had the luxury of my own room since returning from military service and found my desk and the associated privacy a big assist towards efficient and effective learning. Friday nights, as always, were reserved to observe the Sabbath with the family. Sometimes, as during our initial U.S. period, we attended services at B'nai Abraham, where Rabbi Joachim Prinz continued to offer fabulous sermons and Cantor Abraham Shapiro lifted cantorial music to new heights.

My GI bill monthly maintenance allowance of about $65 was shared with the family. During the winter and summer vacations of my first two college years, I was able, with a good word from my father, to obtain a helper's job at the Loewengart company, his New York employer. One summer, I managed to obtain a position as electrician's helper in a Newark industrial plant; at least this was vaguely related to my college studies. Jobs in general were not plentiful during those years, and part time jobs for students did not abound either.

During our first date in December 1996, Bea and I saw the movie *The Jolson Story*; accompanied by friends who provided the luxury of car transportation, we moved a "No Parking" sign near Radio City Music Hall to obtain a precious parking space without cost. Next, we saw *Stairway to Heaven* at a New York luxury theater, which provided very comfortable seats and refreshments. We had a most wonderful time and dated frequently throughout my college years, but I always had to compete with Heinz Jaffe and other young men for Bea's attention. She was not yet ready to make a permanent commitment. In this interim, I also occasionally dated a few other young women but really had no interest in these potential alternatives. I fell deeper and deeper in love with Bea and spoke to her frequently by phone. Although this represented only a second choice to meeting in person, it served its purpose to tide me (us?) over the time spans occupied by my intense academic schedule and Bea's choice of alternating her dating partners. At intervals, we also saw each other at birthday and New Year's parties, which took place at various homes such as the Bravmanns, Strauses, Meinhardts, and Jordans, as well as ours. On Thursday evenings, our refugee youth group met regularly in the social environment of the Jewish Unity Club, where we enjoyed discussions, dancing, playing bridge and ping pong, singing while gathered around the piano, and listening to occasional lectures. I became president of that group, and Bea subsequently did also. On Sunday afternoons, we cheered for our soccer team and, in a way, tried to make up with all these activities for the years we had spent in the service.

Through my association with this group and particularly with the Jaffe brothers, my interest in opera skyrocketed. Occasionally, I stood in line with friends at the old Metropolitan Opera house on 39th Street to obtain one of the very limited number of standing room tickets. When we succeeded, we lined up in back of the last row of orchestra seats and sat down on the floor during intermissions. There was a certain elitism involved with this arrangement, aside from the fact that this admission cost only one dollar. During these years, I saw some of the greatest operatic talents of our time: Enzio Pinza, Jussi Bjoerling, Leonard Warren, Ljuba Welitsch, Salvatore Baccoloni, Licia Albanese, Jerome Hines, Richard Tucker, Rise Stevens, and Eleanor Steber, to name just a few of the luminaries. We started to collect 78 rpm records of our favorite artists and relished listening to them in each other's company. For me, and certainly not me exclusively, the favorite and most talented and most gifted operatic singer whom I ever heard in person was the Swedish tenor Jussi Bjoerling, whose recordings have given me sacred moments of joy throughout my life.

May 15, 1948, was a glorious day in the history of the Jewish people, and I was privileged to experience it. About two millennia after the Romans conquered Palestine and drove out most of the Jews, after this land of our ancestors was passed from conqueror to conqueror and the Jews were scattered in many countries of the world, there was again a land which the Jewish people could call their own. When dispersed as a minority, they frequently suffered terrible hardships, expulsions, and even death while always dreaming of better days to come and the possibility of reestablishing a Jewish homeland in Palestine. Now, like a miracle, this dream had become a reality. Now Jews needed no longer worry about second class citizenship and even worse, about the whims and prejudices of their country of residence, about closed doors and visas and immigration quotas. What a wonderful bright hope for the future after inquisitions, expulsions, pogroms, the Dreyfus affair, after six million of our people were slaughtered by Nazi Germany.

Maybe this latter and ultimate evil motivated the world body, the United Nations, to grant a homeland to any Jew who desires or requires it. Such a quid pro quo analysis is a "maybe" at best, because the Zionist dream of Theodore Herzl was born and enunciated a half a century prior to this founding event, i.e. long before Nazi Germany marched to the genocide drum. Furthermore, the world which, to a large part, stood by silently during the Holocaust cannot consider the realization of the century old yearning of the Jewish people to return to Zion as a compensation for the brutal extermination of six million of our people.

We were elated, of course, in spite of the fact that we lived in a great democratic country that cherishes freedom and justice. Six Arab armies immediately attempted to wipe out the fledgling Jewish state, but, like the Maccabees of ancient times, the Israelis repulsed their onslaught with courage and sacrifice. We hoped for Shalom, a chance for the Zionist pioneers and the survivors of the Holocaust to live and build in security and peace.

I achieved considerable success in my academic studies. In my junior year, I ran for and was elected president of the AIEE (American Institute of Electrical Engineers) student chapter. Such a leadership task was good experience for me. As part of a student show, I played the role of the town barber in Rossini's opera *The Barber of Seville* in miming the "Largo al factotum" aria while accompanied by a recording of Salvatore Baccoloni. During this 1948–49 year, I once became the victim of a pedantic academic action. Having completed the required chemical experiment with three of my partners, we left the lab to return to our respective homes to generate the required report and perform other studies. On the following day, we were notified by the instructor in charge of the lab that he would fail us for the semester because we had absented ourselves without his permission. We tried to explain and prevail on him not to be so harsh in his actions, but the best we could rescue from the situation was a grade of a "D" for the course. My report card for this semester contained seven "As" and the one "D." Since the year's grade for chemistry consisted of the combined record of the chemistry lab and the subsequent organic chemistry course, I attacked the latter with ferocious determination and scored 100% in each test. Our pedantic instructor had no choice but to award me with a "B" grade for the entire year.

In my senior year, I was invited to join Tau Beta Pi, the engineering honor society. During a week or two preceding the final interview and subsequent election, I was required to carry a self-made wooden replica of the

Graduating from Newark College of Engineering with the BSEE degree, June 14, 1950. "Lu(d) is perseverance and doggedness personified" (Yearbook quote).

Tau Bet key around my neck. In June 1950, I graduated with honors, having achieved a scholastic average of 3.64 of a possible 4.

The engineering job market was tight. While school was still in session, some companies visited NCE for recruiting purposes. Among others, I signed up for an interview with Curtiss-Wright Corporation (aircraft engine division) representatives. Just before graduation, I was informed of being accepted for a job as test engineer with a weekly compensation of $61.60. One day after graduation, on the 15th of June, I entered the huge plant, which had employed up to 20,000 people during the war and was located in Hasbrouck Heights near Lodi, New Jersey. When we completed our undergraduate studies, only one third of the members of my class had succeeded in obtaining engineering jobs. Shortly thereafter, the Korean war broke out, and, within one month, everybody had obtained employment. In a cynical observation, one could ask if war is an essential prerequisite for nearly full employment. I sincerely hope that this is not the case.

I initially commuted with Otto Hamburg, a fellow graduate and also a refugee from Germany, who possessed the essential car for the half-hour drive. Otto had just gotten married and was frequently a bit late in the morning, explaining his tardiness with a multitude of reasons except the right one. He was a bright engineer and I enjoyed his company during our joined travel. I was assigned to participate in the testing of Ram Jet Engine Controls. Ram Jets were being developed for the military at that time to serve as propulsion for supersonic missiles. The inlet shock wave at the transition from supersonic to subsonic flow created high downstream pressure which was then heated by a burner to provide the desired thrust. The controls job involved the fuel/air control and the optimal positioning of the shock interface. As a young engineer with limited industrial experience, I had some difficulties with union rules and practices. My co-workers, including the technicians, were nice enough people when they were around. But the union-affiliated technicians spent considerable time washing their hands before the morning start, before and after the breakfast break, before and after lunch, before and after the afternoon break, and before quitting time. In my frustration to get a few things accomplished on the test stand, I helped myself to their tools on occasion. This resulted in a union grievance when discovered, because engineers were not allowed to perform the work assigned to technicians. Somehow I got around this dilemma by appealing to the good nature of key individuals.

In the fall of 1950, I started to attend NCE graduate school at night in order to broaden my skills in automatic control theory, servo-mechanism, transient and stability analysis. The program would eventually lead to a master's degree. In the following spring, my parents bought a cute little house on Weequahic Avenue in Newark. There I had a beautiful room at my disposal which was at least double in size to that on Custer Avenue. As a veteran, I was able to assist my parents by facilitating this purchase with my GI mortgage privilege, which required only a 4.5% interest rate for the loan plus a modest down-payment. The refugees of 1939 had taken root in their own soil and my mother enjoyed planting her little garden.

THE FOUNDING OF A FAMILY

In the spring of 1951, Bea decided not to continue her relationship with Heinz or anyone else besides me. I was absolutely elated, in seventh heaven! Heinz told me subsequently that since Bea would not marry him, he was glad that I was going to be the one. This sensitive expression was a most generous sentiment on part of this fine man. The long five years of competitive courtship had now culminated in the well-founded hope that Bea and I would share the future of our lives.

By the summer, I had saved sufficient funds to afford a new car, a Chevy sedan with standard gear shift. This new dimension gave me much more flexibility and convenience, particularly for dating Bea, for commuting to work, and for traveling to night college. On the 21st of November, Bea and I became engaged. My mother had expressed some concerns that I could not afford, in a financial sense, to marry Bea, but I had no doubts, and Al fully agreed with my judgment. It was the best decision I ever made in my life. Our parents were aware of our intent to announce the engagement on the 21st, the night before Thanksgiving. Bea was alone in the apartment and looked great in a red velvet dress. Settling down on the sofa, we listened to a recording of *Rigoletto*. After a while, Bea asked when I was going to give her the ring. In embarrassment about my forgetfulness, I took it out of my jacket pocket and put it on her finger, a special moment in our lives which was sealed with a kiss. After seeing my parents and sister, we returned to Bea's home, where my mother-in-law-to-be greeted me from the top of the stairs with the exclamation: "Here comes our new son". There was much joy all around. I became better acquainted with Bea's brother Bert and his wife Eunice, with whom I shared a close friendship in the many years since then. To be in love, to plan for married life, those were such great times. In our honor, there were a number of parties, one at Lena Kaufman's house, who was a sister of Bea's mother and another one at the Weinbergs, a sister of Ary Kaufman. The latter lived in a rather unusual South Orange home dubbed the mushroom house because of its unique shape.

My new in-laws were very fine people. Bea's father, who was educated in Wuerzburg, had been a cantor, religious school teacher, and congregational bookkeeper in Konstanz from 1920 until emigration in 1938. Before being called to Konstanz, Jacob Bravmann had had a similar position since 1910 in Neidenstein, a small town near Heidelberg with a high concentration of Jews. It was there that he met his future wife, Flora Jakob, who came from a sizable family and was helping her parents in running a family restaurant. Jacob and Flora left Konstanz together with Bea in the summer of 1938 to immigrate to the U.S.A. The synagogue had already been severely damaged by the Nazis in 1936 and restored thereafter, only to be totally destroyed after their departure during Kristallnacht. Bert had already emigrated in 1933 at the urging of his parents, who, with good foresight, saw no future for a young Jewish man in Germany. After immigrating to this country, my father-in-law was not able to secure a cantor's position, in part due to limited command of the English language and no familiarity with Yiddish. Thus, he took care of his family's needs by working as a bookkeeper. Let me observe here that the immigrants who fled from Nazi Germany during those years universally did not request or depend on public assistance. They were all industrious and proud people who preferred not to lean on their affidavit guarantors for any help beyond the first few months of their U.S. residency.

During this joyful time for Bea and me, my friend Al sustained a serious loss with the death of his mother. She was still in her forties, and we were once again reminded of the fragility of life. The privilege of living should never be taken for granted.

Our wedding took place on a hot and sunny day, the 8th of June, 1952, in the large Reform Temple B'nai Jeshurun in Newark. My in-laws had frequented this synagogue because of the Kaufmans' long-term affiliation with it. Al Meinhardt served as best man and Bea's friend Lore Frank as maid of honor. Al and I were very nervous and had difficulty, with our shaky hands, to affix each other's boutonnieres. The beautiful ceremony, conducted by Rabbi Eli Pilchik, took place in the main sanctuary in front of the ark. Surrounded by family and friends, I remember the sacred moment when Bea, accompanied by her parents, walked down the center

Father Jacob chanting the blessing over bread at our wedding banquest.

aisle and I took her hand. My tenseness continued throughout the ceremony, causing a premature "I do," but I did not mind at all pronouncing it a second time. Bea looked radiantly beautiful, a projection of the life ahead which she created for us both. In honor of the occasion, Bea's parents donated precious Torah ornaments to the temple. Had they not brought these ritual objects along from Germany, then these adornments would have been destroyed during Kristallnacht. After a very nice reception in the temple's Goetz Hall, we gathered for a family dinner at the Essex House Hotel in Newark. At the end of this eventful day, Al and Lore brought us to New York City's Pierre Hotel. When registering for the first time as

Bea and I joined for life: Temple B'nai Jeshurun,
Newark, NJ, June 8, 1952.

husband and wife, the clerk informed me that our reserved double
room was not available and we could occupy a honeymoon suite instead at the same price. It was a very spacious accommodation, and
in the morning I was watching Harry Truman on the living room TV
when Bea awoke. Then we embarked on a lengthy train ride to Miami because I was still a bit leery of travel by plane. Within a few
years, this reluctance had to give way to pragmatic necessity. For
our honeymoon, we stayed at the San Souci Hotel, at that time one
of the newest on the beach front. Aunt Paula resided nearby; she
had moved there for the better climate and had established the
"Knitting Nook," living in a back room of the store. Her marriage
with Lew Levi had disintegrated into separation. She loved meeting
Bea, especially since she had not been present at the wedding. To
no one's surprise, the weather was very hot and we spent most of
our time either on the beach or in an air conditioned environment.

Our first home, located at 18 Marshall Street, Apt. 7N, Irvington, was a modern and bright apartment consisting of two good-sized rooms, a small kitchen, and bath. What fun we had decorating the place! Bea did a great job, and we had very happy times. Early on, Bea bought me a croton, which we called a bacon plant because of its appearance, and with that our common interest in gardening had begun, although I may have been also inspired by my mother as well as by Meta Sander during my earlier years in Suhl.

Since graduating from high school in 1946, Bea had worked for the Bureau of Service to the Foreign Born of the National Council of Jewish Women in Newark. Besides secretarial tasks, she had done a lot of work there helping refugees, i.e., Holocaust survivors, also known as displaced persons, with their immigration problems and assisting them after arrival on these shores. She frequently went to piers on the Hudson River to welcome and aid these newcomers.

After two years of the experimental test activity at Curtis-Wright, I was promoted to the project office for ram jet design and development, a much more challenging assignment. Our primary customer was the U.S. Air Force, which wanted to utilize the ram jet engines for propelling its missiles at three and a half times (Mach 3.5) the speed of sound. Although I enjoyed the technical aspects of the work on jet engine controls, I was not particularly thrilled about the exclusively military aspects of my efforts. By 1954, I advanced to section head and became responsible for all technical aspects of ram jet controls. The organization was anything but optimal because, while supervising 10 people, I had three bosses and thus became the "neck of the chicken," with the inherent difficulty of managing all the swallowing. But alternate employment opportunities were difficult to find, and I decided to make the best of it. The position involved some air travel, at times under rather adverse weather conditions. Once, when departing from Cleveland after visiting the government NACA facility, my plane skidded off the icy runway. The pilot just made a second attempt and, thankfully, he succeeded. North American Aviation, later known as Rockwell, was the missile builder and therefore the prime contractor of the project. I routinely visited Downy, California, together with two or three of my CW colleagues, for coordination and review meetings. The attendance was rather one-sided; it was not unusual to be faced by 20 or more NAA interrogators during these sessions. During these years, I had a few original ideas. After considerable

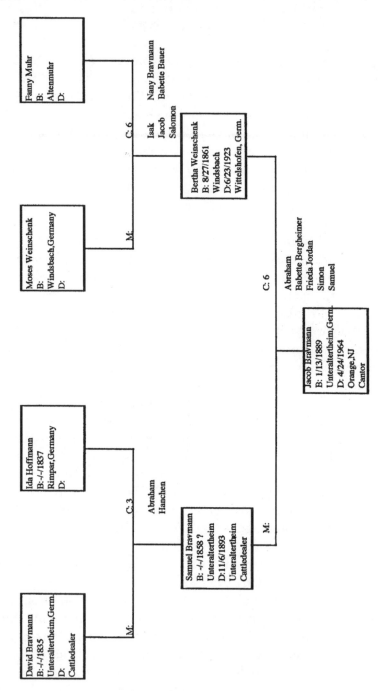

Family Tree of Bea's Father

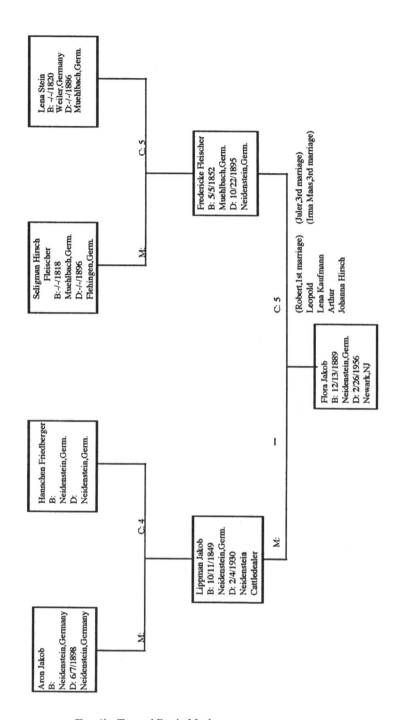

Lena Stein
B: -/-/1820
Weiler,Germany
D: -/-/1886
Muehlbach,Germ.

Seligman Hirsch
Fleischer
B: -/-/1818
Muehlbach,Germ.
D: -/-/1896
Flehingen,Germ.

C: 5

M:

Fredericke Fleischer
B: 5/5/1852
Muehlbach,Germ.
D: 10/22/1895
Neidenstein,Germ.

(Robert,1st marriage)   (Juler,3rd marriage)
Leopold   (Irma Maas,3rd marriage)
Lena Kaufmann
Arthur
Johanna Hirsch

C: 5

Flora Jakob
B: 12/13/1889
Neidenstein,Germ.
D: 2/26/1956
Newark,NJ

Hannchen Friedberger
B:
Neidenstein,Germ.
D:
Neidenstein,Germ.

C: 4

Lippman Jakob
B: 10/11/1849
Neidenstein,Germ.
D: 2/4/1930
Neidenstein
Cattledealer

M:

Aron Jakob
B:
Neidenstein,Germany
D: 6/7/1898
Neidenstein,Germany

M:

I

Family Tree of Bea's Mother

work and interaction with the company's patent attorneys, these were eventually issued as three U.S. patents. So I became one of a multitude of small inventors, and I enjoyed this feeling of participation and contribution.

In 1953, Bert and Eunice decided to initiate adoption proceedings and thus Peter Bravmann entered our lives. This four months old happy little fellow immediately became the focus of our family's love and affection. We enjoyed him from the very start and could not spend enough time playing uncle and aunt. Being the first one of the next generation of our small family, he was the recipient of everyone's adoration. He loved to eat and smile; all of us thrived on it and so did he.

During the summer of 1953, Bea and I took the first of many auto tours to become acquainted with diverse corners of our world. On this initial one, we explored the Montreal and Quebec City area of our Canadian neighbor. French-derived national pride conveyed the impression that General Montcalm had been the prevailing hero of the battle on Quebec's Plains of Abraham, although in fact British General Wolf was victorious. We were fascinated by the quaint and beautiful old part of Quebec City and enjoyed the delectable French cooking of the region.

Touring was not on our vacation menu for the summer of 1954, when we joined friends Bob and Milly Rush on the Hyannis beaches of picturesque Cape Cod. Bea spent a disproportionate amount of time sleeping, and the Rushes could not understand why, but I certainly could! It was the beginning of Bea's pregnancy with Danny.

Danny was almost that intended spring baby, being born on the 7th of March, 1955. What a great, great day for Bea and me and the entire family. After receiving the confirming telephone call from Dr. Goodman while pacing the floor of our apartment, I rushed to see my mother, who met me with tears of joy in the front of her house. Then we brought the wonderful news to my parents-in-law, who had been kept unaware of Bea's hospitalization so as not to worry them. Finally, I saw my radiant wife and our little son. What love had wrought; the whole family was elated. After the Bris, which was performed by Rabbi Friedman in Beth Israel Hospital, we made a triumphal return to our apartment. Danny was a lively little fellow from the very beginning. When he was two weeks old, I scolded my mother for not supporting his head while holding him.

"He is holding it on his own," she proudly replied, "he doesn't need my help." Stiff necked already?

A few months after this happy event, I finally graduated from NCE with my master's degree in electrical engineering. Except for the first semester of night college in 1951, I enrolled for only one course at a time so as to ease my schedule. Courses in servo-mechanisms and automatic controls had proven to be particularly interesting and were most useful for my professional needs. Now I could spend a bit more time with my little family, and we enjoyed walking Danny in his carriage through the beautifully landscaped area adjacent to the nearby Oraton Parkway. This lovely oasis was about to become the victim of the Garden State Parkway construction, a small example of the price we have to pay for the vast urbanization, the convenient transportation, and the mushrooming population growth of our world.

It soon became clear that our honeymoon apartment was a bit too small for three. Early one morning, when I tried to retrieve Danny from his carriage in the living room, our son had disappeared. After a momentary concern, I reached into the storage pouch at the bottom end and found him sleeping soundly in these unintended quarters. We decided to move into a garden apartment in Belleville (271 Branch Brook Drive) near our friends, the Wertheims. This attached unit was built on two levels and provided our offspring with his own room. Once, we carelessly left the screen of a casement window ajar, and Danny received his share of mosquito bites. My mother-in-law threatened, only half in jest, to take him away from us if there would ever be a recurrence. We were living just north of beautiful Branch Brook Park, an oasis blessed with impressive landscaping, including the largest collection of Japanese cherry trees on the East coast. It was fun to take Danny there, even though he was still too young to take advantage of the lovely playgrounds.

On a fall day of 1955, I was suddenly smitten with an intense headache, which our physician quickly diagnosed as polio. He was attuned to this dreadful disease because of another recent patient; therefore, the quick recognition. This sudden turn of events was a tremendous shock for the whole family and friends. My illness, which fortunately turned out to be of the non-paralytic strain, occurred just prior to the advent of the Salk vaccine. For about two weeks, I was hospitalized in the Essex County Isolation Hospital in Belleville. While I was initially lying there on blanket covered

NEWARK·COLLEGE·OF·ENGINEERING

THE·BOARD·OF·TRUSTEES
UPON·RECOMMENDATION·OF·THE·FACULTY·OF·THE·COLLEGE
HEREBY·CONFERS·ON

LUDWIG · MUHLFELDER

THE·DEGREE·OF
MASTER·OF·SCIENCE
IN·ELECTRICAL·ENGINEERING

IN·RECOGNITION·OF·THE·COMPLETION·OF·THE·COURSE·OF·STUDY
PRESCRIBED·FOR·THIS·DEGREE
GIVEN·UNDER·THE·SEAL·OF·THE·COLLEGE·AT·NEWARK·IN·THE
STATE·OF·NEW·JERSEY·THIS · NINTH · DAY·OF · JUNE ·
NINETEEN·HUNDRED·FIFTY·FIVE

FOR·THE·TRUSTEES   PRESIDENT

FOR·THE·FACULTY   PRESIDENT

FOR·THE·GRADUATE·DIVISION   CHAIRMAN

The MSEE degree was earned during five years of night study.

wooden boards, a precaution against potential deformation, I listened to a man dying of bulbar polio in the very next room. It was a frightful and depressing episode. All those who had had recent direct contact with me received injections of gamma globulin. Our friend Ushi Wertheim was particularly concerned, because I had just given her a congratulatory kiss upon the arrival of her second child, son Eric. Luckily, no harm was done, and I returned to work shortly after release from the hospital. Occasionally, since that time, I feel a slight stiffness in my neck, which may be an after-effect of my illness or possibly a manifestation of my personality.

Bea's second pregnancy began just before my mother-in-law's sudden passing on February 26, 1956. She had suffered from hypertension and had seen her doctor just a day prior to that fateful stroke. After ordering immediate bed rest, the doctor carelessly had permitted her to walk home. Bea had visited with her mother on that final day, and when I picked her up in the early evening, Danny responded by waving what turned out to be a fond farewell to his bedridden maternal grandmother. We were utterly unprepared for her death, which occurred an hour or two later. I kissed her forehead as she lay there on her bed in the stillness of eternity. Our lives had now entered a new chapter: the caring for the old, an area to which Bea gave so much of her energy and her love. We are solicitous of the aged in our family to enhance their remaining days and years, knowing that the time will come when we have to bid them a permanent farewell. During the next few decades, Bea took loving care not only of her aging father but also of my parents and a number of elderly people of my family, an unusual and kind forthcoming for which I will always be very grateful. We now entered a time of change and transition. In the early summer, Bert and Eunice bought a house in Livingston, which at that time still had a distinctly small town suburban character. Father Jacob decided to live with them for the time being until we could arrange otherwise. He desired eventually to reside with us. The handwriting was on the wall: with Bea expecting our second child in the fall, we required more room to accommodate a family of five. New residential developments were springing up in various suburban settings, and after limited investigation we put a $25 deposit on a house being built in Cedar Grove that was modified to provide a fourth bedroom. Danny, now in his second year, became very agile, roaming around the apartment and chinning himself on the drawers of the kitchen cabinet. He managed to get past the guard gate of the bedroom level and fall down a flight of stairs without significant damage. When he once accidentally banged his head in the crib during the night, he quickly got accustomed to his mother's solace, for he repeated this now deliberate performance for the following two nights. No response was the solution to that potential habit. During the summer, we took him to Cape Cod and a well-appreciated introduction to the beach. He loved the sand and the hole I dug "to China." Mrs. Wagner, our once-a-week domestic help, accompanied us to assist in caring for Danny. The Bravmanns as well as the Rices, Eunice's brother and family, were vacationing there also and a fine time was had by all.

The construction of the Cedar Grove house progressed at a snail's pace and the builder attempted to escalate the price tag. We asked for the return of our modest deposit and embarked on a new search for an abode. The impending birth of our second child made this an urgent matter. Aside from inspecting houses being offered for resale, we scanned the real estate adds in the paper. In the columns of the Newark Evening News, I spotted an offer for a four-bedroom Livingston residence with a 30-mile view. By that time, Bea's delicate condition made it difficult for her to travel, so I made a solo appointment with the agent to take a look at 15 Orchard Lane. I returned to my anxious wife with the message: "It's a great house but we can't afford it." The asking price was $28,500, and my salary was about $6,000 per year. Bea and I had targeted a maximum of $22,000 as an affordable purchase price. On the following Sunday, the entire family assembled at 15 Orchard for an inspection; they admired and approved. Bea was particularly impressed with the layout of this four level split and the living room fireplace. I had my eyes on the half acre property and was thinking "garden." While Bea was sitting on the porch steps and conversing with the real estate agent, she inquired why this house, built only the previous year, was being sold. "Mr. Anderson suddenly died of polio" was the explanation. Possibly, this was the man whom I heard in distress in the adjoining room while in the Belleville Isolation Hospital. Life plays peculiar tricks! With everyone's approval and my father-in-law's offer to help with the one third down-payment, we made a $24,000 counter offer. A few days later, the agent informed me by phone that Mrs. Anderson would accept $24,500 as the sale price. "Sold" was my spontaneous reply, and we were on our way to becoming homeowners.

A few days later, on November 6, Barry was born. His birthday coincided with Eisenhower's reelection as U.S. President. That cute little fellow with those dark brown eyes looked like Bea. There was great joy in our hearts, and we felt immeasurably blessed. Barry was ingenious right from the start, finding a little hole in his hospital pajamas to suck his thumb. After the Bris, which was again performed by Rabbi Friedman, we brought our little bundle to Belleville. This new life gave us a tremendous lift after the void created by mother Flora's passing. Bea, on behalf of the new brother, presented Danny with a pack of candy. Within a few minutes, little Danny, at the ripe age of 20 months, placed one of these chocolate goodies in his brother's crib. We were touched by this sensitive gesture, a symbolic act indeed, for the two brothers have been bound in a lifelong friendship.

FAMILY, GARDEN, AND GROWTH
AT 15 ORCHARD LANE (1956–1964)

With our relocation to Livingston, a new and significant chapter of our lives was initiated. We moved into 15 Orchard Lane on December 27, 1956, and at this writing, more than 40 years later, Bea and I are still residing at the same address. The opportunity to transform our own house into a sacred home was both challenging and uplifting, but we were, of course, unable to predict the future and the many and primarily happy years that we would be privileged to live there. Baby Barry began his residency there with a severe cold and breathing disorders. We had so much space at our disposal! Even our one car looked a bit lost in the two-car garage! Most appropriately, the first of many celebrations in our new residence was Danny's second birthday: all these kids accompanied by their proud mothers. During that first and many a winter thereafter, I did lots of snow shoveling, clearing that 50-foot driveway; a 125-foot sidewalk, and a 60-foot front walk that parallels the house. We had fun sleigh-riding on the nearby West Orange golf course and building snowmen in the front yard. In the spring of 1957, we started to transform the yard into a garden. The tragically brief occupancy of the prior owners had not permitted any landscaping improvements beyond the basics provided by the builder. There was no lawn to greet us, only lots of rocks and miserable clay soil. We started modestly by planting a few trees and bushes, removing an apparently endless number of stones and boulders, and planting grass to prevent further soil erosion. But even during this incipient year, I dug a few small beds for Bea to plant flowers and vegetables.

On a nice spring day, a young boy rang our doorbell, identified himself as Jay Fortgang, one of our new neighbors, and offered to sell me for 10 cents a tiny bag of top soil with the admonition: "you need it." I promptly accepted his proposition and thus began an extended friendship with his family, a relationship that contains many fond memories. To this day, we are still in contact with Lucille, Jay's mother, a charming and talented woman, an excellent gardener, a wonderful hostess, a good friend both on sunny and rainy days. Later, they moved to Westport, Connecticut, where we spent a number of memorable Thanksgivings as friends and guests.

Bea's father moved in during the summer of 1957. We all called him Bampa, because his first grandson Peter had given him that endearing name. The presence of this gentle and loving man was wonderful for all, especially the boys. Father Jacob had great interest in his grandchildren and the garden. As an old lover of the agricultural avocation, Bampa drew up a detailed plan for an all-encompassing apple orchard in our backyard and presented it proudly to us. I convinced him to do something less ambitious so that the children had a place to play. We very amicably settled on five fruit trees instead. He was a very fine human being and also added a wonderful dimension to our Shabbat and holiday joy as loving father and grandfather. As a former cantor, he was our resident expert for all religious practices and Jewish history. He was always patient and loving with our children.

In 1957, we decided to join Temple Emanu-El. This Reform congregation had been founded only two years previously and was most compatible with our religious approach and our objectives for the children. Having settled in Livingston, we decided to join almost immediately, although our offspring were too young to attend religious school, because it was important for us to belong as part of our Jewish commitment. For Bea and for me, it was a special privilege to have this opportunity, remembering the destruction of the Jewish communities and the synagogues of our youth. Many Jews in the U.S. choose no religious affiliation until required as a mandatory prerequisite for the Bar or Bat Mitzvah of their children. About one half of American Jewry belong to the unaffiliated category. I am of the strong conviction that Diaspora Judaism can only survive and prosper in the presence of a viable synagogue structure. Whether one affiliates with the Reform, Conservative, Orthodox, or Reconstructionist movement is not as important as it is to support a Synagogue in the first place. Father Jacob enrolled separately in the single membership category.

Aunt Paula visited us every year from Florida for about two months during the late summer and early fall, a period that also en-

compassed the High Holidays. This aunt of mine was a real character. She unreservedly loved each of our children, every one of whom
received a knitted apparel as a gift at each of her annual visits. All
of us were quite fond of her in spite of some inherent idiosyncrasies.
She had no children of her own and no husband in fact; we were her
family, and visiting with us was the highlight of her year. Year after
year, Bea was particularly hospitable to this blond old lady . Paula
called Barry "My Precious"; she was especially smitten with that little fellow with his deep and searching dark brown eyes.

During these years, we could not afford extensive vacations, but
we managed on a few occasions to rent a small house for a week at
the New Jersey shore. This was a wonderful time for our little family. The children loved the beach, of course, and we were able to re-
lax in this ideal environment. There was many a hole in the sand,
which I dug "to China." For extensive sightseeing travel, we had to
wait for the children to grow up.

Home ownership and ever increasing interest caused us to become more and more involved with gardening. The children, even at
a relatively young age, learned and loved this activity by working
with us from planting to reaping: flowers and vegetables and fruit
trees and shade trees and berry bushes and grapes; the backyard
was our vacation land. During the late fifties and early sixties, I
built a large picnic table, a sandbox, and a tree fort, installed a swing
set and assembled a prefabricated small log cabin. Quite frequently,
we organized picnics in our garden or in the Bravmanns' backyard.
Bert and Eunice also became interested gardeners, though they
were not quite so intense and expansionist as I. Especially memorable were our excursions with them to the Stokes State Forest in
northern New Jersey. Bert was a gourmet chef in grilling hamburgers and steaks. The liquid refreshments for the adults enhanced the
jovial atmosphere, and both young and old had a grand time.

In January of 1959, we invited the entire family to join in celebrating Bampa's 70th birthday. Father was surrounded by those he
loved, and there was a reflection of joy and serenity in his eyes. Naturally, he received many lovely presents, but the most important
one did not arrive till the summer.

This was the year of Bea's third pregnancy. The baby was due
in August and a long hot spell had preceded the birth. In these days
before air conditioning, Bea found it taxing to take care of a busy
five-person household. On a sweltering July afternoon, Danny

brought a severely injured bird into the house with the announcement that it was going to have a baby, whereupon Eunice turned to Bea and exclaimed: "If that bird can have a baby, so can you!" And she did on the 19th of August on the stroke of midnight. It was touch and go whether we could make it in time to Newark's Beth Israel Hospital. Within a half hour after our arrival, Dr. Goodman gave me the wonderful news of Leslie's birth. The overjoyed mother and her little daughter were doing just fine. When I returned to our home in the very early morning hours, Bampa stood at the top

With Leslie's arrival, the family is complete. Flanking new sister are big brother Danny (left) and little brother Barry (right), September 1959.

of the stairs in tense anticipation: "It's a girl, Bampa," I exclaimed, and the old man was full of joy that he now also had been blessed with a granddaughter. A few days later, there was a triumphant entry into 15 Orchard Lane. The reception committee, lined up on our driveway, consisted not only of the family but also of our neighbors including next door's Bette Wilson and the children of the street. Leslie moved into the room adjoining our bedroom, and the boys from then on shared a room next to Bampa's, half a flight upstairs. The two brothers were proud and solicitous of their little sister. As siblings, they developed a deep friendship and have maintained a profound and warm relationship to this day.

After the birth of each of our children, Bampa established an insurance policy with prepaid premiums as a headstart towards their eventual college education expenses. Some years later, we cashed in the net worth of these policies and invested this liquidation together with occasional savings of our own in mutual funds. Even Bampa made further contributions to these education funds of his grandchildren whenever he celebrated a milestone birthday, the last one when he reached the 75th. This farsighted and generous gesture did not go unnoticed with Bea and me. It was an example for us to follow just as, in a more global sense, our parents' conduct and values represented an important guide how to travel the path of life.

In the fall of 1960, Danny entered kindergarten, and with that event, which was important to the entire family, the formal education of our children had begun; it was not to end until 24 years later. Danny was particularly interested in and fond of animals. To enable him to observe and care for his wild friends, we purchased a Havahart trap and I built a large cage. Our zoo population varied from raccoons to rabbits and even skunks. Danny eventually would release these animals to return them to their free environment. Once, he proudly invited my parents, who had just arrived in their car, to view recently captured skunks in the cage at the far end of the property. Choosing caution as the better part of valor, my mother exclaimed: "I can see them from here." A few years later, Danny wrote a composition in school deploring the hunting and killing of wildlife as a sport and not merely for food purposes; he was a sensitive and sensible little boy.

One of the national bellwether events of these growing years was the 1960 election of John Fitzgerald Kennedy as President of our country. He was a bright, young, and energetic individual. A man with a vision, he was a leader who appealed to both the young and the older citizens of our nation and our world, a poetic orator who generated confidence and hope for the future. We were elated that the insidious prejudice against Catholics holding such a high office was overcome with his election, but just barely. Hopefully, this event signaled not only the decline but the elimination of religious, racial, and ethnic precondition as qualification for governmental, educational, or commercial positions. Ability and character should constitute the only prevailing requirements.

One of the important reasons why our house is a home derives from the Jewish traditions that we perpetuated within its walls; the Shabbat and the High Holidays were and are always special, prepared with great love by Bea and observed with joy and reverence by those who dwell therein. For the welcome of the Shabbat, Bea bakes the Berches (German Jewish Challa), with its distinctive crunchy crust, and sets the festive table in the dining room. For some years, the wine for the Kiddush was even homemade and thus of marginal quality, as pointed out repeatedly by our children. Before the meal, parents bless children and grandchildren, and at the conclusion of the dinner we recite the Birkat Hamazon in gratitude for our food.

The Passover Seder, with its dual message of liberation and nature's rebirth has always been an uplifting and festive occasion for our immediate and extended family and both the Jewish and Christian guests, whom we invited to share this occasion with us. To tell the story of the Exodus from Egypt and Israel's crossing of the Sea of Reeds and the Sinai desert has a particular emotional impact for refugees such as Bea and me

Lighting Hanukkah Menorahs at 15 Orchard lane in order of age: Bampa Jacob, Pa Julius, uncle Lothatr, uncle Max, daddy Lu, Danny, Barry, and Leslie, December 1961.

because of the poignant parallel to our personal history. In this century, the remnants of our people, the Jewish people, crossed the rivers and mountains of Europe and the Atlantic Ocean or the Mediterranean Sea to live again, to live again in freedom.

In the decade of the sixties, we transformed our grape arbor into a Sukkah, a booth decorated with the gifts of the harvest, where God's universe served as our roof while we celebrated the Jewish Thanksgiving. While the observance of the High Holidays are by their very nature primarily synagogue-oriented, Bea made sure that our home always reflected the festive and profound nature of these solemn days. For the children, the greatest fun were the eight days of Hanukkah with the nightly lighting by all participants of their own Menorah (in sequential order by age), the joyful singing, and the multitude of presents. No matter how modest, Bea made sure that each of our children would receive a gift on each of the eight nights of our festival of lights.

We never forgot how precious our religious freedom is and always appreciated being able to observe those special days with family and friends. Bea for all these years had such great love for her family and for her heritage to make it all possible, to make it so very special. She transformed our home into a sanctuary, where the Shekhinah, the Divine Presence, dwelled within our midst.

Similarly, we celebrated each birthday with joy and with love, and particularly for the children with parties and presents. I am a strong believer in the observance of anniversaries such as the day of our birth and the day of marriage. It is a privilege to reach these milestones and we should never take our passage for granted. Although we have to be grateful for every single day of our lives, anniversaries deserve more than a passing glance. Besides the joy of celebration, we should also take out some time for reflection of our infinitesimal existence within the infinity of God's universe.

During the winter of 1960–61, our family faced major health problems. I was stricken with infectious hepatitis and spent six weeks in semi-isolation in our recreation room. Bed rest and the passage of time were the only two prescriptions for recovery. Previously, I had contemplated leaving my position at Curtiss-Wright, but the company was most considerate in continuing my salary for the entire three months duration of my absence. Thus, I put that intention on hold.

Simultaneously, Leslie became seriously ill with symptoms of high fever and excruciating pain. The problem was diagnosed to be a one-sided valve malfunction between the urethra and kidney. This put a tremendous burden on Bea to care for both of us and simultaneously manage the normal needs of the household. Leslie underwent two major operations in 1961, each followed by extensive recuperation periods. Fortunately, she did not lose one of her kidneys as at one time appeared necessary to Dr. Fury, the very competent surgeon who changed his mind during the second operation. Since those critical times, Leslie is very much improved but has to be somewhat careful for her entire life. For the whole family, but particularly for parents, this health crisis of our child was of immeasurable concern, and we are thankful that medical science was able to help.

Within this timeframe, we were notified by the township that the houses on Orchard Lane had been reappraised for real estate tax purposes in response to one or more complaints. This was a period of rapid inflation of property values, and the entire township had been reappraised just a year or two previously. All residents of the street were up in arms for being singled out for such a review in the prevailing inflationary environment while the rest of the town could maintain the status quo. An attorney of the street collected a fee from each resident to prepare an appeal to the county. However, one by one, each homeowner lost heart and interest in this aggravating matter, and within a few months, I, stubbornly, was the only remaining complainant. I decided to represent myself and managed to convince the county at a hearing in Newark of the justice of my case. Thereupon, the township appealed the matter to the state level. Fortunately, I was still permitted to be my own attorney. Once again sacrificing some vacation time in order to attend the hearing in the West Orange townhall, I waited with several hundred others for my case to be called. Suddenly, there it was as I heard the clerk announce: "Township of Livingston versus Muhlfelder," followed almost immediately by Louis Bort, the town's attorney, with: "Township of Livingston withdraws." Not being familiar with procedures and pleased with my success, I rose and proclaimed loud and clear, "Muhlfelder accepts," to the amusement of the entire assembly.

The boys were able to assist us in various tasks, including the painting of rooms of the house starting in the early 1960s; their skill and contribution improved as time went on. We believed it to be beneficial to have our children take on tasks that were compatible with their understanding and physical limitations. Even if we could have afforded to compensate others for these services (which we could not), such an alternative would have been a disservice to the development of a sense of responsibility within our children.

For a window limited to a few special years, I loved to bathe the three children together when I came home from my office. We also had lots of fun playing on the living room floor, where all three climbed on my back while I crawled on all fours. Leslie and at times her brothers took delight in hiding in my bedroom closet when I returned from the office at the end of the day, I always managing to be startled, after which they gave me great hellos. Bea or I put them to bed each night with the children's prayer Hamaloh Hagoel, which both of us were taught by our mothers in another time and another place.

In September 1961, Barry entered kindergarten, another milestone. He was a bit immature for this step and, in retrospect, it would have been more desirable to delay his initiation to formal schooling for another year. Nevertheless, we wondered what his inquisitive and unique mind would do with academia. What a cute boy as he marched off to the bus stop with his jacket and with his dreams. During these years, Barry gave ample evidence that he is a unique individual. For example, he 1) cut his own hair, rather unevenly; 2) explored our toaster with the tip of his nose, with long term after-effects; 3) painted the Wilsons' car partially white, not an appreciated neighborly gesture; 4) challenged his mother with a multitude of questions: how far; how big; how high; how deep; how heavy; how small; how many; how fast; and why? why? why?

The fall and early winter of 1961 was a time of historical family significance for us, for uncle Lothar and aunt Hannah visited us for the very first time. Not having seen them since 1936–37, when they emigrated separately from Nazi Germany to the British mandate of Palestine, resulted in an emotional and momentous reunion. Almost a quarter of a century had passed, and monumental events had shaken the world. Many millions had died in the war and the Holocaust, multitudes had been displaced, but here they were, reunited, three brothers and three sisters as three couples, plus all the other family members. No-one needed to be reminded that fortune had been kind to us.

Our guests loved to explore the metropolitan area and enjoyed becoming acquainted with my good wife and our children. When visiting the Bronx Zoo together, Leslie pointed in surprise to a gorilla, exclaiming: "That's a funny looking man." When Bea pointed out on the way from the zoo how poor people had to live in the slums of New York while we were so fortunate to have a beautiful home in a nice town, Barry observed: "But look how close they live to the zoo."

The motivating factor for our Israeli guests to remain with us through the unaccustomed chill of December was my father's 70th birthday. Their presence at this event, celebrated in a catering establishment, was a special present indeed. Pa, as our children called him, was a young 70, still working at least part time and agile and alert. During that month, we also observed Hanukkah together in our house. It was quite a sight, when we lined up (only the males at that time) in order of age to recite the blessings and light our Menorahs.

By the summer of 1962, we saw a considerable improvement in Leslie's health. On her third birthday, she looked like a precious doll in her starched white dress. We spent a week at the Jersey shore near our friends Bruce and Marion Frey, who taught me how to water-ski and thrilled the kids with boat rides in the bay of Lafayette.

After a relatively brief courtship, Al Meinhardt married Evi, a charming and delightful young woman from Chile, on September 15 in Temple B'nai Abraham. The Meinhardts had been affiliated with this Temple for many years. I served as best man, thus reciprocating the honors of our own wedding of exactly a decade earlier. As we were gathered in a study adjoining the Bima just prior to the ceremony to sign and witness the wedding certificate, Rabbi Prinz started to sing "La donna e mobile" ("Women are fickle") from Verdi's *Rigoletto*, and in full voice Cantor Shapiro joined in. It was a jovial and surprising interlude, maybe to relieve the tension of the moment. Al had become a pivotal member of his father's leather goods business during the prior decade and in that capacity spent a considerable portion of his time on the road.

At 15 Orchard Lane, family life was happy and tranquil. Often, my parents, sister, and the Bravmanns and other relatives, as well as friends, joined us to share happy moments, the celebration of the little milestones of life, the observance of various secular and religious holidays. The garden was becoming more beautiful with each year, and the children participated in its upkeep and enhancement.

Bampa's health was becoming more frail. He had suffered from the relatively intense pain due to kidney stones for many years. Every one of his birthdays we accepted as a gift with profound gratitude. He was a wonderful companion, guide, and friend to our children. His love and knowledge of nature was transferred to them not just by teaching but by innate interest and personal example. In a similar vein, his love of Judaism was intertwined in his teaching of the Hanukkah blessings, his dignified chanting of the Sabbath and holiday melodies, and his participation in the preparations for Passover and the enhancement of our Seders. He relished reading to his grandchildren and encouraged their development by giving ardent recognition to their accomplishments. He was our children's friend and companion, even when at times confined to bed rest because of pain or fatigue. His serene, calm and patient demeanor was a most welcome and beneficial addition to our rather busy and at times hectic atmosphere.

In January of 1964, we celebrated Bampa's 75th birthday. Bea prepared a wonderful party for family and friends. It was a bittersweet day. Three months later, he decided to enter the hospital for a risky but necessary kidney stone operation. He confided to me that he knew the risks but could no longer stand the pain. Though the operation was successful, he died a few days thereafter during a choking episode while still in intensive care. We all realized the magnitude of the loss; even Leslie at four-and-a-half had tears in her eyes. Our children realized that their grandfather would never come back. But I have no doubt that he lives to this day in the deepest recesses of their hearts. Thankfully, by his example, he left a special impact on the children. As long as we live, he will live in our memories as a warm and sensitive man, who loved his family, had a special appreciation and respect for nature, and enhanced the joys of Judaism within our home. He was a blessing to our family.

My parents sold their home in the summer of 1964 and moved to the same apartment complex where Bea and I first resided after our marriage. Time takes its toll, and one of the arts of living is to adjust gracefully to the aging process which sooner or later we will all experience. To grow old while having reasonably good health and retention of our normal mental faculties is a real blessing and a profound privilege, a condition that is not to be taken lightly or considered an entitlement. We have to make the very best of each day.

In this sense, I have often quoted from "The Paradox of Time" by Henry Austin Dobson:

> Time goes, you say? Ah no!
> Alas, Time stays, *we* go;
> Or else, were this not so,
> What need to chain the hours,
> For Youth were always ours?
> Time goes, you say? Ah no!

As so often happens, when signs of the aging process become most visible, we receive a compensation. And so it was in 1964, when our friends Al and Evi Meinhardt were blessed with parenthood with the arrival of son Edward. In great joy, we all welcomed that little boy.

FROM JETS TO SATELLITES:

A TRANSITION IN MY CAREER (1957–1962)

Curtiss-Wright began to decline markedly in 1957, when the Nava-ho missile contract was canceled by the Air Force. Instead of air-breathing ram jet engines, the rapidly evolving rocket technology took over the propulsion for the intended missile function, while the commercial turbo-jet engine technology was in the hands of the British, General Electric and Pratt & Whitney. Curtiss-Wright had missed the boat by not initiating their in-house turbojet develop-ment immediately after the termination of the war. A series of staff reductions appeared unavoidable. The marginal top management did not bode well for the future of the company. Changing jobs was a serious consideration, but inertia and health problems got in my way of action. Once, I had just about committed myself to accept a position at Picatinny Arsenal but changed my mind at the last mo-ment because of a reluctance to "retire" to a government job and a militarily oriented one at that.

By 1962, it became more and more noticeable that Curtiss-Wright was declining at an accelerating rate. I saw my professional career detrimentally affected. It was not just my own professional ambition and pride that were at stake but much more my responsi-bility to provide for my family. I had hoped that my firm would grow and expand and thus create opportunities for young people such as me to work themselves upward on the proverbial ladder. But in-stead of climbing up, I was watching my firm sliding down, and I was not willing to go along for the ride.

With urging from my former colleague Mike Cutler, I submitted my resume for spacecraft attitude control design and development at the RCA Astro Electronics Division near Princeton. This division was founded in 1958 by the world-famous communications pioneer David Sarnoff in order to assure participation in the new space ven-

146

ture. This initiative was not necessarily intended for a quick return of direct profits but instead addressed the priorities of corporate prestige and the possible development of products and techniques that might also be suitable for more earthbound applications. Sarnoff was a man of great vision, already having seen in the 1920s to 1940s the full possibilities of using radio and TV for popular entertainment. After serving Radio Corporation of America as president since 1930, he became chairman of the board in 1947 and projected his pioneering spirit to the many who were part of the RCA team.

The plant was a good hour's drive from our house. Only a few years old, the space industry had to generate new technology at a rapid rate to enable the development of earth observation, communication, navigation, and scientific spacecraft. It was a challenge that I heartily welcomed. The interview resulted in an attractive offer. Apparently, my automatic controls experience was enough of an asset to overcome my limited knowledge of space technology. I started the RCA job on December 3, 1962, and car pooled with Mike Cutler, who had previously switched from Curtiss-Wright to the Astro Division. We decided against relocating to the Princeton area, although RCA offered to compensate us for all associated expenses of such a move. The family had established nice friendships and community ties in Livingston, and I was not inclined, at least for the time being, to interrupt that environment. Right from the start, I found the work at RCA most interesting. My supervisor, Harold Perkel, and my new colleagues appeared to be pleasant, bright, and motivated people. The plant was modern and growing by leaps and bounds, and the work did not consist only of military applications, which was much more to my liking. I was a happy trooper.

I joined Astro as a senior engineer in a group of eight people, which was responsible for the attitude (pointing) control and the stabilization of the spacecraft. My background was in the automatic controls field, which, up to 1962, I had applied primarily to jet engines while at Curtiss-Wright. Now I had to switch and adapt my skills to the spacecraft field, and there was considerable new technology to be absorbed and created. After all, this whole space business was still essentially in its infancy. So it was only a partial catchup game for me; the other and even more interesting part was growing up together with this new and fascinating technology.

The first artificial satellite, Sputnik 1, was launched by the Soviet Union on October 4, 1957. It weighed 184 pounds, transmitted

*At the NASA Goddard Space Flight Center near Washington, DC, during a
critical launch phase of a TIROS meteorological satellite, January 1970.*

its radio signal for three weeks, and reentered the earth's atmosphere after three months. The first successful U.S. satellite, Ex-
plorer 1, was not sent into orbit until January 31, 1958. This
spacecraft weighed only 31 pounds and discovered the famous Van
Allen radiation belt. By the time RCA, with NASA (National Aeronautics and Space Administration) sponsorship, launched its first satellite on April 1, 1960, 46 launches had been attempted by the U.S.
and the U.S.S.R., but 20 of these had failed to achieve orbit. This pioneering RCA satellite, known as TIROS 1, was the very first meteorological spacecraft ever and transmitted about 23,000 earth
images during its the 100 days of operation. The new space technology was rapidly being utilized for exploration, meteorological and
earth observations, navigation, and communication. I was fortunate to be able to participate in its infancy.

Besides generating new designs that, we hoped, would satisfy
our customers' needs, i.e., space missions, I quickly became involved with the generation of proposals and technical presenta-
tions. Our government customers were NASA, the U.S. Air Force,

and the U.S. Navy. The commercial space applications field was still evolving at that point, but it was obvious that there would be great opportunities for navigation and communication applications.

In the late summer of 1963, I was sent on a business trip to Seattle to work with representatives of Boeing on a possible joint venture to explore the moon. Although this cooperative effort failed to materialize, I was compensated by my exposure to this beautiful northwest corner of our contiguous U.S.A. With a few colleagues, I traveled to the 6,000-foot level of magnificent Mount Rainier and entered an ice cave in the late summer. Maybe the moon just had to wait while I was still exploring the earth.

As I gained more confidence and experience, I became involved in the training of new or less-experienced engineers and in the interfacing with other skill areas such as structures, power, thermal control, communication, and propulsion. I welcomed this opportunity, which allowed me to become much broader and more system oriented. But my primary interest was and always remained the attitude control and stabilization area. In its simplest sense, this specialized field uses various apparatus such as earth, sun, and star sensors and gyroscopes as eyes to "see," specialized electronics or somewhat later computers to digest this information, i.e., to think like a brain and thus issue commands for appropriate action in accordance with embedded control algorithms, and finally to act in response to these directions by actuating components such as high speed wheels, small jets, and electromagnets, all of which were the arms and legs of our satellite.

When my supervisor, Harold Perkel, resigned from his position in 1970 in order to start his own business in an unrelated field, he proposed to our management that I be his successor. I was quite surprised, very pleased, and finally overjoyed when I was approved for this position. This was a most important step in my professional career. One has to consider that I was already 46 years old and it was essential that I be able to expedite my advancement within my chosen field of endeavor. Now I had this chance, and I was determined to take full advantage of this fortuitous opportunity.

My approach to my new job was twofold. First, I had to work diligently and with sensitivity to gain and deserve the confidence of the seven engineers for whom I was now responsible and who just yesterday were my co-workers. Secondly, I had to demonstrate to my management that I was deserving of the trust they had placed in me. It was important that my Attitude Control and Stabilization group would not stand still but would further grow into a creative and reliable organization of the RCA-Astro team.

But before jumping too far ahead, let me first return to my involvement with our synagogue, Temple Emanu-El of Livingston, for, along with family and career, synagogue was a major part of my life.

IN THE SERVICE OF TEMPLE EMANU-EL

During the first seven years of our affiliation with Temple Emanu-El, i.e., since 1957, our primary synagogue interactions involved the religious school attendance of the boys and Bea's participation in the work of the school committee and the women's club. Occasionally, we would attend Erev Shabbat (Friday evening) services and, of course, those of the festivals and particularly the High Holiday services. But it was difficult for us to attend regularly while taking care of our small children.

A special congregational meeting was called in the winter of 1962–63 to consider the renewal of Rabbi Rose's expiring three-year contract. A substantial majority of the board of trustees was not in favor, and the congregation was split. After some officers and trustees had addressed the assembly, I was chosen, by the random selection of slips placed in a box, to give brief extemporaneous expression of my feelings on the matter. My recommendation not to renew the contract was well received by many, but a female member reprimanded me with the words "Why don't you go back where you came from?" I guess if one takes a controversial position in public, insults such as this come with the territory. By a relatively close vote, the board was sustained and we had to search for a new rabbi. A few months later, Rabbi Kenneth Rivkin was elected as our new spiritual leader. Bea and I took a liking to him and his family from the very beginning of his tenure.

About a year later, I was nominated to serve for a one-year term on the 1964–65 board. I was pleased, surprised, and elected. Soon thereafter, I found out what was expected of me, when the new president Curt Lilienfeld appointed me chair of the ritual committee. This was a key position for which I had little experience except for my family background and general exposure to synagogue services. After only one briefing by my predecessor, I was responsible for the organization and staffing of my committee, which was charged, in

conjunction with the rabbi, with taking care of the proper functioning of all services, the Minyon (memorial) services for the bereaved,
the Bar Mitzvah scheduling and training, the honors (Aliyahs) extended to deserving congregants, the assignment of ushers, the issuance of admittance tickets for the High Holidays, and a multitude
of other related functions, including the pertinent budgetary responsibility. Besides the rabbi, the temple also employed a cantor
and a professional choir. This sounded to me like a full-time job, and
it soon seemed that it almost was. Not quite, however, because I
still had to make a living and also placed high priority on spending
quality time with my family.

At that time, the congregation consisted of about 400 families
with approximately 600 children and was growing larger with every
year. We lived in the suburbs, which during the 1950s and 1960s experienced a substantial population influx from the cities, consisting
particularly of young families. Our congregation was organized
along democratic lines, as one would expect to be the case for most
liberal congregations. The board of trustees functioned as the governing body and was supported by at least a dozen committees. One
would expect this to be one happy family, but that did not hold true
throughout. Dedicated people have different opinions on how to
achieve a common goal, and an involvement with a religious organization at times causes emotions to prevail over reason. This is
particularly true when most of the participants are volunteers.

My first exposure to such an environment involved the attempt
of my committee to institute Bat Mitzvahs for interested and qualified girls. We naturally already observed the traditional Bar Mitzvah ceremony for the 13-year-old boys and thus believed such an
equalizer to be well received. We had the rabbi's support as a matter of principle, but as the father of three daughters he also had personal interest in the proposed change. The board was split. Change
is not always easy, and tradition was once again invoked to fend off
progress and a more just society. When a past president exclaimed,
"We are dealing here with a vociferous minority," I retorted: "We
are a constructive majority." And we were! The matter was approved both by the board and by the congregation. I was proud of
our accomplishment: the reduction of gender inequality, which had
been ingrained over the centuries as an orthodox dictum within Judaism. It was and still is a cause worth fighting for. The antiquated
practice of excluding women from the Torah reading was also dis-

continued at my initiative and our rabbi's consent. A rumbling of surprise swelled from the congregation when the first woman received such an honor during our 1965 High Holiday services.

In 1965, I was reelected to a two-year term as trustee and subsequently served a second year as chair of the ritual committee. Just prior to these 1965 High Holidays, our professional choir confronted me as ritual chair with a threat of non-participation unless granted an incremental compensation in addition to the yearly adjustment. For a number of reasons, we could not give in to such intimidation. After my negotiating efforts came to naught, I informed the four singers and their attorney that, if they were to carry out their intention, the congregation would just have to manage the services without them. Fortunately, they finally saw the error of their ways and honored their contractual arrangements, while the ritual chairman breathed a sigh of relief.

In mid-1966, the president appointed me to chair the religious school committee, a change and a challenge that I welcomed. I had inherited responsibility for a school, which was led by an administrator whose qualifications as principal were marginal at best. Not a happy situation, but the man was in place and under contract. The temple year had barely gotten under way when the president resigned for business reasons. Of the four vice-presidents, one was elected to take the vacated top position, and I in turn was offered a vice-presidency. This step appeared premature, but the unusual circumstances persuaded me to accept. However, in my new position, I also continued to head the school committee. To serve a congregation or other organization at this level requires personal sacrifice, but much more accommodation and sacrifice by one's spouse and offspring. My family was marvelous in their support and understanding during these busy temple years. After I returned from my office in the early evening hours, it required much patience on their part to tolerate my numerous phone calls (we had only one number, so I was blocking the line) as well as my frequent attendance at various temple meetings.

After serving as vice-president for nearly three years, I was elected to the presidency for the 1969–70 year. By that time, I felt I was well prepared for this challenge. Our friendship with Rabbi Rivkin made it easy to achieve a sense of cooperation. At my June 1969 installation, I included these remarks:

"I hope that I will be able to wield this gavel with all the intellect and heart at my disposal. Tonight we observe another one of these occasions, which symbolizes the continuity of our people. In 1955, 11 inspired families joined hearts and hands and founded this congregation. . . . We can best show our gratitude to all . . . who labored with them, by continuing the task, by providing the link from the yesterday to the tomorrow. . . . We will continue – as a Temple family – to make our silent prayer a very audible reality – until Thy bidding shall at last become for us a hallowed discipline, a familiar way of life, so that we may live on in deeds that bless other lives, and leave behind us the heritage of a good name – the name of Israel."

Our congregation was social-action-oriented, and this approach was much in concert with Bea's and my philosophy about Judaism. The words of prayer have to be transformed into deeds of compassion, justice, and peace. Thus, we were concerned with the lot of the Soviet Jews trapped behind the iron curtain, which was maintained by the Communist dictatorship. This problem was close to the heart of our rabbi, who was born in Russia and entered the U.S.A. at the age of one. For many years, Bea was intimately involved with the work of our social action committee and its many causes, including the reducing the ever-escalating drug problem, to which it dedicated its efforts by assisting in rehabilitation and education activities.

In 1969, our national movement for Reform Judaism, the Union of American Hebrew Congregations (UAHC), convened its biennial convention in Miami Beach. For Bea and for me, it was a unique and new experience to attend such a meeting. Meeting with more than 3,000 Jews who have a similar approach to Judaism made a tremendous impact. Just to pray with such an assembly, to chant the Shema in unison with three thousand voices (Hear, O Israel, Adonai our God, Adonai is One), sent chills down my spine. These were the years of crisis for our Soviet Jewish brothers and sisters. Thus, we participated in a candlelight march in their behalf on the streets of Miami Beach. A futile effort? We could not give up in spite of an apparently hopeless situation in light of Soviet intransigence and antagonism. Who could have or would have foretold the miracle of liberation that was in store for our Jewish people in future years? During this biennial, we were also privileged to hear an address by Elie Wiesel, the first and foremost major Holocaust writer. He held us spellbound for over an hour with his poetic and chilling memories and reflections of the Holocaust years.

On Rosh Hashana, near the beginning of my second year as president, Rabbi Rivkin announced that he and his family would make Aliyah in 1971. We were sorry to lose our rabbi and see our good friends move half way around the globe, although we fully empathized with their decision to live in Israel and raise their family in the land of our ancestors. During our congregation's farewell salutation, I included the following thoughts, among others, in my address:

"I am sure that I can speak for many of our congregants, who could not have accepted your leaving as graciously if it were not, that as a Rabbi in Israel, you are going to Israel. There are some, very few, who act in accordance of their convictions, who do not compromise for the sake of comfort, who do not dream for the sake of escape. Most of us have visions and objectives which are too limited in order to understand: how one can leave the comfort of today for the challenge of tomorrow, how one can leave the most powerful nation in the world for the most inspired people in the world. Our Rabbi has made this choice, and for that reason alone, all of us can be very proud."

After their emigration, we stayed in contact with the Rivkins and visited them several times in Jerusalem. Whenever they temporarily returned to the U.S. to see their family and for business reasons, they stopped by to share precious days with us in New Jersey.

Now we needed a new rabbi. I did not have the nerve to ask someone else on the Board to head the rabbi search committee, which had a formidable task indeed. Thus, I assigned this task to myself and appointed dedicated and capable people to serve with me on the committee. We considered about two dozen applicants and met with about half. Finally, after several months of interviews, verification of references, visits to other congregations, and what seemed to be endless agonizing, we decided to ask Rabbi Peter Kasdan to serve as our new spiritual leader. He was a personable and principled young man, having been ordained at Hebrew Union College five years prior to assuming the Livingston pulpit. The congregation had expressed a desire to engage a rabbi who was youth-oriented and thus would have rapport with our ever-growing youth population. After resolving that formidable task, the nominating committee requested that I serve a third year as president to help the new rabbi and thus bridge the gap of the transition. How could I refuse?

During my three years as President, our religious school grew to over 700 students. To serve such a sizable enrollment, we had to schedule one Saturday and two Sunday sessions in addition to the midweek afternoon Hebrew classes. It became difficult to accommodate our expanding congregation because of physical limitations of our building, a structure that had been intended for a smaller population. Consequently, we enlarged the temple plant by enclosing the rear courtyard, thus providing an additional large multipurpose area and giving our library a room of its own. After all, we had to give pragmatic recognition to our historic mission as People of the Book. Aside from expanding our space, we also placed emphasis on enhancing the quality of our services and school. We enlarged our adult education program, since learning is not just for children but also for their parents. The adults who drop off their children in the temple parking lot to attend religious school should not merely expect them to live by the motto of "Do as I say" but rather "Do as I do."

During a tribute service dedicated to me in June of 1972, I included the following in my address to the congregation:

"I thank you also because by serving my people I could best serve America. I do not subscribe to the melting pot theory – our best contribution to American life can be made by applying Jewish values. We Jews have a contribution to make, not by dissolving into the American melting pot but by being ourselves, by being a stimulus for progress – a call for justice – to speak up clearly and work diligently for our unique value stance, which has been tested in the crucible of history. Yes, we are Jews because Israel's message is the most ancient and the most modern. We are Jews because the Shema speaks of the oneness of God, and thus hopefully the oneness of mankind. We are Jews because we were given for a light unto the nations, and we dare not fail lest darkness envelops the earth. Thus we are enjoined to carry out a dual obligation – to be a link and to be a light. To be a link in the long chain of Jewish history, to teach Torah, these words, these thoughts, these ideals, this way of life to our children. . . . But while we are here, while we number our days, we also have the second obligation: to be a light, to reach out laterally to the citizens of our country, and translate our prayers and aspirations of Tzedakah, of justice and of Shalom into the fabric of the society of today. . . . Thus I am grateful to have been blessed to serve this congregation."

THE SECULAR WORLD, 1950 TO 1973

Let me pause here to reflect briefly on some of the events of the political world from the time I started to work professionally (1950) to the year following my temple presidency. For me, it is impossible to restrict my vision and my interest exclusively to family, to synagogue and to employment-related activities. At this juncture of my life, as our children were growing and maturing, as we appreciated the joy of living in our own beautiful home, there were national and world events that touched me.

Admittedly, I was disturbed and disappointed during the 1952–56 period by the political campaigns leading to the election and re-election of Dwight D. Eisenhower, the general who had led the successful Allied invasion of Europe that resulted in the defeat of Hitler's Germany. I am leery of military figures serving in public elective office. Exclusive military experience, even if followed by a university presidency as in Eisenhower's case, is not a comforting background for being top executive of the U.S.A. Both Bea and I would have much preferred his opponent for both campaigns, Adlai Stevenson, who had intellectual depth, had new and progressive ideas, and projected a warm and sensitive image. But the majority of American people preferred the war hero, the patriot, the father figure. We were disappointed and learned that elections are not determined by just one section of this vast country, in this case the East, and that the nearly unanimous choice of our circle of friends and family is not a reliable barometer for the eventual election result. Bea shed some tears for Adlai Stevenson and what might have been, but in a democracy it is important to accept the result of all the people and take comfort that there will always be the opportunity of another election.

Eisenhower was not a great President: one could not point to any memorable accomplishments, but neither were there any real disasters attached to his tenure. However, he deserves considerable

157

credit for his vision, which was that this country's security was the total product of our economic, intellectual, moral, and military strengths. As he wisely observed, there is no way in which a country can satisfy the craving for absolute security; but it can easily bankrupt itself, morally and economically, in attempting to reach that illusory goal through arms alone.

Senator Joseph R. McCarthy was a prominent politician during the fifties, which many label as the McCarthy era. This designation is a very negative one, for the man was a demagogue, who deviously used his office and political power to mislead many American people. He reveled in labeling any liberal human being a Communist, having no conscience or hesitancy to fabricate false reports and misleading information to destroy the reputation, the careers, and the very freedom of many of his fellow citizens. His sick mind appeared to be a danger to our America. For people like me, who vividly remember our experience of Nazi Germany in the 1930s, McCarthyism was a scary and dangerous era indeed. His kind of America would have been comfortable in the fascist environment of Hitler and Mussolini. Democracy was severely threatened by his outrageous tactics and his unsavory goals. In spite of that, he had the support of many gullible people. I and others like me were frequently criticized for opposing this man, and it took an unusually long time for Eisenhower to assert himself constitutionally to isolate this cancer from our midst and to clarify what McCarthy really represented. But this action was only taken when McCarthy falsely accused the centrist establishment of Washington. Better late than never, freedom was preserved, and lies and deceit were exposed for what they were: fraudulent and without foundation.

To preserve freedom and democracy, one cannot simply sit back and hope in the presence of danger. These threats can be external, such as the German Nazi effort to subvert the world, or they could develop within, such as the creeping sickness of McCarthyism. Silent and inactive observers cannot survive in either case. The democracy called the U.S.A., now well over 200 years old, is not guaranteed to continue unless its citizens, as custodians, stay alert and preserve free speech and justice for all.

In 1957, I was on a business visit at Wright Patterson Air Force base in Dayton, Ohio, when we received the news that Joseph McCarthy had died of natural causes. One of the officers with whom we were interfacing remarked with obvious cynicism: *"They* are dancing in the streets of New York tonight." Had he realized that I am of the Jewish faith, he might not have made this gratuitous remark in my presence. But I did not mind hearing it, for it was a final confirmation of what McCarthyism represented.

During the 1960s, the U.S.A. passed through a sad and most disturbing period, a time of political assassinations. Of course, both American and world history is replete with such violent and despicable actions. But if these foul deeds happen in one's own lifetime, they have a vastly different impact than when we meet them in a history book.

The first leader to be murdered in this decade was President John F. Kennedy. I was sitting at my desk at RCA Astro on that fateful Friday afternoon, the 22nd of November, 1963, when the news came. I was still sitting there about an hour later, for my mental paralysis induced by that shock must have had a similar effect on my body. The world was never to be the same; with JFK died many hopes and dreams. No doubt, as a human being, he had his own faults and frailties, but he had a vision of a better world that he transmitted, with great eloquence, to all. He hardly had a chance to translate any of his dreams into deeds. Although from a very wealthy background, he tried to have compassion and understanding for all and to act accordingly. He came from a Roman Catholic home, but his heart encompassed those from all creeds. He was white, but he reached out with sincerity to all races.

It was so sad for our kids who understood, though did not fully comprehend, the implications of this assassination. For our children, the innocence of youth and the hope for the future received a disillusioning blow. Justifiable or not, JFK, with his vigor, eloquence, and idealism, represented a breath of fresh air on the American political scene, and young people, even children, as well as adults, sensed that and responded to it in a positive way. The violent destruction of such a living symbol was equivalent to extinguishing their guiding star. Like a wounded animal, I went into hiding the entire weekend by painting our living and dining room, as if this mundane exercise could possibly distract my troubled mind. Bampa was hospitalized just then and Bea immediately went to see and console him. When she entered the room, he said: "I knew you would come."

We felt frustrated and guilty that we couldn't shield our offspring from the irrational actions of humankind. Their future, the tomorrow of the younger generation, was even more affected by this revolting event than our own, but it appears impossible to give absolute protection to the top officials of any nation against such sick and dastardly deeds. Leaders like JFK have an innate need to reach out personally to their constituency, and when they give their lives in this perilous attempt, they die like soldiers at the front, they die in action for a noble cause: the advancement and betterment of humanity.

Only five years later, a black American or, as in more current usage, an Afro-American, an American prophet, the great Martin Luther King Jr., was similarly and cowardly struck down. While JFK was still alive in 1963, this man immortalized himself and his cause in keynoting the March on Washington on behalf of racial equality in this land of the free and the brave, where there is to be liberty and justice for all. "I have a dream," he boomed out over the gathered multitude at the Lincoln Memorial, that his children and all of God's children would live and play and work together in complete harmony. For many years, it has been traditional to include Dr. King's words in the Passover Seder of my family and our temple family, for Passover is a festival of freedom and deliverance. King was a great leader, and his death created a big gap in the Afro-American and, for that matter, American leadership, thus giving some others with blurred vision, vitriolic speech, and violent bents an opportunity to step into the void. Of course, this was the intent of the assassin and his cohorts: to undermine the racial harmony that Dr. King attempted to further. Hopefully, his dream will find its ultimate fulfillment within the next few generations.

Finally, and just two months after King's death, JFK's brother Robert was also murdered while engaged in a promising campaign for the presidency of his country. He was a man with considerable ability, the last of the leaders of that period to whom I could relate with enthusiasm. Like his brother John and his friend Martin Luther King, he too died young. We were killing the American soul with the repeated murders of our most promising and most dedicated leaders. There is a song that was composed after this period: "Only the good die young." One could ask with justified cynicism, whether only the Nixons of this world have the privilege of surviving and growing old. We were utterly devastated and feared that American democracy was once again endangered. While we shared our pain with our children, we tried not to let despair overwhelm their hopes for a better and less violent future.

The incipiency of the U.S. intrusion in the Vietnam conflict already occurred under JFK, who authorized the participation of some 18,000 advisors. In retrospect, this was an ill-advised and highly questionable action. However, under the leadership of Presidents Johnson and Nixon, the scope of this incursion was vastly increased to more than 600,000 troops. These two men and most of their advisors, notably Secretary of Defense McNamara, constantly justified this escalation with the need to fight communism in the Far East in order to keep the so-called house of cards from collapsing. Partially, this logic was based on illogical thought processes, but a good part of the debacle was founded on outright deceit of the American people. By their own accounts, which are now in the public domain, both McNamara and Johnson admitted to having been convinced at that time that our bloody intervention in that Far East country was based on false premises. Nevertheless, they moved forward unabated.

Johnson manipulated the Congress with the Gulf of Tonkin incident, an essentially fabricated story of a North Vietnamese attack in international waters. Once having the foot in the door by this devious means, he, the President, poured more and more troops into a bottomless pit. Not only that, but we even resorted to the use of chemical weapons. The whole affair was not only immoral but illegal as well. The "favorable body count" reports of the North Vietnamese versus the U.S. and Allied fatalities was a revolting parameter of the moral fiber of the U.S. administration.

Under the guise of patriotism, most of the U.S. population was deceived, and when it woke up very late it was primarily due to the protests of the younger generation. Thus, when individuals like me would not support the war, they were labeled as unpatriotic. As it turned out, those who opposed this undeclared war were acting in America's best interest. A disproportionate number of U.S. soldiers shipped to Vietnam came from the poorer part of the population, while those with means were more often than not able to receive deferments for a variety of questionable reasons.

Of course, I was outspoken in denouncing this whole action. My car pool partners, with whom I commuted to work, threatened to expel me unless I ceased to protest in their presence. Although I never would honor their request to become a silent bystander in the face of gross injustice, their threat was never carried out.

In 1967, the UAHC biennial was convened in Montreal, Canada. This is the North American synagogue organization of Reform Judaism, a movement in which I was to become active in future decades. Under the leadership of its president, the eminent Rabbi Maurice Eisendrath, a resolution on peace in Vietnam had been circulated in preparation for consideration at the biennial. My temple's board took the unusual step to obligate the congregational delegation to oppose this resolution on the floor of the assembly. Normally, such decisions are left to the good conscience of each delegate. I made it very clear that I could not comply with the board's restriction, having found the Vietnam intervention morally an abomination as early as 1964. This action was not only terrible for our soldiers who had to fight there but also a disaster for the indigenous population of this unfortunate land. How can people who pray daily for Shalom vote against peace, and particularly under these terrible circumstances? Therefore, I refused to go to Montreal, and although the temple's delegation was not unanimous in its opinion on this matter, our entire delegation remained home rather than force someone like me to vote against his or her conscience. As Jews, we consistently pray for Shalom, for peace, although world events such as the Nazi era unfortunately thrust the almost unavoidable burden of war on us as well. In the case of the Vietnam nightmare, which represented no significant threat to the Western world, the Jewish community was tenuous and primarily silent on the issue of war and peace. Our acceptance within American society apparently led to the distorted view that we had to adhere to the "popular" position of blindly supporting this ever-escalating military action. I believe that the need to be part of the "in" group deluded my temple board of that time to forego the perspective and judgment afforded by being somewhat apart. The Jewish community is to be a light to the nations and not allow itself to be seduced, as part of the comforting mass of the secular majority, to enter a jungle of an immoral and inhuman morass.

The poisonous intolerance of that time extended into every facet of society and was spread by slogans such as "America, love it or leave it," the loving, of course, implying the support of the ever-escalating Vietnam misadventure. Once while at work, I entered the Astro Space cafeteria and was confronted by one of the senior secretaries of our staff. "Look at that pig, Lu," she called to me while pointing her finger towards the lunch crowd sitting at tables. "Whom are you referring to?" I asked. "The one with the long hair" was her ready reply. And there at one of the nearby tables, I noticed a man who was well dressed in suit and tie, with meticulously combed long dark blond hair, a visual symbol of identification with the peace movement of the time. I turned towards my observant challenger to point out that "in the country from which I emigrated, many men used to maintain rather short haircuts and dress in neat black or brown uniforms and eventually kill millions of innocent people. The length of a person's hair is not a good measure of an individual's character or basic decency." There was no reply, and I left her standing in the aisle.

President Johnson finally became a victim of his own irrationality. The protests, primarily of the young, eventually found resonance across generation gaps, and Johnson saw the handwriting on the wall. His chances for reelection in 1968 had diminished to political hopelessness. Richard Nixon was chosen to succeed him, but not with my vote. This man was already a well-defined and dubious character when judged by his service in the House and Senate after World War II and as Vice-President during the Eisenhower years. True to form, his promise to end the Vietnam war and to bring peace to that part of the world as well as to America was deviously turned into an extension and expansion of the hostilities. Our troops were even ordered to enter neighboring Cambodia. By the time he became President, the U.S. had already sustained 31,000 fatalities in Vietnam; Nixon's intransigence was to add another 24,000 U.S. fatalities to this tragic total.

But finally it stopped, not because of the idealism of the Washington administration but because the American people became more and more disenchanted. Furthermore, one should not forget that in spite of tremendous application of American military force including chemical weapons, the North Vietnamese were winning the war. Eisenhower once cautioned never to get involved in a war on the Asian continent. To this day, I have great compassion and empathy for all the soldiers our government sent into this disaster, to suffer there, to die there in vain. Furthermore, one should not forget the destruction and the suffering visited upon Vietnam itself, and the approximately three million victims among the Vietnamese people. The United States of America lost more than a war in this misguided venture; we also suffered a diminution in our ability to lead and in our moral purpose. Even long after this war had finally come to an end, our leaders never dealt with it honestly and never acknowledged responsibility for the deceit and arrogance that led to this disaster.

There is a most moving memorial in Washington, located close to the magnificent one of and for Abraham Lincoln. It was erected in honor and in memory of the approximately 58,000 U.S. soldiers who were killed during the Vietnamese carnage. They died while fighting for an unjust cause, they died while following the orders of their Commander-in-Chief, the President of the U.S.A. Whenever I visit this memorial, my soul cries bitter tears; they died because of the poor judgment and the unbridled ego of our political leadership. I hope that there also exists such a memorial in Vietnam for all the Asian fighters who were slaughtered, whether they were communists or not, they were all human beings.

In the Pirke Avot, the Hebrew scriptures (Mishna 300 BCE to 200 CE) also known as "Sayings of the Sages," we read: "The sword comes into the world because of justice being delayed, because of justice being perverted, and because of those who render wrong decisions." This applies particularly to Vietnam, although the root causes of World War I and II also come under such scrutiny. However, in the South Asian conflict, much of the responsibility pertains to our own country, to America, to Washington D.C., whereas the world conflagration of the 1930s and 1940s had its origin with evil Nazi leadership leading to the utter perversion of the German people, while European democracies stood by far too long in unfathomable paralysis and acquiescence. After the tragedies of Vietnam and the three assassinations, it was amazing that any decency and hope survived for America.

Will Shalom ever come? Only if humanity will make it possible. The "Gates of Prayer" liturgy, which was issued by the rabbinic arm of the Union of American Hebrew Congregations in 1975, includes the following challenge: "We live in two worlds: the one that is and the one that might be. Nothing is ordained for us: neither delight nor defeat, neither peace nor war. Life flows, and we must freely choose. We can, if we will, change the world that is, into the world that may come to be, as we were taught from of old."

Now I will turn to Israel from my 1973 perspective. Twenty-five years had passed since its modern founding. I am an American Jew or a Jewish American; in any case, I am concerned with the welfare of the U.S.A. and the State of Israel. After the Holocaust, there is no need to justify the existence of a Jewish state, the land of the Jewish people as home for all Jews who require or desire to dwell there. Thus, my family and I, as well as millions of others, both Jews and non-Jews, were and are closely linked to Israel's survival, and particularly at critical and historical moments such as the wars of 1956, 1967, and 1973. Each one of these conflicts was thrust upon the Israeli people by Arab aggression, each had the elimination of the Jewish state as its ultimate goal.

In the period just preceding the 1967 conflict,the Six Day war, I felt very lonely because of the world's inaction in the face of the multitude Arab threats , including the closing of the Straits of Tiran. The world seemed to be paralyzed, hypnotized, immobilized for an intolerably long moment. I was afraid that we might witness the nightmarish end of a beautiful dream. But part of the world took note of the Soviet involvement in the Arab lands, and the Israeli army fought with heroic determination to counter that threat. Particularly in 1973, the U.S.A., after a brief initial hesitation, was steadfast in meeting its commitment of support and thus enabled the Israeli people to beat back the mortal danger .

I vividly recall, how we received word during our 1973 Yom Kippur services (October 6) of the unprovoked surprise attack by Egypt and Syria on Israel. It was clever and simultaneously despicable for these Arab states to choose our holiest day of the year to once again attempt to push the Jewish nation into the sea. Based on the prior outcomes of the 1948/49, 1956, and 1967 conflicts , my congregation's initial reaction to this stab in the back was one of confidence in Israel's ability to prevail. In fact, Bea and I had sensed a certain overconfidence bordering on cockiness of Israel's population while we visited there in the early spring of 1973. After significant initial Syrian and Egyptian penetration and and Israeli casualties, the Jewish state prevailed and, in its counter attack, came close to capturing both Damascus and Cairo. Only American diplomatic pressure and Soviet threat precluded such an embarrassing outcome.

Israel was and still is the home of many Holocaust survivors, including at that time my mother's sister Johannah, who married my father's brother Lothar, a man who had been incarcerated in Dachau for six terrible months. After reaching "safe haven" in Palestine in the mid-1930s, my relatives, who lived near Haifa had to survive Arab terror for more than another decade until independence in 1948 led to some measure of stability.

I agree with Abba Eban that "national suicide is not an international obligation". Already at the conclusion of the Yom Kippur war (1973), I felt that real peace could come to the Near East only if cooler heads prevailed, and if Israel's former adversaries did not view each negotiation and each treaty as a step towards the ultimate demise of the Jewish state. I am a proud citizen of the U.S.A., but I am also, and without any conflict, a Jew who is dedicated to the survival of Judaism and the security and the development of the State of Israel.

We cannot and should not isolate ourselves from the world, because we are its citizens and guardians, if for no other reason than for the sake of future generations. In concert with other peoples of good will, we should and we can strive for a better and more peaceful world.

OUR CHILDREN GROW, MY PARENTS PASS

(1964–1977)

Having leapfrogged somewhat in terms of my career, temple involvement and world events, let me now return to our family's development beginning with the mid-sixties. The formal educational phase of our children was now in full swing; Leslie entered elementary school in 1965 and loved it from the start. For two years, all three were attending the Mt. Pleasant school simultaneously.

Danny took a particular liking to animals and sports. Because of his maturity and fair-mindedness, he developed into the "judge and jury" of the backyard activities. Was the ball fair or foul? Was the runner safe or out? All eyes and ears turned to Danny. Kids of the neighborhood liked to play in our yard, especially the Wilsons (four boys, one girl). As the boys grew older, our backyard was transformed into a baseball diamond. I offered a prize to the first young athlete who would break one of our windows, an offer to remove the tension of playing in such proximity to our house. But no baseball ever crashed through one of our windows. The boys hit the walls and eventually batted their round missiles into the neighbor's yard, but I never had a chance to present my promised reward. Danny also became involved with Little League baseball; win or lose, he loved to participate in the game. In his junior high school years (grades 7–9, Mt. Pleasant Junior High School), he joined the wrestling team and was awarded a varsity letter in that sport. His promising career was cut short, however, when he dislocated his knee during a match. He was a good sport and took the disappointment in stride. For a while, he also applied himself diligently in trying to master the flute, and he deserves an "E" for effort. During this period, he initially became acquainted with Richard Katz, the son of our friends Marion and Peter. Danny always loved people, and many responded most positively to the sincerity and warmth of his personality.

As he entered his teenage years, Danny became more interested in history and social studies and extended that interest to the current political scene. Thus, he became involved with the circumstances, consequences, and protests of the Vietnam war. For him, turning swords into plowshares and spears into pruning hooks was not merely a religious slogan but a deep-seated conviction. This filled me with pride and satisfaction. In his high school years (1970–73), Danny took a liking to history and the humanities. After school, he supplemented his allowance by working in a local clothing store. Instead of struggling with the flute, he now developed some affinity for the guitar. Together with a few friends, he formed a small band that sometimes played at social functions.

During these teenage years, he and his siblings became good friends of Richard Katz. A most gifted musician, particularly as pianist, Richard gave us much pleasure and love over the years, much joy with his great sense of humor, and much comfort with his sincere devotion to our family. Richard and Danny developed particularly close ties, and this friendship strengthened the bonds among all members of the two families. This Katz-Muhlfelder relationship has immeasurably enhanced our lives and our living.

Throughout his development, from grammar school through high school, Danny maintained a considerable interest in sports and became an enthusiastic ice hockey player. There was many a winter day when he and his brother would spent hours competing in a pickup ice hockey game on nearby Kean's Pond. Barry played goalie and, matching his brother's enthusiasm, required several stitches in his face for selfless defense. Danny joined a teenage hockey league for a while, uniforms and all. The only available icetime in the South Mountain arena was at two or three o'clock in the morning, and his dedicated mother provided the transportation at this ungodly hour. In the summer of 1970, he even spent two weeks at Tam O'Shanter, a Canadian hockey camp. As spectator, he rooted (and still does) for the New York Rangers in the winter and for his beloved Yankees the rest of the year.

Barry brought an independent and inquisitive spirit to his classroom work. He was a scientist from the word "go," and nothing was going to deter him from soaking up esoteric technical information. As the youngest of his class, he was not the most secure and best-adjusted little boy. But by and by, this matter became less and less significant or noticeable.

Barry gained stature with his scientific experimentation and, at times, eccentric approach. As part of the backyard gang and under the tutelage of a protective older brother, he thrived in the Orchard Lane environment. Bored with math as presented in fifth grade by Mrs. Moritz, he received a "D" for the course although he could probably have taught it. When he spent sixth grade at Hillside School with a most creative teacher, Mr. Axtel, he blossomed, aced math, and improved his performance in all other courses. Furthermore, he rediscovered the solar system during these early school years and wrote a booklet detailing the size and orbital characteristics of the planets. With great interest and even greater concern, we watched and prayed when he at times took over Bea's laundry room in the basement to conduct unspecified experiments. The odors were ominous, but nothing drastic ever happened. We all survived these explorations, and eventually Bea was able to fully reclaim her rightful territory. In junior high school, he became a member of the mathematics league and was narrowing the gap with respect to my own background in that skill.

Being mathematically inclined, he also displayed interest in music. He started to play around with his maternal grandfather's Shofar, with which he filled the house with popular rather than ritual music. Anyone who has tried to play the Shofar will confirm that this is a difficult instrument, particularly without a mouthpiece. But Barry was persistent and learned on his own to master it. I still hear him blowing "Yankee Doodle Dandy" to the consternation of my mother. Eventually, he also learned the ritual of the High Holiday sounds and participated a number of years in the youth services at the temple. He excelled on this difficult and ancient instrument to such an extent, that he was once invited to blow the ram's horn on these holiest of days for the entire congregation. Bea suffered from phlebitis at the time, but momentarily sneaked into the service to hear her son. He was spectacular, and his parents, President Lu and wife Bea, were very proud of him. Barry was probably the only individual who ever learned to play the trumpet via the Shofar.

Being scientifically inclined made him also sensitive to health hazards. Thus, he translated his teacher's admonition on the dangers of nicotine into an unusual action in our home. Bea had been smoking modestly for a number of years, consuming no more than one pack of cigarettes per week. Barry, however, felt that even a single smoke was one too many and consequently used a pin to perforate his mother's pack in the kitchen drawer. Bea reprimanded him for destroying someone else's property, but she eventually and fortunately relinquished the smoking habit.

In high school, he was submerged in math and science, with resulting superior scholarship in these areas. His friendship with Paul Monroe was, in good part, based on their common scientific interest. Late at night, these two would jointly tackle Russian math and logic problems via telephone. This type of exposure also generated Barry's desire to excel in bridge, an infatuation that was right up my alley. To save money for his college tuition, Barry decided to cut lawns in the vicinity. At first, he did not have a mower of his own, so he had to requisition my machine at frequent intervals. Although inconvenienced here and there, I was proud of his intense determination and his lofty goals. I once asked him if he would consider a career in engineering as I had chosen. He looked at me in disbelief: "To get up at the crack of dawn and return late afternoon, five days per week to be locked in this schedule, not for me. I want flexibility!" So eventually, he became a physicist, not an engineer. But he is locked in, five days or more per week, nevertheless.

Leslie was and still is a wonderful and warm individual. School was one great party, one big social get-together, one big ball. Aside from her popularity and social attributes, she also showed considerable promise in the visual arts. To this day, we have pictures from those early years decorating our walls. When I view them, I smile with appreciation and nostalgia. She was a sensitive and vivacious little girl. In our backyard, she loved to play house in a little prefabricated log cabin that I had erected under the trees. There Leslie practiced her beauty parlor skills on neighbor Janie Gartenberg, who lost part of her beautiful blond hair in the process. Yes, eventually it grew back. Almost from the start of her schooling, Leslie showed considerable aptitude for the spoken and written word.

Like her brother Danny, she enjoyed participating in various sports and received the President's Physical Fitness Award while in junior high school. With unbridled enthusiasm, Leslie inspired her junior high football team as part of the cheerleading squad. Often, she would enter our house performing a cartwheel. When I tried to imitate this maneuver in our living room, I deservedly hurt my wrist. But that was not my only body part to suffer pain. Both in junior and senior high school, Leslie befriended a number of football players, who at times visited our home. Their handshakes were without mercy; in fact, the pain I sustained from their enthusiastic squeeze sometimes lasted till the following day.

Leslie's having so many friends naturally resulted in many parties, some in our house. Usually, these various logistical aspects were coordinated by Bea, who was and is a most understanding, compassionate, and loving mother. But once, we returned on a Friday night from temple services, and observed that our dead-end street was packed with cars. Bea commented that someone must be having a party. As we tried to pull into our driveway, it became clear that the "someone" was Leslie. She had spontaneously invited a few friends, word spread, and the whole affair got out of hand. It seemed to me that we had at least fifty youthful guests in our various rooms. There might have been more, because our arrival caused a rapid exit through the rear door. No harm was done, but it sticks in my mind when I think of Leslie's growing-up years.

Like her brothers, Leslie at times also worked after school or on weekends to supplement her allowance. Her employment was either at the local clothing store or at the Livingston Mall.

Scholastically, our three children established a good record, usually maintaining their place on the honor roll. Bea and I placed emphasis on learning to the best of each one's ability, although I do remember that I would reward them monetarily for their report cards in accordance with achieved grades. Not the best idea I ever had! However, I had an opportunity to correct this faulty emphasis on at least one occasion, when Barry and Leslie, when about 11 and eight years old, confronted me with the observation that their scholastic effort is made primarily to satisfy their parents' needs. Quickly reestablishing my composure, I explained that their schooling up to high school graduation was not negotiable. However, what they derive from this for possible use in later years is their business; their mother and father had completed their education long ago, and whatever one learns is of direct benefit to the individual involved. They should not feel that they are doing their parents any favor by studying since they will be the primary beneficiary of this effort. The two looked at me thoughtfully with the big brown eyes they inherited from their mother and never brought up the subject again.

All three attended our temple's religious school, which met for the lower grades early Saturday morning and for middle and upper grades on Sunday morning in double shifts. In preparation for Bar/

Bat Mitzvah, they also attended mid-week afternoon Hebrew classes starting with fourth grade. Our involvement with temple had a
positive influence on their attitude towards this parochial schooling. There may be a tendency on part of the students to become a
bit frustrated by a perceived intrusion on their leisure time. But I
believe our children appreciated this exposure, especially as the result of the emphasis that was placed on religious observances within our home.

As part of their involvement with Judaism, each of the kids celebrated the Bar/Bat Mitzvah in our temple, and each of these occasions was a momentous event for family and friends. For Danny's,
I was vice-president of our congregation, for Barry's, I officiated as
president with a kiss instead of the customary handshake on the Bima, and for Leslie's the years as officer of my temple had already
come to an end. As parents, Bea and I were proud of each one of
them. A few generations ago, Bar Mitzvah was a relatively minor
life cycle event, a milestone that one observed as part of growing up
as a Jew. It is a sacred moment in a young person's life, and I am
gratified that girls have, in the second half of this century, finally
been given equal treatment, at least by liberal Judaism, with the
equivalent Bat Mitzvah ceremony. Unfortunately, too many American Jews consider the Bar/Bat Mitzvah event as the closing act of
their children's Jewish education, thus giving the wrong message to
their progeny and keeping them from developing a mature appreciation of their religion. Even as they place importance on secular education, many parents leave the pursuit of post-Bar/Bat Mitzvah
Jewish studies to their children's discretion. In too many cases, this
does not prevent the celebration following the Bar/Bat Mitzvah ceremony into an excessive and distasteful party and sends the second
wrong message to the children. I am in favor of celebrating milestones within reason, be they of a religious or secular nature, but
such an observance should not destroy the sanctity of the moment
and should be properly scaled to the age of the celebrant.

Upon completing 10th grade, each of our children was confirmed and continued to attend our religious school through 12th
grade and thus graduation. During their teenage years, each one
was also active within the temple youth group (TEMTY); Danny
served as a vice-president, and Barry was treasurer during his senior year. After our treasurer – and apparently absent-minded professor – departed for college, we found some cash and checks stored

in various places, apparently for safekeeping, in his room. These funds, which belonged to TEMTY, were returned to that organization, though just a little late. I assume young Barry was chosen as treasurer because of his mathematical skills, not for his meticulous attention to financial details.

During these years of growth and study, our three offspring became more and more involved in a love of gardening. They really could not help it; their father was properly dubbed by their mother as a "gardenoholic", and the mother was also infatuated with this wonderful outdoor activity. They particularly enjoyed working alongside me, and I relished this as well. Danny acquired his horticultural skills early and with considerable enthusiasm and thoroughness. After regular school hours, he participated in a gardening course under the tutelage of Mr. Walters, a wonderful old gentleman and a horticultural expert. Danny's positive contact with this teacher resulted in our whole family's becoming friendly with him, and we visited him a number of times in his home near the Great Swamp reservation. There is still, to this day, an exquisite miniature lilac growing in our garden that Danny received as a gift from Mr. Walters.

Our home was a busy one, with three lively and involved children, temple activities, including many meetings and several Rosh Hashana receptions during my presidency. Besides all that, Bea was always a hospitable and welcoming hostess in arranging numerous gatherings for my extended family. Particularly on my mother's side, there were a number of sisters, Selma, Claire, Hannah, and Paula, who had no children of their own and thus had particularly great joy in visiting with us and being able to touch and share the lives of our three kids. Bea had endless patience and energy, and thus we celebrated many family birthdays as well as other special occasions and religious holidays in our home.

In 1966, my sister Ellen married Jacob Singer. It was almost a miracle that Ellen, after so many obstacles and illnesses and handicaps had reached this privileged milestone. We were particularly pleased that these two people had joined in a partnership for life. This occasion prompted Lothar and Hannah to make their third visit to the U.S.A. Bea arranged for a special reunion party in our home for all nine Franks and their spouses They were all happy to be briefly reunited , all nine, the only time in decades and then never again. However, some still disputed passionately about events in

their common youth and about who had the most favorite status
with their mother. Most deservedly, my grandmother Regina was
held in the highest esteem by all.

In December 1966, we celebrated my father's 75th birthday (in
a nearby catering establishment). Lothar and Hannah had extended their visit to be present for this milestone before returning to Israel. We were, of course, touched by each of these special occasions
but celebrated every birthday of the young as well as the old, independent of whether they completed a half or a whole decade.

By the mid-sixties, we no longer had to limit our summer vacations to the Jersey shore. At that juncture, even Leslie was old
enough to travel and see more of the world. Thus, we ventured to
Cape Cod in 1964, where we met Bert, Eunice, and Peter. Our days
were interspersed with picnics, youngsters partially buried in the
sand, digging holes to China on the beach, visiting with Eunice's
family, the Rices, rowing on a lake, and indulging in New England
clam chowder. Unfortunately, for part of our stay, Leslie suffered
from a high fever due to her kidney problems. She was a good trooper and we made the best of the situation. Ridiculous as it might
sound for a vacation environment, our children helped us while
there to write about 1,000 names on the temple's High Holiday admission tickets, an obligation I inherited as ritual chair.

That same year, we explored the New York World's Fair in
Flushing Meadows near Max and Claire's home. The look into the
future was impressive, especially for the children. In the huge
crowds, Barry became "lost" again; this was not his first excursion,
but after some anxious moments he was found. Actually, Barry usually knew where he was, only we didn't, and that was the problem.
Relatively speaking, these were still safe times. Today, in the late-
nineties, the world is a much more dangerous place for children who
go off to explore on their own.

In 1965, we visited New Hampshire, where Puppu and Pa (the
endearing names given to my parents when Danny first started to
talk) spent a summer recess, and subsequently stopped for a few
days at Lake George. At Carney's Cabins on the lake, we met Toni
and his wife, a couple from Brooklyn with a warm and earthy demeanor. They were childless, and he just loved our kids. This simple
and kind man was always full of fun and energy, moving with agil-
ity in spite of his considerable body-mass. Again and again, he
threw Leslie into the water, calling her "mosquito" because of her

relatively tiny size, and she relished every moment. Later that year, we sent Barry to camp Minnisink for a week. He was lonely and unhappy there. Not quite ready for this kind of experience, he still preferred the comfort and security offered within the family unit.

In connection with a 1966 business trip, our family of five spent two memorable summer weeks in California. I was committed to present a paper on the utilization of magnetic control in space at an American Institute of Aeronautics and Astronautics (AIAA) conference in Seattle. This was the first plane ride for our children, and it was memorable to observe their reactions of awe and excitement. In the Los Angeles area, our crew enjoyed Marine Land and its acrobatic dolphins, but Disneyland with its rides and fairylands was the most fantastic for the kids. To this day, Leslie's talks with special emotion about meeting "her characters" such as Mickey Mouse and Donald Duck. This was followed by a visit to Universal Studios of Carl Laemmle vintage, Santa Barbara with our room at poolside and its famous Moroton Bay fig tree, Hearst castle with its impressive surroundings and vulgar excesses, the rocky and picturesque coast visible from Highway One, beautiful Carmel and historic Monterey, Yosemite National Park with firefalls and the big redwoods (we still drove through one) and Half Dome I called Moses, and Lake Tahoe via a precipitous Route 9 approach from the Nevada side. Finally, we ended up visiting Bea's uncle Juler and wife Helene in San Rafael. Despite being blind, Juler operated a stationery/newspaper store in a Sacramento government building, where the kids helped this blind man during a memorable few hours. In San Francisco, with friend Curt Servos as guide, we explored Golden Gate Park and Bridge and went on the traditional overcrowded cable car ride. Interrupted by an airplane strike, we changed plans and I traveled without the family to the Seattle conference. Together, we finally reached home again, after a fantastic experience for all five of us.

Except for two more vacation stays at Lake George in 1967 (Toni again) and 1968, and brief visits to the New Jersey shore, a number of years had to pass before we embarked on our next major vacation. This 1967–73 period brought us joy and gratification primarily through home-centered events such as Danny's and Barry's Bar Mitzvahs and my leadership involvement with Temple Emanu-El. Furthermore, extensive vacations during those years were somewhat incompatible with our budgetary capabilities.

The nine Franks at Orchard Lane in 1966. L to R., back row: Max, Betty,
Hannah, Selma, Paula, Hedwig; front row: Minna, Anny, Claire.

In February 1972, my parents joined us for a service in our synagogue. Their 50th wedding anniversary coincided with a Shabbat,
and so we all prayed in gratitude and thanksgiving. As a surprise,
Rabbi Kasdan asked them to rise during the service, and he pronounced a special blessing for my aged parents. In my mind, I can
still see them standing there, holding hands and thanking God on
that sunny and beautiful day. Afterwards, we marked this anniversary with a lovely party in our home.

About half a year later, mother suffered a severe stroke during
a summer stay in a Catskill resort. Following hospitalization and
stabilization, she was transferred to a nursing facility in Parsippa-
ny, not far from Livingston. A gradual but limited improvement
gave us some hope and even permitted a one-time visit to our home
in the latter part of December 1972. However, it was most likely
during those particular few hours in our midst that mother, having
regained a modest command of her mental faculties, recognized the
full extent of her limitations, the marginal quality of life that was

to be hers at best. Within a short time after that visit to our home, mother stopped taking nourishment and passed away on the 2nd of February, 1973. I mourned, we mourned. My father, who had lived with us during these trying months, appeared lost, an understandable and natural reaction. My sadness was mitigated to a considerable extend by the comfort of knowing that mother was now relieved from her suffering, both physical and emotional. Beyond that, I was grateful that she died a natural death in 1973 rather than suffering a brutal end at the hands of the Nazi henchmen in 1942, the year that the residual Jewish population of Suhl and all other German towns was deported to the extermination camps in the East. No foul and despicable Nazi hand had violated the woman who bore me and raised me and brought me to the freedom of America. Death has its tears and death has its gratitude.

My father dissolved his apartment and moved to our home. He was warmly received by a loving family, and especially by a caring and sensitive daughter-in-law. In spite of that, he tended to be depressed at times, though Bea tried valiantly to cheer him up and help him adjust to the new chapter in his life.

One of my mother's last thoughts focused on Danny's hoped for acceptance to Rutgers University, our state university. She had difficulty pronouncing the name, asking frequently: "Will Danny go to Rogers?" Shortly after her passing, Danny did indeed receive the acceptance with which she would have been very pleased. Enrollment at a quality school with a modest tuition requirement was good news for all of us. It was the beginning of more than a decade of college activities for the Muhlfelder family.

Danny was certainly a happy trooper at Rutgers. He had a number of good friends there and enjoyed his courses in history, political science, and horticulture. He was not sure where all this would lead, but there is little doubt that he received a broad liberal arts education. There is an advantage in such an approach rather than specializing too early in one's college career. Unfortunately, financial limitations and the materialistic objectives for quick success cause many young people to forego or cut short the liberal arts exposure identified with the educated person, opting instead for early specialization, for example in technology, law, and medicine. During my professional life, I met many engineers who were well versed in math, science, and modern design techniques but had inadequate

1966 visit to Disneyland

skills in English. This constituted a constant handicap and a detriment to their career development.

In 1974, Barry graduated from high school and began his physics studies at Rensselaer Polytechnic Institute in Troy, New York. Our sprouting scientist had found a very good school, and we were confident that he would blossom in this challenging environment.

Three years later, Leslie chose to enter Lafayette College in nearby Easton, Pennsylvania. Of a number of options open to her, she deliberately picked a small school for her undergraduate studies. She concentrated on courses in political science, literature, and economics. When she moved into her first dormitory with a multitude of "essentials," I became a stevedore carting load after load up to the fourth floor (no elevator) on one of the hottest days of the year. The boys had required considerably less baggage.

In June of 1976, we celebrated aunt Betty's 90th birthday in our home. She was comfortable with us and loved Bea's hamburgers. It is an interesting family statistic that of the nine of the original 12 Frank siblings who survived beyond 1920, all except my mother passed the 80-year threshold, and three made it into the nineties. I hope that such quality longevity is transmittable to succeeding generations.

In 1976, my father was in his 85th year, and his brothers Lothar and Max were in their seventies and doing reasonably well. But the blessing of longevity is not without limits. In 1974, while Pa was on summer vacation in the Catskills, he suffered an embolism in his left leg. With the marginal medical attention available in that region and without our immediate presence, his problem was initially misdiagnosed. We transported him by ambulance to Livingston's St. Barnabas Hospital as expeditiously as possible, but precious time had been lost and the leg had to be amputated above the knee. After recuperation, he was fitted with a prosthetic device and returned to our home. Amazingly, at age 83, he learned to walk again, stairs and all. We marveled at his dexterity and nimble movements and at his determination to overcome this handicap. During the summer of 1976, father's heart weakened and his general state of health declined. After some hospitalization, he was transferred to a Livingston nursing home, where he died on Labor Day, September 6.

When I was still a boy in Germany, I reflected on the finality of life and came to realize that even my father, whom I so adored, would someday be no more. That thought panicked me; I was unable to visualize this world and my life without him. When we carried him to his grave and said Kaddish in praise of his long life, I felt relieved that he was at peace and suffered no more from the physical ills of his waning years. The panicky boy from Germany was now a man with young adult children of his own, and the departure of the last of my parents was not only deeply mourned but also accepted in reflective gratitude. "L'dor vador," from generation to generation. Julius Muhlfelder was blessed with a long life and was spared from being slaughtered by the Nazi henchmen.

WE VISIT ISRAEL (TWICE)

Danny's acceptance to Rutgers cleared the deck for undertaking our first trip to Israel with him during the waning months of his senior high school year 1973.

Selma agreed to run the house for my father, Barry, and Leslie. Thus, the three of us joined a small group tour organized by our temple and set out to travel to the land of our ancestors for a memorable 10 days. I still recall my deep emotion when seeing the shoreline of Israel from our El Al plane for the first time and stepping on the soil of our forebears a short time later. For the 11 of us from New Jersey, it was an emotion-packed experience, as it must have been for millions of others during this century. We traveled in two limousines with two excellent guides to view the ancient and the new, the excavations and ruins with such great stories to convey, the kibbutzim and towns built by this century's pioneers, the fields that had been transformed from barren desert into productive farmland and green forests, the ancient and historic coast with its mix of the ancient and the modern, the memorials and the museums, Jerusalem of gold with the contrast of the old walled-in city and the modern western part housing the 20th century influx as well as the government structures of the reestablished Jewish state. We saw and touched and heard and experienced all that and so much more. The people, too, left a lasting impression; we were taken by the drive and enthusiasm and dedication of these modern Jews, who had accomplished so much in the face of apparently insurmountable odds. Yes, we also saw the ultra-Orthodox who condemned the existence of the state; and we were aware of the Arab masses, who had not as yet accepted the 1947 partition and the rebirth of the land of the Jewish people.

The euphoria of these 10 days could not be diminished, however, by the fundamentalism from within nor by the unresolved hostility from without. Although threatened from all sides, Israelis were extremely confident that they would be able to defend themselves and maintain their homeland in the midst of a hostile Arab world. In fact, at times we felt that their attitude bordered on overconfidence.

Of course, we met and visited with our friends, the Rivkins, in Jerusalem. They were struggling with their beginnings and loving it. Their apartment was and still is located across from Ammunition Hill, where heroic deeds took place during Israel's War of Independence. During our weekend in Haifa, we spent some precious hours visiting Lothar and Hannah in their little house in Kiryat Bialik. When Lothar made Kiddush, nostalgia and gratitude nearly overwhelmed my emotions.

During an overnight stay at kibbutz Hagoshrim, serendipity took over. Prior to our departure for Israel, Bea expressed the hope that somehow she could locate three people from Konstanz, her town of birth, people who had immigrated from Germany to what was then the British mandate of Palestine. Talking to the bartender at Hagoshrim, I mentioned that I originally came from Suhl, a fact that caused him to shrug his shoulders. However, when I followed up that my wife, the cantor's daughter, had emigrated from Konstanz, he volunteered with enthusiasm that the daughter of the former rabbi of that town is living in Hagoshrim. Thus we had found one of the three people Bea had hoped for, and the reunion was a special experience indeed. Hava Kohne Rachmilevitsch then gave Bea the Tel Aviv addresses of the other two ladies on Bea's wish list, and those we visited before departing for the U.S. These were the aunts of Werner Merzbacher, an acquaintance of Bea's from her youthful Konstanz days. Thus, through this fortuitous meeting during our Israel trip, Bea reestablished contact with Werner, who now lived in Switzerland with his family. During succeeding years, we became good friends of these special human beings and spent a number of lovely vacations at the Merzbachers' condo in Davos.

The Golan Heights towered over Hagoshrim, where I observed numerous bomb shelters. Hava explained that the members of the kibbutz had to seek frequent refuge in these underground places because of numerous Syrian bombardments between 1948, the founding year of the state, and 1967 when the Heights were captured by the heroic Israeli army following the Syrian attack of that year. It seems that no matter where Israel borders on the Arab world, the country and the lives of its citizens are threatened by their neighbors. In spite of that apparently ever-present obstacle, miraculous progress has been made to rebuild the country, to make the desert bloom, to remember the biblical past with dignity and pride, and to develop a thriving modern society under democratic rule. Since that time, Bea and I have returned a number of times to Israel, but this initial trip was the most memorable since it was the first.

A few months after this first visit, the Arab world, led by Syria and Egypt, launched a surprise attack on Israel, the Yom Kippur war. Their initial success was quickly reversed and turned into defeat by the heroic Israeli army, but at considerable human cost to the young Jewish state. When will Shalom ever come? When we learn to respect each other and share the riches and the beauty of this world.

During November 1976, the World Union for Progressive Judaism, which is the umbrella organization for liberal Judaism, convened in Jerusalem. Bea and I decided to serve as delegates to this extraordinary meeting, thus embarking on our second trip to Israel. Leslie stayed temporarily with Bert and Eunice, and 15 Orchard Lane closed down for a month.

During our entire three-and-a-half week stay in Israel, the weather was nearly perfect. We lived at Hotel Rivkin in the Ramat Eshkol district of Jerusalem. It was wonderful once again to share extensive quality time with our good friends. Our 1973 visit had been quite rushed, and now we had adequate opportunity to explore the wonders of this city in greater depth. Helen and Ken served as expert tour guides and great hosts. While there, we also had the chance to visit with my mother's youngest sister, Anny, and husband, Heinz Ronberg. They used to live in Connecticut and, upon retiring from their wholesale coffee business, had made Aliyah in the early seventies. The Rivkins had just been blessed with their first grandchild. Ayelet was adored by all as the first of the next generation as well as the first native-born, the first Sabra in the Rivkin clan.

After exploring the Dead Sea area, including the nature oasis of Ein Gedi and the spectacular and historic Masada fortress, we headed north towards the Golan and the Galilee. When ascending the Golan Heights, we could appreciate how the Syrians could bombard the Galilee valley with impunity until 1967. Traveling along the eastern rim of Lake Kinnereth, Bea and I turned into a banana plantation to take a picture. As Bea posed in front of a tree, an Israeli on a tractor approached to inquire about our intentions. He probably thought we were stealing bananas but only found enthusiastic American tourists. After exploring the excavations of Megiddo, the palace from King Solomon's period, we returned to Kiryat Bialik and another memorable Shabbat with Lothar and Hannah.

While in the Haifa area, we stopped at the Leo Baeck School to say Shalom to its head master and our good acquaintance, Rabbi Bob Samuels. This secondary school is affiliated with our liberal religious movement and does a fabulous job in educating not only Sabras but also immigrant children from Ethiopia and the lands of the former Soviet Union. Although the school is very effective and of great benefit to Israel, it receives little if any financial support from the state. The Orthodox establishment is recognized as the official religion of all Israeli Jews in spite of the fact that 80% of all Israeli Jews are secular. Conservative and Reform rabbis still are not authorized to officiate at life cycle events such as conversions and weddings, even now as we observed the 50th anniversary of the rebirth of the modern Jewish state. I hope, some day all this will change and the Reform and Conservative branches of Judaism will not be discriminated against any more for the sake of political expediency. It appears incredulous that Israel grants equality to all religions except liberal Judaism.

After returning to Jerusalem, we were welcomed by our former Rabbi Rivkin in full battle dress, steel helmet, Uzi weapon slung over the shoulder, and all. He was on duty as a reservist at the Allenby bridge. His appearance was worth a good laugh, for Ken was incompatible with his military attire and looked like a contradiction in fact.

Helen suggested that we join her on a three-day bus tour, which she conducted for academicians as part of her job with the American Professors for Peace in the Middle East. We stopped at Tel Aviv University and then traveled north to the Lebanese border, the so-called "Good Fence" utilized to support the Lebanese Christians. Subsequently, we entered the West Bank area that Israel occupied during the 1967 Six Day war. We were received in the city hall by Basam Al Shak'an, the mayor of Nablus, the largest town of the area. Tea was served, and the mayor's Arab remarks were translated. He was, without question, a PLO sympathizer but could not, in view of the Israeli occupation, admit to being an official member of that terrorist organization. Before concluding the meeting with the group, the mayor invited questions that he answered in English. One professor inquired which part of the land could be allocated to Israel as part of an eventual peace settlement. Al Shak'an hesitated for just a moment and then answered, "Tel Aviv, maybe." This "Tel Aviv, maybe" pronouncement has remained impregnated in my mind ever since. I would like to believe that the Arabs would be willing to share this historic land with the Jews instead of making the destruction of Israel their ultimate goal in accordance with the PLO charter and other pronouncements by Arab heads of state. But I am very uncertain with regard to my premise. For the sake of Shalom, we have to hope for the best for the sake of Israel and for the entire Mideast.

Our next three-day excursion had its inception once again in Jerusalem. It was a commercial sightseeing tour led by a talented Syrian Jew. Traveling south via S'de Boker, David ben Gurion's home kibbutz where he had lived in utter simplicity, and Avdat, a Byzantine and Nabatean way-station in the Negev desert, we viewed the spectacular red sandstone formations of the Solomon's pillars before reaching the resort port of Eilat on the Red Sea. Because the Sinai peninsula had been captured by Israel in response to the Egyptian provocation during the 1967 Six Day war, we were able to continue southward along the coast all the way to Sharm el-Sheik and the straits of Tiran, where we saw the ruined Egyptian gun emplacements. The area that we traversed was rugged and beautiful and spectacular in its almost pristine state. The Sinai was eventually returned by Israel as part of the peace settlement with Egypt. After returning to Eilat, we enjoyed a swim in the pool of the Laromme Hotel with its unique island bar. Before departing from this lovely resort, we were thrilled to view some of God's most beautiful creations: the tropical fish of the Gulf of Eilat. Both in terms of unusual shapes and colorful iridescence, these creatures constitute a spectacular exhibition of the grandeur of nature.

When we returned to Jerusalem, the time had come to attend the Congress of the World Union for Progressive Judaism. We remembered the past when we paid homage at Theodore Herzl's grave and said Kaddish at Yad Vashem, the national memorial for the Holocaust's six million victims. At the Hilton Hotel, we heard numerous reports and addresses, including those by Abba Eban and Yitzhak Shamir. Joined by the Rivkins, we attended an elaborate dinner at the Knesset, where we listened to Prime Minister

Yitzhak Rabin, who was then serving the first of two widely-separated terms in that burdensome office. We met with progressive Jews from all of the world's continents, and it was enlightening and thrilling to be exposed to the eloquence and enthusiasm of those in leading positions. However, the emotional highlight of this gathering was the dedication of the first Reform (i.e., progressive) kibbutz in Israel, Kibbutz Yael in the Arava, one hour's drive north of Eilat and a fraction of a mile from the Jordanian border. Hundreds of delegates were bused south for this special occasion. With blue and white flags flying, with saplings being planted by each participant, with Mezuzahs ceremoniously being attached to the doorposts of the new houses, with song and with dance, we celebrated this historic day. Leading an emotional procession, Rabbi Alexander Schindler, the president of the UAHC, presented a Holocaust Torah scroll from Czechoslovakia to the young kibbutznics of Yahel. This was one of these times when all participants were aware that they were witnessing and making history.

Now it was time to leave and to pronounce "L'Hitra'ot," till the next time! On our way back to the States, we stopped off in Switzerland for a few days. Quite a contrast to Israel, and not only in terms of the weather. First, we spent a few delightful hours with Barry's friend Paul Monroe, who was studying at the Technische Hochschule in Zurich. This was followed by a brief hello with Werner Merzbacher, a friend from Bea's youth in Konstanz. During the war, he lived in the New York area. At that time, I also got to know him when he visited New Jersey, first alone and later with his wife Gaby. Our reunion in Werner's office was brief, but it was obvious that we would make up for lost time in the future with these warm and interesting people.

From Zurich, we drove north to Kreuzlingen, which is contiguous with Bea's hometown Konstanz across the Swiss-German border. We were hosted by old friends of the Bravmann family, Margot and Herbert Dreyfus. It was a nostalgic time for Bea, the first visit since 1938 to the area of her childhood. In the early part of this century, the Jews of the two adjoining towns had combined to form one congregation in spite of the international border in their midst, and Bea's father functioned as their cantor and religious school teacher. But, with few exceptions, the Jewish congregants of Konstanz had either emigrated before 1940 or were deported and perished in the Holocaust. Thus, the old friends who joined us during our stay at the Dreyfus residence were essentially all from the Swiss side of the congregation, from Kreuzlingen. For a brief and uncomfortable hour, Bea and I crossed the border for a quick look at Konstanz. In place of the destroyed synagogue, an ugly modern commercial structure had been built. We located a small sign on its facade, acknowledging the house of worship that once stood there. The building was erected after the war by a Jewish survivor and immigrant from Poland, who had purchased the property and included a small prayer hall within. Next door, Bea pointed out the Gemeinde Haus, the congregational residence, where the Bravmanns used to live on the third floor, the place where Bea was born. It was raining and drab on that day, and after viewing the harbor area, Bea suggested that we return to Switzerland, which I readily accepted. The memories were too painful, and Bea's exposure to the changed Konstanz was too sudden. Would the passage of time ever heal? The future might tell, but to forget the past, never!

We concluded our extensive vacation trip with a short tour of northeastern Switzerland. The formidable Saentis peak was engulfed in fog, but the dining at the peak, reachable by cable car, was delightful anyhow. We were the only guests and Bea correctly stated that the Swiss do not know how to make a bad meal. On our way, we paid a call on some other old friends, the Hilbs of Herisau. I still recall that Dorle, whose maiden name was Gump, described to us how the Swiss authorities caught Jews who fled across the border from Germany or Austria and returned them to the Nazi authorities. Switzerland is a beautiful country, but it does not have a Statue of Liberty. From there, we made brief stops in Arosa, an unforgettable fairyland with a new blanket of snow, and at the Valduz castle in tiny Liechtenstein.

The end of a memorable few weeks had arrived, and we were welcomed at Kennedy airport by Danny, Barry, and Richard, and at 15 Orchard Lane by a large "Welcome Home" banner, which I believe was Leslie's handiwork. We were a few months away from Danny's graduation from Rutgers, Leslie's graduation from Livingston High School, their parents' 25th wedding anniversary, and a new phase of our lives as "empty-nesters."

PROFESSIONAL CHALLENGE, SUCCESS,
AND INVENTIONS (1970–1989)

Within the years immediately following my 1970 appointment as manager of Attitude Control at the RCA Astro Space Division, I was notably challenged by the initiation of two important satellite projects.

Prior to my employment with RCA, i.e., December 1962, the division was already involved in the development and application of weather observation satellites. Both NASA and the U.S. Air Force were significant customers for this type of space application. A decade later, however, there was a need to improve the precision of the meteorological observations by about one order of magnitude (factor of 10) and to accommodate a multitude of instruments on one spacecraft. Such a requirement placed a particularly stringent demand on the attitude control subsystem, which could only be satisfied by providing precise three axes pointing instead of the previously utilized spin-stabilized orientation. But we welcomed the challenge and, after eliminating Boeing from the competition, worked intensely and creatively to come up with the proverbial new mousetrap. Together with my people, I thrived in that kind of environment. We took advantage of the latest in technology, including spaceborne computers and star mappers, to attain our goal.

By 1976, we were ready with our first new DMSP (Defense Meteorological Space Program) spacecraft, but serious problems developed during the orbit insertion. A gas leak caused the satellite stabilization to be out of control. Although located in proper orbit, the spacecraft was useless in this spinning state. We worked tirelessly in close cooperation with our Air Force customer to generate a rescue plan, i.e., reestablish an attitude (stability and pointing) that is compatible with mission requirements. After six long months and a number of lengthy stays at the customer's facility in

Astro Space General Manager Vollmer congratulating me on my tenth US patent at RCA, 1979

Omaha, Nebraska, we finally succeeded with ingenious on-board computer reprogramming to establish and maintain the desired conditions. This was not an 8 am to 5 pm operation but rather a continuous and time-consuming effort. I was fortunate to work with excellent and motivated people. About three months after the mishap, I had been able to devise a rescue method involving interactions with the earth's magnetic field. Having first been verified via computer simulations by Roger Hogan, a member of my group, this technique enabled the satellite recovery and its restabilization. The two of us eventually received a U.S. patent for this effort. Since that time, numerous environmental observation satellites have been built by the Astro Space Division and successfully utilized for many years by various customers, such as the U.S. Air Force, NASA, and NOAA, the National Oceanic and Aeronautic Administration, but none gave me a greater thrill than the first one.

During this same timeframe of the first half of the seventies, we became involved with another challenge, geosynchronous communication satellites. Both the weather satellites and the earlier communication spacecraft operated in relatively low orbits of a few hundred miles altitude, with the plane of the orbit path steeply inclined with respect to the earth's equator. For communication purposes, it is particularly desirable for our space-born relay station to be in continual contact with a well-defined area of the earth. This is not possible with low altitude orbiters that regularly disappear over the horizon and subsequently reappear for a limited earth-contact period. Initial work had been accomplished by some of our competitors to design and operate spacecraft that appear to be sus-

Plaque commorating my tenth patent at RCA, 1979

pended at a particular spot above the equator. This trick is accomplished by placing a spacecraft into an equatorial orbit that makes exactly one revolution per day. For RCA to progress in the space communication business, it was essential to exploit that type of mission. So there we had our second challenge of the 1970s. Up to that point, the initial attempts had utilized spinning satellites for this purpose. But that approach represented significant limitations for absorbing sufficient solar energy for the generation of electrical power and for the accommodation of ever more complex antenna dish arrangements.

What we needed was a three-axis body-stabilized spacecraft, with its antennae permanently pointing at Earth while its power-absorbing solar array was continuously pointing at the sun. This was recognized by one of my former supervisors, Jack Keigler, a brilliant scientist and a first-class human being. Aside from this welcome challenge of creating the first three axis Satcom, as we dubbed it, my involvement in this specific technology also resulted in the special benefit of working hand-in-hand with this talented and highly ethical man, a relationship that resulted in a lifelong friendship as well. Although Jack was not always fully appreciated by the company staff, his beneficial impact on this technology was indisputable. Together with a Canadian colleague, he subsequently received the prestigious RCA David Sarnoff Award for his contributions. When working in unexplored territory, one has much more latitude, more opportunity to be creative. And so we found out again that necessity is the mother of invention. This was a wonderful time. I was gratified to play a leading role and simultaneously contribute a number of ideas that evolved into U.S. patents. Eventually, I was awarded 13 patents while at Astro, thus making it a total of 16 together with the three dating back to my Curtiss-Wright days. Some of these were individual creations, and some I shared with other members of the technical staff. When our first Satcom was launched from Kennedy Space Center in Florida in December 1975, it was flying with six patents bearing my name. At our customer's ground station in Vernon Valley, New Jersey, we worked and prayed and improvised and learned during this first launch and the immediately following orbit achievement operations, eventually placing our new "bird" where it belonged and assuming its correct pointing attitude. We were, of course, inexperienced at this, and thus the initial orbit achievement was quite an adventure. Learning on the job is fun and sometimes the only practical way. This first Satcom satellite was a big success and had a multitude of successors to serve our various customers. All RCA communication spacecraft utilized the same basic design but evolved into ever greater sophistication and capability. In total, I participated in 11 such programs, most of which consisted of three satellites each.

On one occasion, our success-oriented expectations received a rude shock. In the process of injecting the third Satcom into its final orbit, the large solid (fuel) rocket motor suddenly ceased to function after about one quarter of its intended firing duration. Within a fraction of a second, the entire satellite disappeared without any further trace of telemetry or radar signature. All signs pointed to an explosion of the rocket motor that had fatally damaged the satellite and sent its remains into a different orbit, a fact verified by later investigations. But immediately after this unfortunate accident, we were all sitting there in shock and disbelief. CBS television crews were permitted to enter the ground station to feed the appetite of the hungry news media. I became an unwitting TV "star," an engineer associated with failure. The world was told that a bunch of smart scientists had "lost a satellite the size of a refrigerator and weighing a ton" and did not have the ability to locate it any longer.

The media took clever advantage of the dual meaning of the word "loss," emphasizing the as yet unexplained disappearance rather than the accidental destruction of the spacecraft. Of course we realized that, more often than not, bad news is good news for the media. But we were disconsolate nevertheless.

In addition to the communication and meteorological spacecraft, we also produced quite a number for scientific and navigation applications. A few of these missions were dedicated to the observation and mapping of the Moon and of Mars. It is most worthwhile not only to utilize space for various purposes but also to contribute to a better understanding of our world. During the late 1970s, I made three trips to Japan with RCA colleagues. This country had taken initial steps to enter the field of space technology and was eager to deal with American firms involved in this evolving field. Most likely, Japan's primary motivation was the rapid acquisition of the latest technology rather than the purchase of a few U.S. satellites; however, the latter was the means to achieve the former. Interestingly enough, the U.S. government tried on one hand to prevent the export of advanced U.S. technology while on the other hand showing tolerance if not interest in the sale of U.S. products to foreign customers. In the process of engaging in the latter, the Japanese also accomplished the former and primary objective, the rapid acquisition of American knowhow. Individual corporate entities are primarily interested in the short-term bottom line and less so in the long-term impact of technology transfer. During our Tokyo and Yokahama visits, we were hosted royally and found the capital city most interesting. I remember buying some gifts for the family, including a colorful kimono for Bea. When dealing with Japanese business contacts, I learned that a smile or a nod did not generally imply agreement or understanding. Each of our three journeys to Japan made a stop in Anchorage, Alaska. I had never used Japan Airlines before, and I marveled at its efficiency and the courtesy of its personnel. Once, a Japanese fellow passenger even gave me a back-rub during one of the long flights.

By 1980, my RCA group had grown both in personnel and diversity, so I sub-divided it into three parts: attitude control analysis, orbit achievement, and systems, each subgroup with its own manager who reported to me. In later years, I was given the additional responsibility for spacecraft propulsion. Occasionally but rarely, one of our space birds failed to achieve its initial orbit or ceased to function after some time in orbit. Overall, we were flush with success. Naturally, my key people and I were frequently involved in the highly competitive bidding for new business acquisitions. The required proposals consisted of many volumes of documentation. Long nights and weekends had to be added to the normal work schedule to get these important tasks accomplished. In the early 1980s, I joined a small group of RCA managers on a trip to Buenos Aires. The Argentinean space agency had extended an invitation, and we hoped to stimulate some business. They were interested in our presentation and we enjoyed seeing this southern metropolis. But there was no funding available for the relatively expensive high technology satellite applications.

AMERICAN INSTITUTE OF
AERONAUTICS AND ASTRONAUTICS

In recognition of his
professional distinction
and his notable and
valuable contributions
the Officers and Directors of
the Institute declare that

LUDWIG MUHLFELDER

has been elected
to the grade of

FELLOW

MAY 3, 1989

Professional recognition by the AIAA, Washington, DC, May 1989

As an unusual side benefit of my activity and as the result of intensive recruiting of additional staff, I played indirect Cupid to four young engineers in my group. Romance bloomed for two charming couples, each of whom had passed the scrutiny of my professional interview some years prior.

In order to keep up to date, I usually attended the annual Guidance and Control conference sponsored by the American Institute of Aeronautics and Astronautics (AIAA), occasionally presenting a technical paper. After becoming a member of this organization in 1964, I served on its guidance, navigation, and control technical committee for a few years around 1980. I benefited considerably from my involvement with AIAA, and I therefore felt that I should perform some service in return.

My career went well until the end of 1985, when I was startled by the announcement that RCA had agreed to be bought out for $6.2 billion by the General Electric Corporation. This appeared to be a tremendous bargain for GE because the sale included NBC, with an approximate evaluation of four billion, plus one billion in cash. Besides that, GE had not distinguished itself in satellite technology,

Managing Guidance, Control and Stabilization at the Astro Space Center, Princeton, NJ, 1982.

but then again the satellite business was not a priority for GE. Quite obviously, I am not a big corporate wheeler and dealer, only a little technical manager. In any case, after the initial shock, I bounced back and tried to make the best of the situation.

Astro was subsequently merged with GE's Space Division in Valley Forge, Pennsylvania, about one hour's drive to the west of the former RCA facility. My new GE supervisor, a real gentleman, interviewed me and requested that I expand my responsibilities by also managing the technical groups of my specialty at Valley Forge, thus becoming responsible for about 75 people. I did my best, although having personnel located about 50 miles apart did not lend itself to an efficient operation. The GE absorption was, in my opinion, not beneficial for our Astro Space Division. An ever-increasing bureaucracy manifested itself in a mushrooming of management reports, regulations, and meetings and therefore eclipsed the prior emphasis on technical excellence and creativity. My personal overhead charges tripled at that time and thus exceeded those devoted to the core technology area of the business. A further detriment was an ingrained atmosphere of internal intrigue and politics at all levels of the organization, something that we had been not used to at RCA.

GE had been one of RCA's space technology competitors since 1960, but only in the government business area. They had little success or capability in the commercial aerospace sector. Their CEO, Jack Welch, was nationally known as "neutron Jack" because of his so-called downsizing and restructuring techniques, a euphemism for layoffs and plant closings. The people were gone, but the buildings were left standing. A number of former RCA divisions quickly fell into this category, but our Astro activity apparently satisfied the GE objectives and was thus permitted to continue its operation, at least for the time being.

In the spring of 1989, I was inducted as a Fellow of AIAA, the highest grade of membership of that organization, during a gala ball at its annual general meeting in Washington. Bea, Danny, Leslie, and Richard Katz were all present during this honorary recognition, which I deeply appreciated. Jack Keigler, one of my nationally recognized sponsors, had preceded me in this attainment.

WORKING FOR TEMPLE AND UAHC (1972–1984)

In parallel with my important professional involvement, I continued to be active within the Reform religious movement subsequent to the end of my presidency of Temple Emanu-El in 1972.

In June of 1972, I participated in the moving installation of my successor, Lou Barnett, as president of our congregation. Merely a month later, on the 4th of July, this dedicated man died suddenly. The personal tragedy and the impact on the temple were both very painful. I wrote for our temple bulletin:

"There are times in our lives when the frailty of our existence demonstrates itself in a sudden and sad event. We love and we labor, we prepare and we plan, we are a link between the yesterday and the tomorrow. In the morning we flourish and grow, and in the evening we are cut down and wither. When will the evening come, and when will the shadows fall? For Lou Barnett, the evening came suddenly. And the shadows of mourning fell upon his home and his temple."

During the following decade, I was requested to chair a number of ad hoc committees such as search and contract negotiations for our professionals, and long-range planning for the temple. The latter was particularly challenging, since it was the first time that our temple had ever undertaken such a farsighted projection. We spent over one year gathering statistical data and other pertinent information before formulating our evaluation and recommendations. Unfortunately, the board made little or no use of the final report. Because of my status as a recent past president and my subsequent involvement with our national body, the Union of American Hebrew Congregations (UAHC), I continued to serve on this governing temple body for many more years.

For years, Bea had been active on our temple's social action committee. She had served as chairperson of that activity, which attempted to help the downtrodden of our society and transform our words of prayer into deeds of helping and healing. In the aftermath of the Vietnam tragedy, there was an opportunity to assist refugees from that war-torn country and to settle them in a better surrounding, our U.S.A. With the enthusiastic help of Rabbi Kasdan, the committee raised the necessary funds within our congregation to give these potential new immigrants a headstart, i.e., the congregation committed itself to be the guarantor for the new arrivals from this distant land. One fine day, our new family arrived, the Bangs with their seven children. Bea and our good friend Anita Smith were particularly involved in settling these newcomers from a primitive and trying past into what was to them a strange and modern western world. To me, and likely others, it seemed that we were making material and humane restitution for some of the pain and havoc that America had inflicted on Vietnam during the war. Somewhat later, a few additional refugees were also received and helped by the social action committee. All of them, including the seven Bang children, became upright and responsible citizens of the U.S. The eventual spouses of these children came from various backgrounds and could found their own miniature United Nations. A number of times, Bea invited this large family to reunion picnics in our backyard, and words of prayer were turned into deeds of kindness. Such social action is really religious action; I was proud of our participation of this project, and particularly in Bea's pivotal role.

In 1981, I served as a member of a cantor selection committee to find a replacement for the retiring individual. After numerous auditions and corresponding interviews, we brought Mikhail Manevich to our congregation. He and his wife Emma had immigrated five years earlier from the Soviet Union, well before mass emigration was permitted by the Soviets. During the investiture service from Hebrew Union College (HUC), it was a stirring moment when, as the first Russian to graduate from our cantorial school, Mikhail was singled out for a special blessing by its president, Alfred Gottschalk: "He will sing God's song for all to hear." And what an impact he made with his voice, with his choir direction, with his teaching, with his concerts, with his personality, with his charming wife and little son Jacob. Our new cantor had received excellent training as a choir conductor while still in St. Petersburg (Leningrad), and he was thus most effective in organizing a volunteer choir, which has been a great asset to our congregation ever since. Our temple emerged into a new and wonderful era.

At the beginning of the 1980s, the temple honored Bea and me during an Israel Bond breakfast, which featured our good acquaintance Rabbi Bob Samuels from Haifa's Leo Baeck school as the main speaker. It was especially meaningful for Bea to be one of the honorees, for my visibility in light of my leadership activities had given me disproportionate credit. The multitude of activities I had engaged in over the years, both professionally and in the Jewish sphere, would not have been possible without Bea's generous support, endless energy, wise counsel, and great patience.

In the mid 1970s, I became involved in the activities of our UAHC region. For administrative and support reasons, our national Reform movement is subdivided into thirteen regions, each with its own professional director and staff. At first, I devoted some effort to religious school statistics and standards, leading to improvements in this important facet. But before long, I found myself involved in MUM (Maintenance of Union Membership) work. The more than 800 congregations of our movement financially support their umbrella organization, including the four HUC campuses, by taxing a percentage of their expenses. That seems straightforward and should not require much administrative work, particularly since there is a professional staff devoted to this function at our national headquarters in New York, the House of Living Judaism. But the necessary yearly congregational documentation does not always get promptly and properly submitted by the congregations, and quite a few of these congregations have problems in adhering to the required dues payments, i.e., they request dues relief. Therefore, each region has its own lay MUM committee, which functions under the auspices of a national body. So that is what I became involved with. It has been said, "Where there is no bread, there is no Torah." Although basically religious in nature, the movement, like any viable organization, requires sustenance in order to carry out its mission. By 1979, I assumed the chairmanship of the regional MUM activity and concurrently became a member of the national committee.

The work was challenging although not always pleasant. Many congregations experienced financial stress and thus required dues relief. Even if all financial information was made available, it was difficult to judge how much relief would be appropriate in each case while simultaneously being fair to the union of sister congregations. Furthermore, some congregational leaders did not hesitate to circumvent the rules of their national organization so as to achieve an unethical financial benefit for the congregation they represented, an action that was blatantly incongruous. Thus people such as I, who were representing the UAHC, had to work with great diligence and patience to maintain a level playing field. We did not always succeed, but we gave it a good try. In addition to the frequent travel within our region, which encompassed the most southern counties of New York state and most of New Jersey, my duties also required a few plane trips per year to more distant U.S. locations to attend national committee meetings. All this volunteer activity had some side benefits in addition to the work. I particularly admired the co-operative effort of so many fine people, who with dedication, intelligence, and generosity both with their time and personal resources labored to further our national religious movement.

In 1984, I was elected to a four-year term on the UAHC national board of trustees. Most likely, this honor was based on my efforts on behalf of the New Jersey/West Hudson Valley Region UAHC Region and my participation on the national MUM committee. I believe that I was the first member of our temple who was given such an opportunity. This was particularly appreciated because most of the trustees of the national board were not only capable and dedicated leaders of our movement but were also in a financial position to contribute generously towards the financial needs of this organization. If the latter capability had been a critical qualifier, then I would not have been nominated and elected to serve.

The board of those years consisted of about 160 members, a body that is too large to permit the flexibility required for short-term decision-making. For this reason, about 20% of the most experienced trustees are organized into an executive committee that meets four times per year. I never served in this particular body. Board meetings took place at six-month intervals. Each year, one of these gatherings was scheduled for the greater New York metropolitan area, and the second one took place in various parts of the U.S.A. and Canada.

For my initial meeting, I traveled to Bar Harbor, Florida, in November of 1984. As a new member, I joined a small group of the same category to receive a cordial welcome and brief orientation. A gentleman sitting next to me introduced himself as Peter Yarrow. Admittedly, I was not tuned in to his great fame and thus gave no cognizance to the wonderful and sensitive artist at my side. I even missed his concert offered during the Sabbath afternoon of the three-day meeting, falling soundly asleep on the beach instead. Since that time, I have learned to appreciate Peter, as well as the other members of his world-famous group, Paul and Mary. When I returned home and mentioned this to Bea, she exclaimed in utter frustration: "Only my husband would sit next to Peter Yarrow and not know it!"

In 1988, I was elected to serve a second and constitutionally final term on the national board. Besides the essential plenary business meetings, there were many opportunities for intellectual stimulation and emotional Jewish experience. It was a privilege meeting with so many bright and capable people. The lay and professional leaders as well as invited guest speakers were usually inspiring and well versed, but none equaled in eloquence and insight our President, Rabbi Alexander Schindler, who served our movement in that pivotal position from 1973 to 1996. He had also fled Nazi Germany in the late thirties and made an outstanding contribution to the North American Jewish community as well as towards greater justice and understanding for all people in both the national and international spheres. From my enthusiasm for this affiliation, it must appear obvious that I tried to be part of each meeting during my eight-year tenure on the board. I missed just one because of a trip to Israel. Bea and I also attended the regional and national UAHC biennials, which took place in alternate years and were always most informative and inspiring events. Acting as delegates for our congregation, we returned home with enthusiasm, observations, and recommendations intended to enrich the programs and practices of our own house of worship.

I continued to serve as chair of the regional and as member of the national MUM committee, and because of my national board affiliation was also a member of the regional UAHC board. In 1985, I also joined the dues policy review committee, a newly formed national body charged with reviewing our UAHC dues structure and formulating appropriate recommendations for potential improvements.

At the regional biennial of November 1994, which was attended by about 500 people, I received a singular Aliyah and Mi Shebeirach (called up for the Torah reading and a prayer for God's blessing) in appreciation of my services. Subsequently, I was presented with a beautiful calligraphy depicting a rendition of the Shehecheyanu, the traditional blessing expressing thanks for reaching joyous occasions. Although the inherent nature of MUM work does not tend to enhance an individual's popularity, it appeared that I still had quite a number of admirers at the conclusion of 15 years of involvement in this area.

Another by-product of my membership on the national and regional UAHC board was a continuation of my active participation on the board of our temple beyond 1984. During this period, I served on three additional cantor selection committees, one as chair, and thus for a total of five since 1964. In some of these cases, the professional change was essential for the welfare of the congregation, and in others the cantor did not seek contract renewal for family reasons or more desirable opportunity elsewhere. After a highly appreciated seven years with our temple, Cantor Manevich accepted a position with one of the largest and most prestigious houses of worship of the Reform movement, the Washington Hebrew Congregation. Bea and I kept in contact with this lovely family and were invited to the Bar Mitzvah celebrations of both sons.

I had no further desire to chair or participate in the work of the standing committees, not only because for me it would be a somewhat repetitive exercise after so many years of service but also of the need to afford younger people this type of exposure and on-the-job training. It is essential for the temple or any organization to maintain a cadre program to develop future leadership. However, as a past president, it was difficult for me to turn down a request from the person currently occupying that position. Thus, I did occasionally get involved in ad hoc jobs such as contract, finance, constitutional revision, and special review (hardship) activities. In addition, when a member family sustained a death, I assisted our professional staff with home Minyan services. The sadness of these occasions is compensated by the satisfaction I derive from performing such a Mitzvah.

In addition to her social action involvement, Bea had served over the years on the religious school committee, the ritual committee, and a number of nominating committees. Therefore, it was no surprise when she was elected in 1984 to the temple's board of trustees, on which she worked with great dedication until 1989. For two years of that period, she even served as a vice-president of our congregation. However, since Bea had no desire to ascend to the presidency, she declined to continue to serve as an officer beyond 1989.

Our second home: Temple Emanu-El, "God is with us."

Starting about 1980, Bea and I participated in a Bible study class that is partially sponsored by the temple and still meets for about six sessions per year. The teacher of this small group is recruited from the Jewish community, and the study is conducted in participants' homes on a rotating basis. While parents and grandparents are eager for their progeny to attend the temple's religious school, most adults make relatively little effort to further their own and usually limited Jewish education. Our Bible study is an attempt, admittedly by only a handful, to counteract this practice. Young people are perceptive and react negatively to the message of their elders: "Do as I say and not as I do." It would be naive for me to claim that the attitude of many towards Jewish education is only influenced by this dichotomy, but lack of knowledge combined with contradictory messages to our young people does not further the study of Jewish scriptures, customs, literature, and philosophy. Either within the temple structure or the general Jewish community, there are many opportunities to further one's knowledge of our religious heritage. Ignorance is not bliss, and without study of our heritage we will find it difficult if not impossible to ascertain what kind of a Torah lives in our soul. Particularly those engaged as lay volunteers in temple leadership need to rise above the necessary though mundane aspects of organization, multiple participation, and budgetary considerations; they have to aspire to be role models of the people of the book and make the enhancement of their Jewish knowledge a top priority. After 17 years of Bible study, Bea and I are still learning.

Since my earliest school years, I have been aware of the centrality of the Torah, the five books of Moses, to my life as a Jew. Thus, Bea and I were grateful for the opportunity offered in 1987 by our temple of symbolically participating in the writing of a personal Torah. A Sofer, a scribe, was engaged to perform this act for which we had neither the skill nor the knowledge. Our participation consisted of selecting and endowing a particular portion of this monumental and holy document, thus giving support to our house of worship to meet its programming and educational objectives. Bea suggested that we select the portion read on the afternoon of Yom Kippur: Leviticus 19–20 entitled Kedoshim (holy or holiness). This was an excellent and most meaningful choice, as some excerpts from "The Law of Holiness," which were addressed to the whole house of Israel, will clearly illustrate:

"When you reap the harvest of your land, you shall not reap all the way to the edges of your field, or gather the gleanings of your harvest. You shall not pick your vineyard bare, or gather the fallen fruit of your vineyard; you shall leave them for the poor and the stranger. . . . The wages of a laborer shall not remain with you until morning. . . . You shall not render an unfair decision: do not favor the poor or show deference to the rich; judge your neighbor fairly. . . . Love your neighbor as yourself. . . . When a stranger resides with you in your land, you shall not wrong him, for you were strangers in the land of Egypt. You shall be holy, for I, Adonai your God, am holy."

Now and then, Rabbi Kasdan gave me, as well as others, the opportunity to contribute to creative services marking special occasions such as temple anniversaries or remembrances of importance to the Jewish calendar. Both on the 40th and 50th commemoration of the 1938 Kristallnacht, I addressed the congregation during Erev Shabbat services. The impact of relating these experiences of and by someone who was there was not lost on those assembled. Similarly, I have been invited, often together with Bea, to speak to our religious school students about our Holocaust experiences. Such an exposure is likely more meaningful to our students than being relegated to textbook descriptions. But we will not live forever, and therefore the written word and video recordings are the best alternative for preserving the history and the lessons of the past. During the summer vacation months, when our Friday night services take place in the Hillel Room instead of the main sanctuary, lay members conduct our worship in conjunction with either the cantor or the rabbi. During most years, I presented one drash, the interpretation of the weekly Torah portion, during that period. Each time, I gain a deeper understanding of these ancient and sacred texts, usually finding within the lines valuable applicability to our own days.

In February 1990, I used the Exodus portion of "Beshalach" for a meaningful parallelism between the ancient Israelites leaving Egypt and eventually arriving in the Promised Land and my family's own exodus from Germany and our resettlement in the United States of America:

"In Egypt our people were slaves, deprived of their freedom, their dignity and their future. In Germany our freedom diminished with each passing day, many of our people were incarcerated in concentration camps and special laws and statutes deprived us of basic rights and invited discrimination and violence. Our people crossed the Sea of Reeds and the dangers of the desert to be inspired at Sinai and reach the Promised Land. My family and other fortunate remnants of the Holocaust crossed the rivers and mountains and borders of Europe, the mined waters of the English Channel and the storm-tossed Atlantic Ocean to be inspired by the Statue of Liberty and the freedom of the American shore.

We read in Exodus that God delivered Israel from the Egyptians. *All* the children of Israel left Egypt, *all* crossed the Sea of Reeds. . . . It was a people of escaping slaves who had not yet experienced their spiritual birth.

When we left Germany, we were part of the People of the Book. Sinai, ancient Israel with its Kings, Judges, and Prophets were part of our history. And although we Jews represented only a fraction of a percent of the world population, our contributions not just to religion but also to literature, science, medicine, music, and philosophy were in staggering disproportion to our numbers. We did not have to stop at Sinai, for we had been there thousands of years ago. . . . We knew the way. But contrary to an entire people crossing the Sea of Reeds, we were a small part of European Jewry crossing the Atlantic Ocean. Although we did not know it at that euphoric moment in our lives, most of Central European Jewry was destined for the Teutonic ovens. It was a far cry from the delivery of an entire people singing in gratitude the Shirat Hayam, the Song of the Sea."

When our rabbi first took charge of our temple's pulpit, he had relatively limited prior opportunity to meet Holocaust survivors. His contacts with people like us and the increased interest in this tragic period generated by an ever mushrooming literature coverage had a most stimulating effect on our spiritual leader. Besides our participation in the annual Yom Hashoah (Holocaust Memorial Day), Rabbi Kasdan initiated the observance of the Kristallnacht anniversary as part of the appropriate Sabbath service and also made certain that the annual confirmation class would receive first-hand reports from Holocaust survivors. In 1989, he originated the idea and located a sponsor for installing a small Holocaust Museum in our temple's lobby. Bea and I agreed to co-chair the museum committee, although it was Bea who really provided the leadership of this activity since its inception. Twice per year we display a new exhibit pertaining to this terrible period of our people's history. Our theme, inscribed artistically above the museum case, is "Zachor, Remember." Not only do we thus honor and preserve the memory of the six million men, women, and children who were slaughtered by the Nazis and their henchmen; we also educate all those who view these exhibits to be ever alert to preserve liberty, further justice, and fight prejudice. We need to trouble the world, a world that often is reluctant to hear and see, to look upon the face of evil and not deny it or relegate it to the amnesia of ancient history. It is certainly true that we cannot exclusively live in the past, but as George Santayana, the American philosopher, poet, and essayist, so succinctly stated: "Those who cannot remember the past are condemned to repeat it."

In 1984, I was invited to join the newly formed Catholic-Jewish Dialogue of Essex County. This group, meeting a few times annually, was about to embark on another attempt to enhance the relationships across religious lines in light of the opportunity provided by the Second Vatican Council in 1965. There and then, in the unprecedented document "Nostra Aetate," "In Our Time," the assembled bishops under the inspiring leadership of the renowned Pope John XXIII had unequivocally rejected the nearly 2,000-year-old accusation of deicide against the Jewish people and forcefully condemned anti-Semitism. More than likely, some of the impetus for this action stems from the Holocaust itself. This systematic murder of millions of Jews in the heart of Christian Europe raised moral questions that are beyond human understanding. The dialogue in which I, together with my respected friend and fellow congregant Gadiel Smith, participated was more at the grass-root level and not unique in itself. However, it appeared to me an opportunity to contribute to better understanding between the two religious groups. The activity was sponsored by the Catholic Archdiocese of Newark and the American Jewish Committee. Over the years since its beginning, we have established a worthwhile relationship between the core participants and, I hope, also had a beneficial effect on the occasional visitors to these interchanges. One has to remember, however, that those Jews and Catholics who show an active interest in such an activity are most likely of a liberal persuasion in the first place and that the jury is still out with respect to the extreme conservative, i.e., orthodox, wings of these religious movements.

In a chapter devoted to my involvement with our liberal religious movement, it might appear somewhat unusual to devote some thoughts to our good and respected friends Gadiel and Anita Smith. But if there is anyone in our acquaintanceship who belongs into this section of the spiritual, then this unusual couple would be my obvious choice. We met Gadiel and Anita during the early years of our temple membership, when Gadiel was vice-president and almost perennial chair of the program committee. But meeting is not knowing; that had to wait until the early seventies when Bea and Anita worked side by side as part of a small group on social action programs such as drug rehabilitation, Vietnam refugees, and rescue of Soviet Jewry. The Smiths, well grounded in Jewish knowledge and intellect, always lived to turn their words of prayer into deeds of kindness. Although family circumstances placed a heavy burden on them, they were never deterred to reach out to those in need. They were the founders of our Bible study program, and Gadiel is most deservedly its resident expert. For years, I have been honored to serve with Gadiel on the Catholic-Jewish dialogue; he represents a most valuable resource to this organization. Both are in their ninth decade now, but their spirits are young and their determination to stay involved with our world is absolutely amazing. Gadiel, though retired as physician from the VA hospital, still tends to the sick and still teaches the interns, while Anita practices Tikkun Olam, the repair and healing of the world, wherever she can. To know and walk alongside such human beings is indeed a spiritual experience.

Most of my congregational life, i.e., ever since 1971, took place within a temple that was under the spiritual leadership of Rabbi Peter E. Kasdan. I still served as president of the congregation during this rabbi's first year at Emanu-El. This man has guided "his flock" with dedication and integrity. He always emphasized transforming our words and prayers into good deeds, to look beyond the temple walls to be a light to the nations and to repair our world. He taught and motivated us not merely by his messages but also by his personal commitment. He is older now and the labor of the years have taken their toll; the peaks and valleys identified with the service of a congregational rabbi and in fact for any spiritual leader leave their marks of joy, sadness, and fatigue. But it must be a great satisfaction for him to look back on more than a quarter century of service with one synagogue, to have shared the smiles and to have shared the tears, to have walked side by side with hundreds of people and touched them with heart and with hand. As our rabbi and our friend, he has enhanced our family's Simchas (joyous occasions) and given support and solace in times of bereavement. We are grateful for both.

In May of 1990, our congregation honored Bea and me for the many years of service during a memorable weekend. Rabbi Kasdan, together with Cantor Hickman, had prepared a most moving Friday evening service for this occasion. We were presented with a Tzedakah (alms) box, a precious work of art, a larger replica of which resides within the sanctuary of our temple. Leslie, as family representative, spoke words of gratitude and praise, and I had a chance to thank the entire congregation. For Bea and for me, it had been and will always be a duty to serve our Jewish people, a people that has suffered so much throughout the ages and particularly in our own time. On the following evening, we were feasted and entertained at a fantastic dinner dance at the nearby Eaglerock Club. All this, including an elaborate journal containing a multitude of well-wishes and praises, was most gracious and generous. A large committee, under the leadership of temple member Janet Wolff, had no doubt labored long and hard to bring forth such a wonderful and warmhearted message of gratitude.

THE EMPTY NEST (1978–1984)

In 1978, Danny, who had lived with us for a year following his graduation from Rutgers when he was settling into his job at L. J. Gonzer in Newark, moved into his own apartment. Barry, who had maintained an excellent academic record and had developed the appearance of a scientist, with long beard and long hair, graduated from RPI and enrolled in a graduate physics program at the University of Rochester. Leslie was in residence at Lafayette College, enjoying her freshman year. And our beagle Mickey, which Danny had picked out of a litter next to a cow-stable and named after his New York Yankee hero Mickey Mantle in 1963, died at the old canine age of 15. Our home at 15 Orchard Lane, which had been filled with the lives of children for so many years, now legitimately qualified as an "empty nest." Unlike those of our feathered friends, however, our empty nest was never lacking in activities. For holidays, particularly the religious ones, and for special celebrations, our children nearly always returned. Besides that, Bea and I maintained an active social life, and we took advantage of our independence to travel.

In the summer of 1978, we revisited the Skyline Drive and the Blue Ridge Parkway. Bea and I had been there before, in 1974, when we traveled through this Allegheny region and marveled at the wonderful forests, the profusion of rhododendrons, the multitude of wild life, and the picturesque views from ragged ridges. I recall that on both visits I saw this uplifting spectacle of nature as a manifestation of God's creative genius and felt that through the beauty of nature I was touched with a supreme invisible and indivisible being that we Jews know as Adonai. In 1975, we traveled on to Nashville to visit with our friends Peter and Marion Katz, who took us to the Grand Old Opry. In 1978, we stopped off in Charlotte to see our friends Betty and Heinz Jaffe, then headed north to visit historic Williamsburg, where we had candlelight dinners in two of its historic restaurants and were transported back to the pre-Civil War period, decor, menu, and all.

Later that year, we returned after a prolonged absence to Cape Cod, where we enjoyed a few pleasant days as guests of Betty and Sam Rosenberg, the family of Bea's sister-in-law Eunice. The Cape had undergone tremendous changes since our last stay, with the addition of a multitude of vacation homes and a proliferation of commercial establishments to service the burgeoning tourist industry. Naturally, the roads were wider and the traffic had increased immeasurably. All these changes are generally viewed as progress but detract from the quality of one's vacation stay. I guess it is an inherent by-product of the 20th century population explosion, coupled with the improved living standard of the average American family. The Rosenbergs' home was fortunately still located in a tranquil and picturesque cove, where one could hibernate for a few days, out of the way of the busy tourist tumult.

As part of my AIAA involvement, we spent 10 days during the summer of 1979 together with our friends Jack and Irene Keigler in the beautiful Colorado Rockies. Prior to the annual AIAA G&C meeting, which took place in Boulder that particular year, we traveled together through this most picturesque region. After the high altitude of Pike's Peak induced dizzy heads and spectacular views, we visited several old and charming mining towns and the Royal Gorge Bridge, which sways in suspension about 1,000 feet above the Arkansas River. These were beautiful and memorable times that we spent with our good friends in one of the most picturesque areas of our great country.

In 1980, we returned to Israel for our third visit to help uncle Lothar celebrate his 80th birthday. He was most appreciative of our presence, and I surprised him with a congratulatory poem written in German. Lothar and Hannah's world was primarily centered in the German Jewish community of the Haifa region, so their command of both English and Hebrew was limited. We had a good opportunity to explore Haifa, its University on the Carmel, and the ancient catacombs and synagogue at Beth Shearim.

Once again, but never enough, we spent precious days with the Rivkins in Jerusalem, admiring the beautification that had taken place under Mayor Kollek's leadership. Aunt Anny had moved to the Wolfson towers overlooking the Valley of the Cross. She relocated there after Heinz had suddenly died at the conclusion of a Shabbat morning service, just as he was folding his Tallit (prayer shawl). Heinz had been a cheerful person, and he concluded his life in the city of his dreams, the city he loved, Yerushalayim. In the old city, we were very impressed with the progress that had been made with the rebuilding of the Jewish quarter, which had been destroyed by the Jordanians during the 1948–67 occupation. We could not resist stopping by the studio of Lea Majaro-Mintz, a seventh generation Israeli sculptress whose work we had grown to admire. She lived and worked in her crowded house that was connected to ancient reclaimed caves that she had discovered in the Jewish quarter of the old city. Her art focused exclusively on the creation of the female form and her garments. During each of our visits (the first in 1976), we purchased one or more unique renditions of the female figure.

From Jerusalem, we made a short trip to view Nathan Rappaport's impressive monument, "The Scrolls of Fire," in the martyrs' forest. These depict the story of the Jewish people in lifelike relief, from Moses smashing the first tablets to the days of modern Israel. Rappaport is the artist who was commissioned years later to create for New York's Liberty Island the moving monument of an American soldier carrying a victim of the Holocaust in his arms. During a brief trip to the Arava, the area between the Negev and the Dead Sea, we returned to Kibbutz Yahel. The young pioneers had made visible progress since the 1976 founding. The little saplings we had planted were now about three feet high. Flower beds cheered up the otherwise desolate landscape. Between the kibbutz and the nearby Jordanian hills, one could see a green oasis, Yahel's fields of fruit and vegetables. Even in these surroundings, we are the People of the Book; the National Federation of Temple Sisterhoods, now known as the Women of Reform Judaism, had donated a spacious study center for the continuing education of both residents and guests.

From there, we joined the Rivkins in an excursion towards the north. After passing through historic Jericho, an ancient spot obviously blessed with water and thus intertwined with greens and blossoms, we inspected Hisham's Palace dating back to the eighth century CE just north of the town. The well-preserved ceramic floor of the bathhouse made the visit especially worthwhile. Subsequently, we passed through the most eastern part of the Jordan valley, which is sparsely populated. From the heights of Fort Belvoir, we had a spectacular view of the valley at our feet and the hills of the Kingdom of Jordan beyond. This is the so-called West Bank area, captured by Israel during the 1967 Six Day war and thus not an integral part of the state. Prior to 1967, it had been occupied by Jordan since the 1948 war of Israel's independence. Continuing towards the northern Israeli border, the four of us stopped for an old-fashioned picnic in a Keren Kayemeth forest. Over the decades since the early part of this century, land developments such as this have been sponsored by the Jewish National Fund, which has reclaimed a few hundred thousand acres of Israeli land, half by drainage, planted well over one hundred million trees, and built many roads in the frontier regions and more sparsely populated areas. This endeavor has been sponsored by all the Jews of the world. Many homes, including Bea's and mine, while still in Germany, contained the traditional Blue Box of the JNF (Jewish National Fund) for collecting the coins required for reclaiming the land, Erez Israel. Over the centuries, this land had reverted to desert like conditions due to the neglect, ignorance, and abuse of those who lived and governed there. With the return and reestablishment of the Jewish state, forests have once again taken the place of desolation, fields of produce flourish in previously swampy areas, colorful flowers and fragrant vines grow where weeds and scrubs used to be the norm. God created the world in six days, and we, as stewards, have to take care of that creation all the days of our lives.

We continued our journey to the Lebanese border and Kibbutz Yiftach, the home of the Rivkins' second daughter Judy and her husband. From there, we could see Mt. Hermon to the east and barbed wire with watchdogs immediately to the west. The kibbutz was only a few yards from the Lebanese border, an area frequented by Palestinian guerrillas. In spite of all possible precautions made by the Israeli army, infiltration by these well-armed and dangerous gangs was still possible. Thus, the kibbutz had to create its own security measures in order to safeguard the lives of its citizens. Bea was quite nervous when she heard the barking watchdogs at night, and she was fully justified with her concerns. Shortly after we departed from Yiftach, we received the news that during the time of our stay there, Arab intruders from Lebanon had invaded a kibbutz a few miles to the north and killed a few small children in a nursery. On our way south, we looked at the ancient ruins of Hazor, the capital of Israel in the 13th century BCE. The contrasts available in Israel could not have been demonstrated with greater clarity, since we had just left a kibbutz that was only a few years old. After a two-day stay at the Plaza Hotel on the shores of Lake Kinneret and a brief tour of the Golan, it was time to bid farewell to our friends and relatives and to say: "L'Hitra'ot, Israel."

From Ben Gurion Airport, we flew to London, for Leslie was spending the spring semester of her junior year studying in England. This was a wonderful opportunity to be reunited briefly with our daughter and see a bit of England for the first time. We were kept busy visiting famous sights in London, including Hyde Park, the Royal Academy of Art, the Tate Museum, the Tower, London Bridge, Buckingham Palace with its changing of the guard, Parliament, Harrod's and high tea, Covent Garden, and so much more. Leslie was a superb guide and host; we stayed near her apartment in a fourth floor flat. The city was overrun with oil-rich Arabs, who had purchased much of the prime real estate and cruised the streets in their extravagant automobiles. Quite a change in so many respects from the Israel we had just left. We took a one day bus tour to Shakespeare country, Stratford-upon-Avon, Anne Hathaway's cottage, Mary Arden's (Shakespeare's mother's) house, and Shakespeare's New Place, with its fabulous vintage garden. It was all very interesting, especially because many of the sights we visited in that short time had in prior decades been in our mind for their historical or artistic significance. This was the last chapter of a great trip.

During Leslie's spring recess, she toured France, Switzerland, and Italy; travel is also a part of a person's education. At the conclusion of her studies in London, she visited Israel for the first time. Aunt Selma was generous to make this possible, and Leslie's stop at Hannah and Lothar's home in Kiryat Bialik is now a precious memory. When she returned to the States, I inquired what she considered the most significant item she had learned on the other side of the Atlantic. "To appreciate what we have in our country" was her insightful answer, which illustrates once again that it is difficult to judge the quality of our lives without having a comparative opportunity.

In the 1979–80 period, we had to bid farewell to two of our loved ones, my mother's sister Paula and my father's youngest brother, Max. Max died of leukemia within about six months after the illness was first diagnosed. He was a good friend, not only an admired uncle. We shared difficult times in Germany during the late 1930s, and we shared much happiness with him and Claire during their frequent visits to Livingston. After his death, Bea and I assisted Claire in being admitted to a senior citizens complex in our vicinity. Thus, I could see her weekly and we were close enough geographically to assist her promptly if and when she required. She was not alone.

Paula lived alone in Miami Beach and had done so for many years. During her final illness, I visited her once for a few days. As I was leaving her hospital room, when both of us knew it was likely to be a final parting, she said: "My special love to Bea for having sent you. Good night, good night darling, have a good trip." After I came to the U.S.A. in 1939, some of the members of my mother's family ominously predicted that we would eventually have to provide for Paula's upkeep during her later years. The implication was clear: Paula could not plan and manage her life to provide a measure of independence and security for her retirement years. Both she and her husband Lew had ridden a roller coaster of success and failure during their productive times, and it appeared to these relatives that the burden of support would sooner or later fall on the rest of the family. I was troubled by these predictions, but subsequent years did not bear out this pessimism. True enough, during Paula's last few years, from age 88 to 92, I organized the family to generate a small monthly stipend for the old lady. But this old lady had worked until she was 88 years old, running a knitting store and living in utter simplicity in a dark backroom of her rented establishment. She never complained, and she cherished the time of the High Holidays, which she annually spent with us in Livingston. We, including each of our children, loved her, respected her, and mourned her. To this day, when we think of aunt Paula and recall her days, her peculiarities, her hospitality, her generosity, her personality traits, and her love, we smile in grateful remembrance.

Starting during this period and extending over a number of years, our friends Phil and Phyllis Lieberman invited us annually to spend a weekend with them at their lovely summer house on Fire Island off the coast of Long Island. In addition to the pleasure of their stimulating company and their gracious hosting, our stay at their place was most appreciated because of the uniqueness of this beautiful spot. Cars, except municipal service vehicles, were not permitted there. That provision immediately and drastically changed the environment into a delightfully relaxing atmosphere. Everyone either walked or used a bicycle. The disappearance of traffic was like a gift from heaven. Furthermore, the resulting tranquility converted most of the summer residents and visitors into

Richard Katz received his doctorate in medicine from the University of Rochester, 1982.

much more amicable human beings. I have always maintained that the pressure of large cities, exacerbated by their inherent congestion, pollution, and lack of elbow room, leads to a dehumanization of those who live and work there. Maybe in terms of economics there is no solution to this problem, which seems endemic to a world of geometrical population growth. But wouldn't it be wonderful if we could all live in a summer house atmosphere?

In 1980, our temple celebrated the 25th anniversary of its founding. To mark this auspicious occasion, Richard Katz was commissioned to compose a special service. That was a great opportunity and honor for our young friend, and we were proud of the fine result. For us, it was especially gratifying to witness how one of our children's generation contributed creatively to the chain of Jewish continuity. In the following year, Richard completed his medical studies at Cleveland's Case Western, and together with his parents we participated in celebrating this milestone. The next phase of Richard's career was to be his internship in Chicago. From Cleveland, Bea and I continued on to Niagara Falls, the justifiably famous natural wonder, which is also a traditional honeymoon spot. Well, for that we were just a little late, but we enjoyed our brief stopover anyhow.

The 1981 year was also graduation time for Leslie. She had opted to pursue a legal career, and there were a number of law schools interested in her. Finally, she chose Georgetown in Washington, D.C., where she found her studies both stimulating and challenging. But to our surprise, she was not particularly fond of living in our nation's capitol. There were no ties that residents had developed with this area; most people were from "some other place." Once, when she was sitting between classes in a poorly lit corner of a hallway, a favorite teacher of hers, Professor Greenhall, passed and inquired: "What are you doing in the dark, Miss Muhlfelder?", whereupon Leslie exclaimed: "That's where I have been the entire semester!" Her subsequent professional career, however, did not reflect her humorous claim of intellectual darkness.

During the summer of 1981, the annual AIAA G&C meeting, which I usually attended, took place in Albuquerque, New Mexico. Bea and I took advantage of this opportunity and combined this trip with a visit to Phoenix, Arizona, an area of the country that was virgin territory to us. The Channins, friends from Livingston, had relocated there, i.e., to the suburban retirement community of Sun City. They were most cordial hosts and appeared pleased with their new and sunny surroundings. From there, we drove north past Sedona with its unusual reddish sandstone to the northern rim of the Grand Canyon. One look from that precipice convinced me that this fantastically beautiful canyon fully deserved its name and its fame. We did not descend to the Colorado River because the return trip was not too inviting: no, thanks, not even via a donkey ride.

In November of 1981, we witnessed our only launch of a spacecraft. This might sound unbelievable because of my profession, but one has to remember that my RCA group's flight support function began only after the spacecraft had been sent at least into its initial orbit. The rocket stages were someone else's business, for example that of McDonnell-Douglas or Ariane Space. Some of our technicians, however, had to be present at the launch site such as Kennedy Space Center in Florida, the AF Western Test Range in California, and the Kourou site in French Guiana in order to assist with final spacecraft preparations and checkouts. After the launch, the work of my people just began, and that was carried out from various ground control stations, with the location dependent on the particular mission and customer.

Thus, Bea and I were invited to be present for the Florida launch of Satcom IIIR, our fourth geosynchronous communication satellite. Prior to that event, we visited the Disney World amusement park near Orlando. We were reminded of 1966, when we took the children to California's Disney Land. The launch itself was tense and awesome; we viewed it from a stand about a mile from the pad. To be present there, rather than watching the event on television, is a whole other thing. The air vibrated, the ground shook, and the Delta rocket with our satellite perched on top took off majestically into the blue sky. Someone took a candid picture of us during those few emotional seconds: Bea appeared to have tears in her eyes, and I, the experienced space engineer, stood there with my mouth wide open. Immediately thereafter, we flew back to New Jersey so that I could participate in the scheduled orbit achievement and station acquisition maneuvers, which were directed from the Vernon Valley RCA Americom ground station. During the typically one-week effort for this type of mission, we were housed in the nearby Americana hotel, which served as local ski resort and potentially but never realized gambling casino. Aside from its modern decor and comfort, it also featured a "Bunny" club, with well-endowed and scantily-dressed young women. I still have a group picture of the unique combination of some of these attractions and us space scientists.

It was around this time that our family began a new tradition. We had, of course, always celebrated all the Jewish holidays, including the children's favorite, Hanukkah. But with our offspring and Richard Katz being dispersed to various locations, it was difficult to gather all for song, candle lighting, and gift exchange in our home on the calendar date of Hanukkah. Yes, although we had eight nights available, we found it necessary to add a ninth, which took place whenever the entire gang could show up at 15 Orchard Lane. This joyful tradition exists to this day. Orthodox Jews most likely would not approve, but that is why we are Reform and try to adapt ourselves to the modern world while continuing the joy of our Jewish heritage.

I might have been short of time with the multitude of activities that I was engaged in, but I always found time for gardening. Bea labeled me as a "gardenoholic" for good reason. Besides all the produce and flowers that grew in our garden, I also engaged in lunch time agriculture on a small plot made available by RCA starting around 1970. The company plowed the soil in the spring and provid-

ed the essential water. During the midday break, the garden fanat-
ics, including me, quickly gulped down a sandwich and ran outside
into the heat to tend to our vegetables. We must have been a peculiar sight gardening in business attire. The produce was plentiful
because our area had consisted of farmland and contained no trees
to interrupt the sun's rays. Once, when my harvest was particularly
plentiful, I loaded it into a wheelbarrow upon returning home and
pushed the whole load into our living room without comment, to the
amazement of our family. Eventually, I abandoned this extracurricular RCA activity because Bea was overloaded with my goodies from
the soil. Aside from that, my colleagues were not eager to enter my
office after I had returned from the field, drenched in perspiration
on the hotter days of the summer.

Returning to Israel in the summer of 1983 gave us another
chance to see the Rivkins and explore Jerusalem, a place worthy of
many visits. We also spent time with Lothar and Hannah, who in
the meantime had moved into a senior citizens residence on Haifa's
Carmel. They had noticeably aged and were comfortable in their
new surroundings. Also on our itinerary was a New Jersey acquaintance, Lance Colie, who was working at Kibbutz Magal, located
near the Green line that marks the border between the 1948–67 Israel and the West Bank. From there, at the narrowest point of the
original Israel, we could see the Mediterranean coast and, in the opposite direction, the hills of the West Bank.

During this visit, we had the unique and joyous opportunity to
participate in the dedication ceremonies of Lotan, another Reform
kibbutz located in the Arava just south of Yahel, which we helped
dedicate in 1976. Together with the Rivkins and their friends Am-
non and Rivka, whose son was one of the kibbutz pioneers, we were
privileged to be present as young and dedicated people were making
history. But one day does not make a kibbutznik. After the festivities, speeches, affixing the Mezuzah, partaking in food and drink,
and joining in song, we left to return to Jerusalem while the hard
task for the young people had just begun. Today, more than two decades later, many of the founders, including Rivka's son, are still
there to build their lives and make the desert bloom. I have always
admired the idealism and dedication of the kibbutz movement. The
capitalistic transformation of much of Israeli society during the last
decade or two has detrimentally affected this type of development
and the kibbutzim network. With the influx of large numbers of im-

migrants, particularly during subsequent years from the former Soviet Union, into a country of limited "Lebensraum" (living space), the idealism and socialism of the kibbutz pioneers is under heavy pressure and might not survive. This would be unfortunate because such pioneering activity is beneficial to the maintenance and enhancement of the human spirit.

In the spring of 1984, we sent out a poetic invitation entitled "It's Party Time," with the following first and last stanzas:

> The Muhlfelders plan a celebration
> To mark three very joyous occasions
> Two of us are attaining advanced degrees,
> While one completes a decade of rings on trees.

> So come and join us on the 16th of June,
> Some flowers will bloom in the afternoon.
> A celebration of love, of labor, of life,
> Please celebrate with us – the Orchard Lane Five.

After nearly six years of graduate work, Barry had attained his Ph.D. in physics, while Leslie had been certified as a full-fledged attorney following her three year stint at Georgetown Law. My accomplishment was simply an aging process, having reached the 60-year plateau. It was a great party, and the weatherman delivered a perfect day. Bea outdid herself with decor, food, and drink, and several of our friends graciously pitched in to help. We were in a most thankful mood, not only because of the various milestones but because Barry had just escaped from great danger. Bicycling near Boulder, where he had begun his post-graduate work at the National Bureau of Standards, he collided with a truck and sustained some painful injuries. Fortunately, he wore a helmet and was thrown some distance off the bike instead of being run over. A little worse for wear, he was with us on our special day and I thanked God with a prayer in the evening preceding the party. Leslie moved to Philadelphia's Rittenhouse Square to start as an associate for Ballard Spahr, a sizable law firm. The youngest guest at this party was Carl Bravmann, who was born just a few months prior and thus became the first representative of our family's next generation. Time marches on! Just shortly after our celebration, Danny was promoted by his firm to a vice-president position, with primary responsibility for temporary placement of technical personnel. There is a German proverb, "Aus Kinder werden Leute" ("children evolve into people"); Bea and I were gratified to experience our children's progress and development.

Shortly after the milestone party, my uncle Lothar and aunt Hannah died in Israel within a two-week span. Being aware of Lothar's terminal illness, I had flown there early in June 1984 to be with him for a few days. I preferred to give him some pleasure while he was still among the living instead of attending the preordained funeral. He recognized that and thanked me profusely. My uncle was brave and shed no tears when I departed. Without him, life had lost its meaning for Hannah. She observed the traditional week of mourning, after which she refused all nourishment. Once again, I thought of the Nazi period; once again, I was thankful that those I loved had lived a generous lifespan and were not exterminated in the Holocaust.

The Orchard Lane Five with Orchard Lane flowers, 1982

WEDDINGS, GRANDCHILDREN, AND TRAVEL (1984–1991)

The years between 1984 and 1991 were full ones for our family. During the summer of that first year, we focused our sightseeing in the northern regions of the North American continent while in the company of our good friends Al and Evi Meinhardt. Following an AIAA meeting in Seattle, we did some touring of that picturesque corner of our country. In 1966, I had been disappointed that an airplane strike prevented Bea from joining me in a visit to that region. So now, we were making up for that delayed opportunity. Bea loved the harbor and the dockside crabs, and all of us admired the formidable Mount Rainier. A side trip by boat took us to Victoria, British Columbia, and the famous Butchart Gardens, a spectacular and opulent display of natural and cultivated beauty.

The four of us then flew to Calgary for the start of a guided tour of the Canadian Rockies. Traveling by bus with a superb Tauck Tour guide, we were relieved of all planning and hustle that are normally a part of a sightseeing vacation. Nature puts on a spectacular show for those fortunate enough to make such a trip. Montana's Glacier National Park, the Rockies' fairytale-like Lake Louise, Jasper, and Banff, are all embedded in my mind as jewels of God's creation; lakes, mountains, waterfalls, glaciers, and wild life all displayed in their pure and unspoiled state. On our return trip, Al arranged for the two of us to visit briefly the cockpit of the Boeing 757 plane while it was cruising along on automatic pilot.

For Thanksgiving, we were all invited to Peter's and Penfield's "Wilder Hill" farm in Shelbourne Falls, Massachusetts, the first of many yearly get-togethers there on this holiday. Bea's nephew had married Penfield Chester in 1979, the bride and groom arriving in the back of a brand new garbage truck, a product of Penfield's father's manufacturing business. On that August day, we had had a grand and unforgettable time, despite the fact that the skies had opened up and rained relentlessly on the ceremony. Together, we remembered the occasion: the tent leaked, the ground was muddy, the barn became the dance floor, and some changed into dungarees. Now, joined by baby Carl and Barry's new love, Debbie Yager, we once again had a grand and gastronomic time. Buggy rides through the charming New England landscape, walks with those we love on winding country lanes, shopping for local goods at outdoor markets, cheering for Peter at horse pulls and equestrian events, and even assisting in cleaning out the stalls; these were the traditional activities that we all cherished and that added a temporary and much appreciated charm. Penfield and Peter were always excellent hosts, and I remember these annual "Wilder Hill" visits fondly.

After such a lovely summer and fall, the winter of 1984–85 had also something special in store for us. Prompted by Barry, our children had presented us, as my 60th birthday gift, a vacation in the Caribbean. We opted for four days in Antigua and found that an escape from the harshness of winter was especially delightful. We have returned to the Caribbean a number of times, although such luxury is not an annual occurrence.

Encouraged by the prior summer's guided tour experience, Bea and I decided on a similar arrangement for a long-yearned-for Italian exposure, as choreographed by the Petrillo organization. For 10 days, we immersed ourselves in the culture, the art, the structures, and the atmosphere of Rome, Venice, and Florence. It was a humbling and inspiring experience to view, particularly within such a concentrated time, the products of so much human talent. Just as Rome was not built in a day, so we found it difficult to do justice to the wealth of art and creativity that met our eyes. Thankful for the opportunity, we hoped to return some day, especially for a more extended stay in Florence to see with greater care that city's cultural and artistic wealth.

From Rome, we flew to Nice to spend a week in nearby Vence with our Swiss friends, Margot and Herbert Dreyfus. We stayed in a lovely villa that relatives of theirs had made available for a limited time. This was the famous Riviera region, the home of huge hotels, lush casinos, and topless beaches. It was also the area of unique light and brilliant color, which had been an attraction for artists like Matisse, Chagall, and Miro. Gallery Maeght, with its Miro garden, was a gem. Marc Chagall's grave, marked by his wife's

1982 Thanksgiving on nephew Peter's and wife Penfield's Wilder Hill farm, Shelburn Falls, Mass. L. ro R.: Leslie with friend, Penfield, Peter, brother-in-law Bert, his wife Eunice, and Danny.

family with a large cross, was disconcerting. Although this artist had treated Christian as well as Jewish subject matter with great skill and imagination, we found the supposed posthumous transformation from his Jewish roots most surprising, to say the least. A more neutral resting place might have been in better taste.

Within this year, Bert and Eunice moved from Livingston to a house in Whateley, Massachusetts, located about 20 minutes from their children. With the arrival of grandson Carl, this was both a logical and beneficial relocation. With advancing age, it seems desirable to live near one's children. The ranch home they selected was situated on a lovely rural lot with an overview of a reservoir in the back and of farmers' fields with Amherst on the horizon from their front windows. We visited there at regular intervals during the following seven years, and it was always a special and relaxing time to be with them, our close relatives and good friends.

In the fall, the family gathered for Richard Katz's wedding. In 1979, Richard had graduated from the University of Rochester, where he had pursued a pre-med curriculum while simultaneously pursuing his musical interests at the Eastman School of Music. His next step was medical school at Cleveland's Case Western University. There, he not only received his medical degree a few years later but also met Stacey, a beautiful and charming young woman who had twice been U.S. ice dancing champion. Now, we were in an art gallery in Chicago to celebrate their marriage. Our family had followed Richard's career with interest and pride; we shared his happiness as he and Stacey set out on life's journey together. As time has passed, Richard and Stacey have become ever more precious to our lives; although they are not our children, they could not be dearer. I will always be grateful that our paths crossed and became intertwined, and I hope and pray that we will be able to share life's ups and downs with them for years to come.

We opted for a Swiss vacation during the summer of 1986, in part because our friends, the Merzbachers, who live near Zurich, made their Davos condo, which they use primarily during the skiing season, available to us. Their generosity permitted us to spend wonderful days in the midst of a most beautiful area. All we needed was a small rental car and some local maps. After feasting on delicious Swiss rolls, we would set out each morning on a different excursion. Since Davos is at an elevation of 5,000 feet, it is from there a simple matter to ascend to one of the nearby mountains by means of cable car or cog railway. From the heights, we could admire the profusion of Alpine plants and flowers as well as the array of snow-capped mountains and the green valleys below. There are numerous and well marked paths, some alongside steep cliffs, which provided excellent hiking opportunities. During our stay, we received the happy news of the arrival of Rachel Katz, who bestowed parenthood on Richard and Stacey and whom we learned to love in succeeding years.

The Davos area had been the studio and the refuge of the German post-impressionist painter Ernst Ludwig Kirchner. This artist, in search of peace of mind and health of body, had moved in 1918 from Berlin to Frauenkirch near Davos. Within the surroundings of his beloved subject matter, he created great art that reflects the tensions of joy and despair within this conflicted man. Apparently unable to reconcile his own fate and the ominous world events of his time, Kirchner ended his life in 1938; he is buried in a nearby cemetery. On the floor above the local post office, quite a few of his creations had been assembled in a small museum. Eventually, the local foundation was able to erect a spacious and attractive building to house this wonderful art, a testimony to a talented and sensitive human being.

A short ride from our temporary mountain home is the most picturesque Engadine region with the world-famous St. Moritz. When we entered this narrow valley for the first time, it was a revelation of fairy-like character. But it was not St. Moritz, located in the Upper Engadine, that impressed us; in fact, this spot was disappointing in spite of its attraction to the world elite. What we fell in love with was the unspoiled beauty of the Swiss National Park and, even more so, the quaint Lower Engadine region. There we "discovered" Guarda, a little village clinging to the steep slope above the valley floor and the river Inn. Its streets are narrow and wind their way between closely-spaced and well-maintained houses. Many of the local residents speak Romansh in addition to other languages. They are proud of their heritage and artistically decorate the outside of their homes with intricate designs and lettering known as scraffity. We have stopped there during all of our subsequent Swiss visits; you have to see it to believe it. The food being served there is, of course, outstanding as it is almost everywhere in Switzerland. Aside from that, the place is a photographer's paradise. God created the heavens and the earth, and in the Lower Engadine humankind did a particularly fine job of complementing the work of the Creator.

From Davos, our journey took us southwest to Ascona on Lago Maggiore, where we briefly visited Gaby Merzbacher's parents in their charming abode above the lake. This is the Italian part of Switzerland and reflects this not only in language but also in appearance and culinary offerings. In fact, from there we briefly traveled through Italy as the shortest route to Zermatt and the Matterhorn. It takes a certain amount of optimism to schedule a one-night stay in nearby Taesch and expect to see this spectacular mountain, which bashfully hides in fog during many days of the year. We were blessed with a fantastically clear day and received adequate confirmation that the Matterhorn is truly deserving of its fame.

After two memorable days in the Grindelwald region, we returned to Zurich to attend the wedding of Phillipe to Claudia, the daughter of our friends from Kreuzlingen, the Dreyfus family. The ceremony took place in a synagogue that was guarded by well-armed police in view of potential Palestinian terrorist threats. The Bima represented an interesting combination of the traditional and the modern, with the rabbi, cantor, and bridal couple invoking the ancient Hebrew blessings while photographers, a video crew and an artist were competing in the crowded space to record the important event. The subsequent celebration in the prestigious Hotel Zurich was quite elaborate and highly entertaining. In accordance with the strictly Orthodox practice of the young couple, dancing with the opposite sex was not part of the program. Throughout the evening, both friends and family presented charming skits and humorous poetic renditions, a practice that is European in nature and in this case served as a superb alternative to the normal dancing interludes.

Shortly after the conclusion of this vacation, Bea departed once more for Europe to participate in the homecoming of surviving Jews of Konstanz, her place of birth. I chose not to accompany her during that week because of my still-retained inability to separate the Germany of the postwar period from the Germany of the Holocaust. Instead, Danny and Leslie as well as Bert and Eunice joined Bea. For Bea and Bert, it was a nostalgic experience to be reunited with old friends and familiar surroundings, while Danny, Leslie, and Eunice had a unique opportunity to touch the past of those they love. Organized and hosted by the mayor and local authorities, this homecoming received its primary impetus from Professor Roy Wiehn, a sociologist of Konstanz University. Bea and the children established close contacts during their stay with this unusual and dedicated man and his lovely and hospitable wife Mirjam. This was to be the beginning of a close and significant friendship between our families for years to come.

In the 1986–87 winter, we discovered St. Lucia, one of the island gems of the Caribbean. Accompanied by Bert and Eunice, we stayed at the St. Lucien Hotel on the northwest coast of the island. The place fitted our tastes and needs, friendly and tranquil, not opulent or boisterous. It offered lovely grounds, a magnificent half-mile beach and a variety of sports. Besides swimming, I engaged in another sport that was a first for me. During the initial few days, I watched with fascination and a little envy the parasailing activity in the bay. Participants were ferried to a platform, from which they took off and landed. Towed by a powerful motor boat, which connected to the person's harness by means of a long line, the adventurous floated for five to 10 minutes under a huge and colorful parachute. Bea could read my mind and eventually my lips, but was not thrilled with my intentions. However, I eventually gave it a try, and the ride was thrilling. I floated like a bird, looking down on our idyllic vacation spot and singing "I float through the air with the greatest of ease." This was a vacation to remember, and we vowed to return.

Illness suddenly struck Bert on July 4, 1987. A serious heart attack was followed by open-heart surgery at Boston's Massachusetts General Hospital. Fortunately, medical science was able to restore my brother-in-law to a reasonably functional state. The signs and the threats of advancing years were beginning to manifest themselves in our own generation.

Meanwhile, the younger generation thrived. With the conclusion of Barry's two post-graduate years with NBS in Boulder, he accepted an offer from Stanford University, where he joined a fascinating space project dedicated to the verification of Einstein's theory of relativity. Dubbed Gravity Probe B, the sophisticated instrument package being developed by Stanford was intended eventually to be flown on a satellite flying in a precise circular north-south orbit about our planet. In order to measure the orbital effect of mass drag and curvature of space as predicted by Einstein, instruments of much higher precision than the best currently available would have to be developed. This appeared to be a very fertile territory for our scientific son.

At the same time, Barry had become involved in a romantic relationship, as had his brother Danny. Danny, who had had a romance during the 1970s and early 1980s that eventually dissolved, rediscovered a grownup Abby, whom he had met when she was still a teenager as a member of our temple youth group. Barry, after completing his formal education, met Debbie during a visit with San Diego friends. Their relationship had become stronger in spite of lengthy geographic separations. We could sense at that time the beginnings of new families and continuity of the generations.

At home, Bea and I were busy at 15 Orchard Lane. For many years since first moving to the home that was to surround us for so many years, we had been aware that the house was not built with a garden in mind. In fact, from the living area, the backyard was visible only from the dining room and a small kitchen window that was blocked by the sink. In addition, our small kitchen precluded Bea, as resident chef, from fully participating in the joys of ever-larger fam-

ily gatherings. After considerable thought, we finally decided to en-
large the kitchen area. We met with a recommended architect, Mr.
Heinz, who appeared to be not particularly interested in such a relatively small job, although for us it represented a huge undertaking.
When Bea described to him her concept of openness and angularity
of this addition, she awakened a spark of inspiration in our creative
professional. The rest is history in the Muhlfelder home. The old
kitchen was stripped down, and the new one, triple in floor space,
contains a lovely multiple window/skylight area with an adjoining
deck. The house was extended into the garden, and the garden had
become part of the house. Bea could now cater to the gastronomic desires of her family and friends without being separated from the ban-
ter and joy of the gatherings. In the process of the construction, it
was possible finally, after 30 years, to complete the unfinished bath-
room on the top floor. The project turned out to be a huge success and
provided much comfort and happiness not only for Bea and me but
for all with whom we are able to share our lives and our home.

The changed house served as a welcome impetus for me to re-
landscape a good portion of the backyard. The lily bed, the Glickson
bed (in honor of our long-term next door neighbors), the kitchen garden, and the shady corner were all added in response to the enhanced home. Finally, the house and the garden were able to
embrace each other, and we were happy with this new romance in
our midst.

In the fall of 1987, we celebrated Bea's 60th with family and
friends. My wife was now 60 years young, certainly in my eyes. As
a birthday gift, my good woman did not care for a materialistic luxury such as jewelry but instead suggested that we take our three
children on a trip to Israel. This was a wonderful way to share the
privilege of having attained such an important milestone. It was a
value judgment that symbolizes Bea's life.

So the Orchard Lane Five set off for the land of our ancestors and
the land of Israel's rebirth. We were equipped with plans, cameras,
enthusiasm and five shirts emblazoned with "To Bea 60." For Barry,
this was his first visit; for our other two offspring, this was the second
time. For all of us, it was so special to be together on this once-in-a-
lifetime journey. We covered the land, from the Golan to Eilat, from
Tiberias to the Dead Sea, from the springs of Banyas in the north to
the pillars of Solomon in the south, from Kibbutz Hagoshrim in the
Galilee to Kibbutz Sode Boker, Ben Gurion's home and final resting

place. We said the Kaddish at the graves of Lothar and Hannah and we sang the Kiddush in Jerusalem with the Rivkins. We stood in silence at Yad Vashem in memory of the six million Jews murdered in this century, and we ascended Masada and recalled Jews of ancient times choosing death rather than Roman slavery.

Traveling south past spectacular Mitzpe Ramon in the Negev desert, we stopped in the wilderness to enable Barry to climb a steep and rocky mountain. Danny went along with his brother, and just when the boys had reached the top, two Israeli Air Force jets skimmed the top of the mountain. The suddenness and the thundering noise were a bit frightening for our two young mountaineers. Barry was the latter to descend, and when he approached close enough for us to see, we noticed that he was carrying two large stone tablets. This was only half in jest, for the significance of this historic land and people must have been on his mind. Here we were, in the desert, the five Muhlfelders, celebrating Bea's birthday and remembering the children of Israel with Moses descending with the tablets from Mount Sinai.

On a memorable Friday evening, we welcomed Shabbat in the midst of the Rivkin clan in the Tel Aviv apartment of Judy, Rivkin's second daughter, and her husband Yoram. Space was at a premium, and a large dinner table had to be transported via a precarious outdoor route through adjoining windows. A unique atmosphere of joy and friendship and gratitude enveloped all participants; life seemed to have been temporarily elevated to another level. We valued the opportunity to become better acquainted with Judy's new husband and sensed a resonance between these two which bode well for their future. Little did we know that their happiness would be short-lived, that Yoram would be fatally injured before long in a rear-end collision caused by a large truck that would not stop. This was a double tragedy: a precious and promising human life had been lost and Judy's search for family happiness had come to a cruel end. Many Israeli drivers are particularly impatient, and the casualty rate of traffic mayhem far exceeds that of its wars.

In the late fall of that year, we joined a delegation of our temple to participate in a demonstration on behalf of Soviet Jewry, the march in Washington. Hundreds of buses brought Jews and sympathizers of other religions from all over the country to the nation's capitol, sending a message to the Soviet authorities to let our people go towards the freedom they were seeking in Israel, the U.S.A., and other countries of liberty. Gathering and marching with hundreds of thousands was an uplifting experience. The participation of the Manevitch family, including their very recently arrived parents and siblings, served as an emotional and symbolic focal point for our own delegation. Although the chances for Soviet acquiescence appeared slim at that point in time, subsequent events dramatically demonstrated that hope backed up by determination sometimes turns darkness into light and bondage into freedom. A mere few years later, nearly a million Jews were able to emigrate and regain the privilege, in fact the right, to live their lives as Jews rather than being culturally and religiously forced towards extinction.

Nineteen eighty-eight started with a new beginning for our family: Danny and Abby announced their engagement. Bea and I had been waiting and yearning for such a step from one or more of our children for some time, but we had to be patient for them to make the proper choice in this matching game. The future appeared bright. The two lovers seemed compatible in many important aspects. Later that year, Barry and Debbie took the cue and also formalized their relationship with the traditional ring. In between these two events, Leslie started to date Dick Freemann, an attractive and warm person whom she had met at the Philadelphia law firm that she had joined in 1984. Dick is a person of profound intellect and engaging personality, and the Muhlfelder gang felt an immediate affinity for him. During this period, Leslie also changed positions, finding the demands and the drudgery as an associate of a commercial law firm not compatible with the personal lifestyle she was seeking for herself in the future. Thus, she became a member of Temple University's small legal staff, a position that provided greater diversity of work and more time to pursue personal interests and activities.

During June of 1988, we returned to Switzerland in response to an invitation for our friend Werner Merzbacher's 60th birthday party. The celebration accurately reflected our friends' lifestyle; it took place in a charming Swiss restaurant in a relaxed and friendly environment. The Merzbachers could well have chosen to opt for an elaborate and formal affair in a plush Zurich hotel, but that would have been incongruous with their refined ways. There was a warm and sincere feeling of joy and gratitude interlaced with poetic renditions. We felt honored to be present.

This time, we stayed in Davos in mid-June, i.e., much earlier than previously. As a reward, we were treated to a spectacular display of spring flowers bursting forth in the higher elevations. These delicate and usually tiny plants show their colors only in the early part of the growing season and often bloom close to drifts of snow. Some hiking paths familiar from prior visits were, in fact, still impassable. But we did not mind the inconvenience and reveled in God's beautiful landscapes.

In Kreuzlingen, we stayed as guests of the Dreyfus family. As old friends of Bea's parents, they once again outdid themselves as the perfect and most gracious hosts. Friday evening contained the charms and the memories of old time Shabbats, especially for Bea because Herbert Dreyfus had cultivated, preserved, and practiced the melodies and rituals as taught by his former cantor and mentor, Bea's father Jacob Bravmann.

In the bright sunshine of the Bodensee region, Herbert guided us through the nearby world-renowned Insel Mainau, a vast estate on the south shore of the lake. This prime property is owned by Swedish royalty and accessible to public viewing on a commercial basis. It overflows with the most magnificent formal gardens and topiary, well-cared for woods with specimen trees, picture-postcard views and the appropriate castle for the royal household. Preferably, one should visit this nature treasure in the early part of the day to avoid the mass of humanity that caravans of tour buses disgorge upon its grounds. The most important thing is not to miss it, and we have always returned for another thrill whenever we visited Konstanz in succeeding years. From there, we crossed the lake by one of the numerous ferries to the castle-capped ancient German town of Meersburg. The steep and narrow streets added a captivating charm, and the promenade alongside the north shore of the lake served as a pleasant rest stop for refreshments.

Yes, we were inside Germany, although still very near the Swiss border, but we felt comfortable within these lovely surroundings in spite of the Nazi past of these lands. No, we were not forgetting, but we were slowly adjusting to new times and the succeeding generations. Rather than viewing this as a questionable rationalization, I would define it as an adjustment of human beings such as we, passing through time without compromising the sacred memories and memorials of darker yesterdays.

Before leaving the Konstanz-Kreuzlingen area, I had the privilege of visiting with Bea the residence of Roy and Mirjam Wiehn, the special people who had been so helpful and cordial during the

1986 homecoming of former Jewish citizens. Their two-story abode
is a uniquely cozy home, with walls and shelves covered with art,
much of it of Jewish origin, Hebrew memorabilia and Israeli arti-
facts, and a wealth of literature. Based on Bea's and our children's
prior experience, I expected to meet two most unusual and forthcoming human beings, and I was not disappointed. I quickly com-
prehended that this fortuitous meeting was likely to be the
beginning of a once-in-a-lifetime experience. Roy Wiehn is a jigsaw
puzzle of many interests and activities: professor of sociology at
Konstanz University, director of the Konstanz-Tel Aviv Universities Friendship Society, the author and catalyst publisher of many
Holocaust books, an outspoken and widely read social and political
man of conscience, and an organizer and active participant of
Tzedakah (righteous deeds) for less-fortunate European Jews who
yearn for freedom and opportunity. Mirjam, a dedicated public
school teacher, is complementing this good work at her husband's
side with a quiet and patient intelligence and the delicate touch
that only a special woman can muster. Those two fine people lived
as Jews, but they were neither born as such nor had formally entered the Jewish faith. But they had entered our hearts and minds
as two special human beings, a feeling we took with us as a precious
memory as we returned to the U.S.A.

On November 5, 1988, Danny and Abby were married in front
of the Holy Ark in our temple. Rabbi Kasdan and Cantor Manevich
performed a most meaningful ceremony for these two young people
and for the many who were assembled in the sanctuary. For Bea
and me, this day was also a threshold of a new chapter in our lives,
a first in a lifetime privilege to walk with one of our offspring towards the Chuppa, the wedding canopy, to witness the emergence
of a new generation. Occasions such as this have a particularly profound meaning for those who survived the Holocaust. The gratitude
and joy of family and friends burst forth in a scintillating celebration at the nearby Bretton Woods catering establishment. We were
not only on cloud nine during this evening to remember but continued on an emotional high for several weeks thereafter. The bride
and groom spent the beginning of their married bliss in nature's
beautiful Hawaii and then settled down in Danny's Montclair, New
Jersey, apartment.

The following winter, we spent another week in tropical St. Lucia, this time without Bert and Eunice because Bert's state of health

required him at that time to remain within easy reach of his doctors. Without family to accompany us, there was more of an incentive to meet other people. Thus we befriended Jean and Mike Brett from Toronto, two fine people with whom we shared days of quality and fun. Once again, I was able to demonstrate that I was still young enough for parasailing.

While walking along the beach, I overheard an older couple conversing in a German that reminded me of the language spoken in the Swiss-German border region of Bea's origin. Bea stopped by to inquire and learned that the couple was of Swiss nationality, the lady was born in Bea's hometown of Konstanz. Her husband, a retired director of a bank, inquired if I would like to go sailing with him on a small boat called a Sunfish. Pointing out that I had no experience, I agreed to accompany him for a trip across the bay. We had barely set out, my Swiss acquaintance handling the sail and I struggling to steer the rudder per his direction, when I inquired how he had attained his skill in this sport. "I just learned yesterday," was his cheerful reply, which instilled a feeling of utter emptiness in me. When it was time to turn around, we ended up in the water but managed to right the boat and continue the journey. No one from the beach had been able to observe our debacle. But as we were ineptly trying to make the final maneuver to return to our starting point, we again keeled over, this time in sight of all beach occupants, including our amused wives. Our lack of sailsmanship had been dramatically exposed. But did we have fun; this was the first of a number of tries for the two of us to navigate the waters of St. Lucia.

Our return flight became an adventure in itself because of the spillover of another airline's strike. In spite of valid tickets, we were bumped off our scheduled plane and delayed a full day, while our luggage had left for the States without us. Our air carrier not only provided us with gratis luxury accommodations during the extra night's stay but also made monetary restitution equal to about three-fourths of our vacation expenses. The initial upset evolved into a most pleasant final day.

During the winter season, I had the opportunity to participate in a musical skit in our temple. I am willing to try anything, better late than never. My part was that of a little boy, and I did not miss a line or a beat. Lots of fun, especially for the amateur performers. For me, it was a welcome interlude to the more serious aspect of serving on the board of trustees.

In the 1989 summer, Orchard Lane was the location for the simultaneous celebration of my 65th birthday and the engagement of Barry and Debbie. Debbie's mother Merle was our honored guest, and it was a joy to have this gregarious lady in our midst. The garden party, under sunny skies and with flowers at their peak, was an absolute delight. Shortly thereafter, we visited Barry in Mountainview, California, and spent a pleasant time with him in his waning days as a bachelor. He found his position at Stanford most challenging and used his leisure time to strive for another demanding goal. Our son had become infatuated with marathon running and eventually achieved a best time of 03:02:39. Though he would not qualify for the Olympics, even this time required substantial and persistent training over many weeks.

Leslie's 30th was celebrated, per her request, at the Jersey shore. Boyfriend Dick joined family and friends in the sunny celebration. Somehow, Leslie could not keep track of her shoes, and pranksters (I being one of them) added to the confusion by placing her footwear on hydrants, lamps, and in tropical fish tanks. Sometimes even adults enjoy reverting to childhood.

In the fall, we all descended on sunny San Diego for Barry's and Debbie's wedding. That gave Bea and me a most welcome opportunity to make the pleasant acquaintance of Debbie's large family. We appreciated their hospitality as well as Rabbi Kasdan's willingness to travel across the country to co-officiate with one of Debbie's rabbinic friends. With the Pacific as a dramatic background to the traditional Chuppa setting, the knot was tied at a La Jolla hotel on October 29. The subsequent celebration in this beautiful setting was appropriately framed by various festive activities before and after the big day. Barry, like his brother, also spent the honeymoon with his bride in romantic Hawaii.

On December 5 of that year, half a century had passed since I first set foot on U.S. soil as a refugee from Nazi tyranny. I never forgot, we never forgot! Joined by Al Meinhardt, my traveling companion on that fateful journey, and our wives, I spent the anniversary day in New York City, both in thankful prayer and in joyous celebration. Al and I have known each other since meeting as refugees in Rotterdam in November 1939. Our lives and that of our wives have become intertwined in a lifelong friendship. It was no mere coincidence that we served as best man at each other's weddings. Our common background, our shared experiences in war and in peace, in joy and in sadness have molded us into an unshakable bond of friendship that easily bridges our individual diversities. I am grateful to have walked for so many years with Al as my dear friend. Life is a great privilege and not to be taken for granted; such recognition is particularly applicable to Holocaust survivors.

Starting late in January of 1990, I experienced great pain in the small of my back and neck region. For the next six weeks, various doctors performed a multitude of tests without being able to pinpoint the cause of the problem. My professional work degenerated to a part-time occupation, and my slender frame became noticeably thinner. Finally, blood culture tests at St. Barnabas Hospital demonstrated that I was suffering from endocarditis, an infection of the heart valve. Since my scarlet fever days in 1939, I knew that I was a heart murmur specimen (mitral valve prolapse), a condition that makes one more vulnerable to infections of that organ. My infectious disease specialist announced, "I have good news and bad news for you. The good news is that we know what we are dealing with and know how to treat it. The bad news is that you have to remain in the hospital for the five week treatment."

After the initial shock, I made up my mind to use this time, which was characterized by intravenous antibiotic infusions at four-hour intervals, to the best of my ability within the inherent restrictions. After only one day of initial treatments, I already felt comfortable. The miracle of modern medicine and science had begun to take its healing effect. Aside from the injections and numerous visitors, there was lots of time for additional activities. With a phone at my side and some office files, including pertinent business mail, on my night-table, I was able to keep up with a good portion of my managerial responsibilities; however, I had arranged to have one of my managers fill in for me in all matters that required on-the-spot attention. This was springtime, and Leslie supplied me with sufficient seeds, trays, and soil to permit gardening activities on the large bay window next to my bed. As I regained more of my strength, I walked the rectangular corridor of my hospital wing with ever greater frequency and speed. In fact, once I almost collided with a justifiably annoyed physician. When my MUM activities, which I chaired for the UAHC Region, required a meeting, I arranged to conduct it in an adjoining conference room. It worked quite well, although I was hooked up to the intravenous gadgetry at the time. Two weeks prior to my scheduled discharge, I returned, with doctor's permission, to our home for a few hours to conduct the Passover Seder. This was a wonderful evening and a great way to return for the first time to home and family after such a lengthy and serious illness. No matter what obstacles life may present, it is important to be resolute and not give up hope. Admittedly, my dear Bea's love and support during this trying time, as well as that of my family and friends, made the carrying out of this resolution vastly easier.

Fully recuperated, I joined Bea, Bert, and Eunice for a visit to Paris in July 1990. This time, I entered this great city legitimately and not, as in 1945, absent without leave from the army. The joy, the beauty, the awe, the enthusiasm, the reverence, the appreciation, and the amazement that the four of us experienced during that week is hard to put into words. The beauty and charm of this famous and historic city formed the appropriate framework within which we found the jewels of the world's great artists. And so we explored some of the artistic wonders of our world, walking in fascination and dreamlike reality through the Musee D'Orsay (twice), the Louvre, L'Orangerie, Picasso, and Marmottan. The latter was an unforgettable climax immediately following our visit to Monet's Giverney home and garden. My brother-in-law Bert was 77 years old then, and his shouts of admiration and ecstasy on the Marmottan's Monet floor were no embarrassment in the stillness and tranquility of this exhibit; these sounds were a sacred expression of experiencing human greatness as instilled by God. Yes, we did take time out to view such famous sights as the Eiffel Tower, Notre Dame Cathedral, Montmartre, the various parks, and the River Seine. But when I think of Paris, the memory of the four of us wandering through the great museums and the gardens of Giverney will always predominate.

From Paris, Bert and Eunice returned directly to the U.S. while Bea and I continued by train to Zurich. Our friends – the Wiehns, Merzbachers, and Dreyfuses once again outdid themselves with their hospitality. We will never tire of the natural beauty of that area and the cozy charm of our Davos hideaway.

The 1990 European trip was wonderful indeed, but it was not our exclusive focus for this chapter in time. Livingston offered its own events. The Katz-Smith family moved from Chicago into our little town, and we were delighted. Richard had accepted a key position at the Kessler Rehabilitation Institute while Stacey continued her studies towards a medical doctorate. We appreciated the proximity of our good friends who had become as close as family.

Danny and Abby bought a house in our immediate neighborhood, a charming place at the terminal end of a cul de sac, directly adjacent to the woods and a brook. The motivation for this expansion was the best news of all: Abby was pregnant and grandparent-hood awaited us in the immediate future. We were very excited, to say the least, and we looked forward to the momentous family event with great expectations. The euphoria was interrupted when Bea, in her Honda, collided with a truck. Fortunately, the damage was restricted to the fright of the

Bea's brother Bert Bravmann and wife Eunice in Monet's Giverney garden during our 1990 visit to Paris.

impact and a badly damaged car. Seconds and inches made the difference during a few dangerous and fleeting moments. We thanked God for our good fortune and bought Bea a new Honda Accord.

On January 23, 1991, my secretary forwarded an important call to my office. It was Danny, announcing with a vibrant voice buzzing with excitement, "We have a beautiful little girl." After accepting a few congratulations as a newly-baked grandfather, I drove directly to St. Barnabas Hospital to meet my new granddaughter, Joanna Esther, and her emotionally intoxicated parents and family at large. Everyone was ecstatic and understandably so; Joanna represented the first grandchild on both sides of the family. As we looked into each other's eyes, I sensed that we would become good friends. This might be the proverbial "wish being the father of the thought," but first impressions count. When she was at the beginning of her second year, Joanna renamed me affectionately "Babops," and we have been close ever since that first day in her life. She is a beautiful and sensitive little girl, not only in appearance but also within her soul.

THE UNION OF AMERICAN
HEBREW CONGREGATIONS
is pleased to present this

CITATION
FOR
RELIGIOUS
LEADERSHIP

to

Ludwig Muhlfelder

*for exemplary service to the UAHC
as a member of the Board of Trustees
from 1984 to 1992 in appreciation
for your labors in the enrichment of
communal life through Reform Judaism*

PRESIDENT   CHAIRMAN
<u>November 1992</u>
DATE

Citation by the UAHC, the North American body of Reform Judaism.

STEPPING INTO RETIREMENT

Late in 1990, at age 66, I decided to announce my retirement from GE so that I could devote my remaining years primarily to my family and to alternate activities and interests. My boss offered me a different position without management responsibilities. Upon asking him how many days a week I would be expected to be present, he said five and I replied: "Wrong answer, I am retiring." And so, the date was set for April 1, 1991, and this was no April fool joke. I had hoped that GE would appoint my successor during the remaining few months of my tenure. No such luck, and so I turned over my responsibilities to one of the managers reporting to me as an interim measure.

Just prior to my final day of work, my many friends and colleagues at the organization honored me at a wonderful farewell dinner. In the presence of most of my family, our rabbi and wife and an assembly of nearly 90 people, I listened to an avalanche of sincere and complimentary speeches. I still recall the enthusiastic and humorous remarks of our former general manager, Chaly Schmidt, who described with effective exaggeration my oratorical contribution in the winning of a key 1980 contract. Nostalgically, I also remember the address by my long-time friend and respected colleague Jack Keigler, with whom I had shared so much professional satisfaction and such a special relationship. It would not be long afterwards when he also decided to retire, but unfortunately in his case for serious medical reasons. A little more than one year later, his productive life would be tragically cut short.

The party concluded with some remarks of my own, with an appreciative glance at the past and an optimistic projection into the future, I offered the following comments:

> To reach the milestone of retirement causes me to be rather introspective. There are no guarantees that one is entitled to reach this privileged juncture on the road of life. In fact, in the springtime of my

existence, I was exposed to two severe winter storms which could easily have precluded me from experiencing the bloom of summer. I was spared from the fate of six million European Jews . . . and survived another storm as a member of General George Patton's Third Army. . . . The 45 years to follow were glorious indeed. . . . During the summer of my life, I had the golden opportunity to participate in a new adventure, to reach into unexplored space, to extend travel to the supersonic, to enable a look at the planet earth from a new perspective, to help link humankind by means of revolutionary sentinels in the sky. To participate, to create, to work hand in hand and mind in mind with others, to help young talent grow – to dream the impossible dream – it was a great privilege indeed.

So my summer is ending. But fall is a beautiful season, and I am looking forward to the future with great expectations. As Thomas Jefferson said, "No occupation is so delightful to me / As the culture of the earth. / But though an old man / I am but a young gardener.

I had worked for the Astro Space Division in excess of 28 years and experienced success and satisfaction during the challenging development of this space business. For this unusual opportunity and for the privilege of participating in the development, the considerable progress and even the occasional disappointments, for all this I was and am very grateful.

Despite my willingness to close the chapter of my career with the Astro Space Division, however, I knew that a sudden transition from full-time work to full-time play would be somewhat drastic. Moreover, I also thought it would be desirable to supplement our fixed income with some additional earnings during the first few years of my retirement. Consequently, LuBea Incorporated was born. This new and tiny company, the name reflecting the ties of our marriage, furnished consulting in my area of expertise to the aerospace industry.

Since retiring, I have serviced a number of clients, including my former employer, the Astro Space Division, and its competitors and customers. In addition, I also did some consulting for Stanford University on a unique scientific space project. Generally, I found my LuBea Inc. work, which involved design reviews, generating design concepts, and verifying that the defined implementations will satisfy the intended mission, challenging and satisfying. Often there was a temptation to expand my activities into the available time of retirement status, but I deliberately resisted this, limiting my consulting to 40 days a year. After all, I retired in order to devote my remaining years mostly to the pursuit of interests outside my prior professional involvement.

Only once did I have some regrets at starting this consulting business. In 1994, a Washington patent firm representing a then un-identified client contacted me for possible technical assistance in my area of expertise. After some thought, I agreed, on behalf of LuBea Inc., to provide this service. Somewhat later, the law firm filed a suit on behalf of its client, Space Systems/Loral, Inc., for patent infringe-ment against my former employer, the Astro Space Division, which in the meantime had been sold by GE to the Martin Marietta Corpo-ration. Four months after the law firm's initial contact with me, the Astro Space Division of Martin Marietta asked me to help in the pending patent matter. I declined because of prior commitment.

I was surprised and shocked to be sued by Martin Marietta three days after I turned down their request for my services. Be-sides me, the defendants also included the law firm, Loral, and an-other consultant. I was accused of violating confidentiality agreements with my former employer and of misappropriating trade secrets. Martin Marietta sought to prevent me from rendering patent advice to a competitor with whom it had become involved in litigation by asserting bogus claims against me.

After months of discovery proceedings, a federal judge in New-ark, New Jersey, dismissed the allegations raised against me, stat-ing that "there is no evidence that there has been any use or disclosure of the confidential information which underlies the state law claims – indeed, Martin Marietta concedes as much." The very firm, now operating under different ownership, which had so sub-stantially benefited from my inventions and many years of faithful service, had filed a suit without merit against me. The gesture did not succeed, but the experience was most painful.

Since then, Martin Marietta has merged with Lockheed, and this corporate entity has announced, as part of restructuring, that the Astro Space Division will cease to exist before the turn of this century: a sad ending for a technology center that had contributed so much to the advancement of the space age.

As I was winding up my professional career, I was also stepping down from my official role in the UAHC. I still had a year to go on my second term on the national board, which expired in 1992. After chairing the regional MUM for 15 years, I asked to be relieved of this responsibility; my successor took over the reigns in early 1995. My service in that position had been long enough, possibly too long, and I questioned whether I still had the patience and perspective required for this difficult task. Simultaneously, I also completed my participation on the national MUM committee. To me, it seems important not only to serve in selected organizations that are worthy of support but also to know when to step back and give other people, preferably younger, an opportunity to contribute their talents.

I remained an active member of the dues policy review committee, which in 1995 consisted of about 45 members. To aid in our search for a more equitable dues structure, I proposed a different approach to the body in January 1996. Rather than basing the temple dues to UAHC exclusively on a congregation's expenses, I suggested a reduction of that component and the addition of a membership-size-sensitive per capita charge. This "blend" approach was eventually chosen from eight proposals and submitted to the national board and the assembly of UAHC congregations (about 850). I was gratified indeed when these international bodies (U.S. and Canada), which considered the proposal at the October 1997 biennial in Dallas, gave their overwhelming approval to this original proposal. For me, it was a special satisfaction to be able to make an intellectual contribution to our liberal religious organization. I hope that the implementation of this dues plan will have a beneficial effect on our entire Reform movement.

As Bea and I looked forward to the 40th anniversary of our marriage, much was happening in our children's lives. Leslie shared more and more of her leisure time with Dick, who had switched positions from the Philadelphia law firm to a become inside counsel of a pharmaceutical company and was at that time living in a rented house near Valley Forge, Pennsylvania. These were years of adjustment and transition for Dick, for he had been separated for some time from his wife and was now in the midst of divorce proceedings. Without being intrusive, Bea and I were hoping that the future would bring happiness for our daughter and her friend, but whether their relationship would become permanent was really in their hands and hearts. We were just very interested and fervent bystanders. In the summer of 1991, Dick bought a beautiful new and spacious house in Wayne, Pennsylvania, and it was no surprise that Leslie, who by now was living with him, planted a perennial garden even before Dick legally took possession of the property.

Barry and Debbie decided to buy a house in preparation for the arrival of their first offspring and in response to Barry's own infatuation with gardening. By California standards, the property, locat-

Fortieth wedding anniversary celebration in Kiawah, South Carolina, June 1982. The family keeps on growing.

ed in Castro Valley, between Barry's workplace at Stanford and Debbie's at Berkeley, had a good-sized lot. A day before my birthday, at least in terms of West Coast time, our grandson Joshua Jacob made his entry into our world. Bea, Leslie, and I were personally introduced to this fine boy, but I am not at all sure if he appreciated my holding him as the Sandek during his Brit Mila, the ritual circumcision performed on all Jewish (and Moslem) males in the tradition of Abraham. So our "little" boy Barry had now become a father, and we were thrilled with all the blessings that came our way.

In the 1991 spirit of expansion and growth, Richard and Stacey became parents of their second child, Julian, during the summer. He had a cute and impish face, prompting me at times to call him "Spitzbub," rascal. As he grew older, he retained that characteristic, which appeals to me and makes me smile.

In the 1991–92 winter, we joined the older and younger Bravmanns for a two week stay in Negril, an inviting vacation spot on the northwest shore of Jamaica. We (Bert, Eunice, Bea, and I) were initiated into the area with a big bang, a head-on collision of our bus with a car on the road from Montego Bay to Negril. Most fortunately, our injuries were minor and essentially forgotten a few days later. The beach was a dream, and I managed to swim a total of 18 miles under ideal conditions. My determination to reach that number was no accident, 18, chai in Hebrew, also stands for life. Even Leslie joined us for a few days to participate in the family frolics.

By 1992, 40 years had passed since Bea and I had joined forces for a life of love and labor, and we resolved to mark this occasion with a week of family fun on Kiawah island off the South Carolina coast. There were 14 of us that June, including the Katz-Smith family who had moved to St. Louis. The kids were appropriately dressed in specially decorated T-shirts: Joanna J-1, Joshua J-2, Julian J-3, and Rachel as Pie (the endearing nickname coined by her father). We were delighted with Abby and Danny's announcement that the family roll-call would increase to 15 by early 1993, great news to top off this anniversary celebration.

The summer was marked by two contrasting visits to our garden. The Keiglers reminisced with us on our deck, recalling the joys and successes of bygone days. It was a bittersweet moment, a farewell for Jack. Fatally ill, he was to die a few months later. He was a fine human being, a good friend, and a highly respected colleague from the Astro Space Center.

A more joyous and buoyant affair was the aptly named Bang picnic for the Vietnamese family whose immigration and initial needs were sponsored by our temple a decade earlier. The original nine had now mushroomed to 18 due to marriages and resulting offspring of the now-adult Bang children. Those of us who helped in the initial adjustment process, particularly Anita Smith and Bea, derived much satisfaction from this family's success, the academic achievements of the children, and the sense of responsibility as good citizens to take care of their own needs and aspirations.

That year, we also welcomed Helen Rivkin for an annual visit that we have enjoyed for some 15 years. The long and expensive trip from Israel was not primarily undertaken as a social call but rather as an essential requirement for Helen and Ken's export business of Israeli books. Even so, it was always a special treat to renew briefly this contact with two people who are very dear to us. During this decade of the nineties, Ken was no longer able to carry on the business because of declining health; therefore, Helen in solo was our yearly guest. She is an unusual woman, the "Golda Meir" of our inner group of friends: strong, outspoken, peace-seeking, warm, highly principled, liberal. Although I do not agree completely with every one of her positions, I highly respect her and cherish every moment we can share. In 1971, Helen and Ken took their three daughters to Israel to assure or maximize their Jewish identity. That move was made with open eyes, which saw the sacrifices in security and standard of living that lay ahead. Twenty-six years later, Helen's vision is undimmed while she functions as the matriarch of her family. To know such a woman is inspiring indeed.

On January 6, 1993, a few weeks ahead of schedule and quite in keeping with the years to follow, Jeremy Micah Muhlfelder arrived on the scene. Joanna had a sibling, and we were blessed with our third grandchild. Within a brief period, the little fellow managed to overcome his somewhat premature status and amused the family to no end with his humorous and determined personality. He had no problem at all carving out a special place and role for himself within our family. The celebration of life continued to unfold. Like most grandparents, we treasure our grandchildren. As one progresses towards the upper numbers in the human lifespan, the presence and interaction with this new generation is a beneficial elixir, somewhat like Ponce De Leon's legendary fountain of youth.

During the summer of 1993, we welcomed special guests for a once-in-a-lifetime occasion. Roy and Mirjam Wiehn spent a few memorable weeks with us not only as tourists and good friends, but also to finalize their long-desired conversion to Judaism. Under Rabbi Kasdan's tutelage, they had been studying for some time to enhance their substantial prior knowledge of our faith. Now, after the final important steps, including circumcision and ritual bath were performed, our small group gathered in front of the arc on the Bima of our Temple. In a moving ceremony, Rabbi Kasdan, assisted by Cantor Dower, warmly welcomed Mirjam and Roy as the newest members of the Jewish people and asked for God's blessing upon them.

We were profoundly touched by this event, which represented a long-yearned-for confirmation of our dear friends' convictions. These unusual human beings had lived and prayed and acted as Jews for years. Roy had studied Hebrew and visited the pioneers of Israel in his youth. The Holocaust literature has been enhanced substantially by this dedicated and talented man, and new bridges have been built between the Republic of Germany and the State of Israel because of his efforts. The Wiehns' Tzedakah, their righteous deeds, took many forms, including numerous trips to the lands of the former Soviet Union to bring food, clothing, medical supplies, and hope to those in need. And now they had finally formalized what they had practiced all along; they had become part of the Jewish people.

President Clinton had dedicated the Holocaust Memorial Museum in Washington the preceding spring, and thus a visit to this place was a natural for us during the Wiehns' visit. I found it to be an outstanding institution for teaching the history of this tragic period of humankind to peoples of all races and creeds. To be exposed to the horrors and the pains of that time in such a concentrated manner is not easy to tolerate, but not to remember and to permit these events to fade into the ever-receding past would be an intolerable act of injustice and irresponsibility. Since that first visit with our guests, Bea and I have returned to this museum several times with groups from our temple.

In preparation for our Washington trip, Roy Wiehn brought home a book from the Metro West Jewish Federation library. This volume, *The World Must Know*, by M. Berenbaum, which depicts the history of the Holocaust, was issued on the occasion of the museum's dedication. As I leafed randomly through its pages, I noticed a picture of thousands of prisoners lined up for a roll-call at the Buchenwald concentration camp. Scanning the rows of men closest to the Nazi photographer's camera, I suddenly saw my father. There he was, in characteristically erect posture, his head shaven, standing during the first of many roll-calls, with an uncertain future and a tenuous life.

The photograph was most likely taken by the German authorities shortly after the November 9–10, 1938, Kristallnacht, when essentially all Jewish males between 16 and 70 were arrested and shipped off to concentration camps. I must admit, that after all these years, knowing that my father was released from this horrible detention after three weeks, after witnessing his living till the age of 84, after all these years I was still profoundly shocked to see him standing there. For days after discovering this picture, I would wake up at night to re-examine and study my father's image with a magnifying glass. What were his thoughts at that moment,what were his fears and his hopes under these trying circumstances? What eventually was the fate of each of these thousands who stood there with him?

As my 70th birthday was approaching, Bea inquired how I would prefer to spend this milestone event. "At home with family and friends" was my spontaneous reply. I could not imagine that there would be a more appropriate location for celebrating this day than that special place where I have spent more than half of my life together with those I love. So Bea planned for a garden party and we hoped for sunshine. There was a bit of a shower just as our guests were about to get seated, but quick action temporarily transferred the festivities indoors. Toasts, speeches, and poems were intermingled with liquid refreshments and gourmet delights. Pleasant weather returned in time to show off my horticultural accomplishments. For dessert, Abby had spent many hours preparing a delicious cake arranged as a miniature vegetable garden, the individual produce meticulously shaped with marzipan. Sharing the occasion with Joshua, who was simultaneously observing his third birthday, was an additional delight. I was touched by all the attention and love coming my way as I reached the three score and 10 mark and concluded my remarks with the following:

On a day like this, there is the temptation to look ahead. We humans may plan, but we cannot penetrate with our vision the mist which shrouds our tomorrows. With deep gratitude for all the love and beauty and opportunity which life has bestowed upon me, and particularly the sacred and precious bond of marriage with Bea, let me conclude with the lines of Robert Frost's inspiring poem, "Stopping by Woods on a Snowy Evening":

> The woods are lovely, dark and deep,
> But I have promises to keep,
> And miles to go before I sleep,
> And miles to go before I sleep.

During the 1994 summer, the magnetism of Switzerland and the Bodensee pulled us once more to that picturesque corner of Europe. On this excursion, we added the old city of Basel to our usual itinerary. While in this historic town, we were hosted and guided by Bea's acquaintance Markus Bergheimer and his friend Barbara. During our traditional indulgence in Davos, we made an overnight excursion to the Engadine fairyland, the Hotel Meiser in Guarda. There, our vacation contentment had reached its ultimate peak. I was always an avid photographer, but in Guarda I became nearly obsessed with our photographic diary. In my happiness and admiration, I seemed to be determined to make time stand still and preserve these precious moments forever in the pages of our photo albums. Let me emphasize here that I only snap the pictures; while it is Bea who, with great care and patience, has assembled many volumes of these photographs into a closet full of albums.

While relaxing one evening in the Davos condo, we happened upon a fascinating television documentary that had been produced by the Swiss TV network. In amazement, we watched a highly critical and damning account of the Swiss history during the Holocaust. Mind you, this was a Swiss product of introspection. We learned, for example, that the big red "J" stamped in passports of German Jews, including my own, was a Nazi response to a Swiss initiative. Upon being implemented by the more-than-willing German government, this "J" enabled the Swiss border authorities to identify readily the Jewish refugees fleeing illegally across the border and return them to the Nazi terror. We were reminded of Dorle Hilb, who related to us this incomprehensible practice during our 1976 visit to the little Swiss town of Herisau. Furthermore, according to the TV report, the Swiss government expressed a willingness in the 1943–44 war years to give safe haven to 50,000 French children, provided that no Jewish youngsters would be included. Bea and I were aware, of course, that Switzerland had permitted some Jewish refugees to enter their country during the Nazi period. But it seemed that the 1933–45 history of that beautiful land is somewhat tainted by insensitivity and anti-Semitism. That constitutes a painful realization about a nation renowned for its democratic institutions, its supposed impeccable neutrality and its humanitarian reputation.

Our Konstanz stay was again an absolute delight thanks to the devotion of our hosts, the Wiehns. Roy treated us to an unusual and meaningful observance of Tishah B'Av, the day of mourning observed by many Jews in memory of the destruction of the first and second temple in Jerusalem. Many modern Jews pay little heed to this day, maybe in part due to the many other sad memorial days that man's cruelty to man has imposed on the Jewish calendar since that ancient time. Roy and Mirjam, as 20th-century Jews, took us for an all-day excursion to the Jewish cemeteries and former synagogue sites, the latter now marked only by memorial plaques, of the nearby communities of Wangen, Randek, Gailingen, Kreuzlingen, and Konstanz itself. A large schoolhouse and the huge Gailingen cemetery attested to the formerly substantial Jewish presence (50% of the population) in that town. On one end of the cemetery, we noted the old and weathered grave markers of the 17th century slowly sinking into the ground, and on the other end we looked in sadness on the final single memorial erected for the 20th-century Jews, those who were deported from Gailingen in 1940 and became victims of the Holocaust. There are no Jews left in that town anymore, only Jewish memories, a symbolic observation pertaining to so many towns and villages of Germany and formerly Nazi-occupied Europe. Tishah B'Av 1994, a most poignant day, observed in a most fitting way.

In the late summer of 1995, Bea's brother Bert could no longer manage to live with Eunice in the Amherst continuing care facility. A series of minor strokes took their toll, and he therefore entered a nearby nursing home. Eunice saw him there almost daily, and we took a trip to Massachusetts at few months' intervals. He always responded with joy on those occasions, although his speech was severely handicapped and his ability to move about quite limited. He could no longer read and displayed little interest in the outside world; even television viewing of his once favorite sports went by the wayside. During July of 1997, his weakened body was invaded by an infection. Medications were only temporarily effective, and he died while we visited Amherst on August 21. Although Eunice, Bea, and the entire family recognized that this ending was really a blessing, it was nevertheless a time of sadness. When Bert was laid to his final rest in a pristine forest, an area in back of the more formal Amherst cemetery, there was an aura of serenity and unusual spirituality enveloping those gathered for the simple graveside services. Even the pallbearers, struggling over the slippery and somewhat uneven ground of the forest, lent a surrealistic feeling to the moment. I added these few words to those of a most sensitive rabbi:

> I called him Bruder – brother
> though he evolved from a different womb.
> He and I shared a common heritage:
> Israel's roots in Teutonic soil,
> Crossing the ocean and surviving the Shoah,
> fighting to preserve freedom
> and eradicate the ultimate evil.
>
> I called him Bruder.
> His sister my wife,
> His wife my friend,
> His town my town,
> my family his family,
> His home my home,
> my garden his garden.

Let us give praise that he escaped the Nazis' clutch and the enemy's
bullet.
Let us give praise for his years of love and years of labor.
Let us give praise for his long span of life and
for the privilege of having walked with him part of the way.
I called him Bruder.

Nineteen-ninety-five was a happy time as well, illuminated by
Leslie's wedding to Dick Freemann. In February, they announced
their engagement after Dick, in a kind and appreciated gesture,
asked us for our consent. Bea and I were delighted not only because
we had waited for this moment for quite a number of years but also
because we had developed a high admiration for Dick. Leslie's man
had to be a special human being, sensitive and steady, intelligent
and patient, giving and firm, warm and discerning, encouraging and
discriminating, challenging and understanding. Dick has all of these
characteristics and then some. Nevertheless, Leslie had difficulty
deciding on a marriage commitment because Dick is her senior by
more than a decade and not a member of the Jewish religion. She finally and wisely decided on her own that with Dick's long-ago enunciated consent, she could create a Jewish home and in love bridge the
perceived age difference with the wealth of qualities that they share.

The wedding took place on Labor Day in the magnificent natural setting of Appleford, an atrium located in Villanova, Pennsylvania. Words cannot do justice to the delicate beauty and the refined
atmosphere that enveloped this entire affair; pictures and video can
do much better. True enough, Leslie planned every detail, usually
with Dick at her side. The preliminaries spanned a few days and appropriately led up to the culminating event. A picnic, a wedding
party dinner, and a brunch all gave ample opportunity for the
guests to get to know each other and establish some bonding on this
sunny weekend. Leslie's gardening skills are partially inherited,
but during the past decade her horticultural finesse has far sur-
passed my capabilities. This was not only reflected in her selection
of the wedding locale but also in the choice of floral displays marking this joyous occasion. Dick and Leslie's friend, Circuit Court
Judge Pollack, presided at the ceremony and added a well-balanced
sense of introspection and humor to these significant moments.
Leslie was radiant as Bea and I were aware of the great privilege of
walking her to the Chuppa, located under the cooling branches of a

huge weeping willow adjacent to a small waterfall. The strains of "Dodi Li, My Beloved is Mine," performed by Penfield, Richard, and friend Bud Mishkin, added a sense of nostalgic holiness to this emotional instant in time. The weather was most cooperative, and the mood of joy, thanksgiving, and hope so vibrantly present during the ceremony, continued to permeate the entire day, the rose-garden reception, a lengthy cocktail hour, and the dinner dance. I recall with much gratitude and happiness the wonderful wedding days of our other children but must admit that the mood and the setting of this September weekend remain especially vivid in my mind.

Shortly before her marriage, Leslie accepted a new position at her undergraduate alma mater, Lafayette College, in Easton, Pennsylvania. The president of the school, an unusual man of vision and compassion, had invited her repeatedly to consider joining his staff. Although her commute is a bit long, she finally consented. As a vice-president of this exclusively undergraduate school, Leslie works as in-house counsel and also as director of human resources. This represents a considerable expansion of her prior responsibilities at Temple University. Dick was pleased with the change and so was I; Leslie had reached a plateau at her prior job, and if one does not progress, one slides backwards. Bea was a bit apprehensive that Leslie's increased responsibilities and the commuting chore would leave little room for the other facets of life. Time will tell.

On the first day of spring in 1996, a tiny flower was added to our family garden, Joshua's sister Mira. Although the existence of children is not always an absolute assurance of the soundness of the marital bond, we felt that Mira's birth was a positive indication that Barry and Debbie, who had been experiencing marital difficulties and spent many sessions with counselors and therapists, saw hopefully into the future and expected to walk life's path together. Bea and I greeted our fourth grandchild with great joy and were present for the religious naming ceremony, which was written and compiled by Debbie. I pray for our children and grandchildren each night that they may be blessed with health and peace. If first impressions count, Mira seems to have Barry's and therefore Bea's dark brown eyes, which view the world with considerable inquisitiveness and intensity. In keeping with our prior practice, we promptly initiated an education fund for our little granddaughter in the expectation that, as People of the Book, our children's children will make the expansion of their intellect a high priority.

15 Orchard Lane in the spring of 1993.

After years of delay, we finally took a trip to St. Louis in the fall of 1996 to visit the Katz-Smith family. They had repeatedly invited us and even insisted on treating us to our airfare. Primarily, we hesitated to accept because of Stacey's demanding professional schedule. Her residency obligations as psychiatrist left almost no time for extracurricular activities. But now she had leapt over this last hurdle, achieved her goal, and set up her private practice. I consider this an extraordinary achievement. After reigning for two successive years as U.S. ice dancing champion and then entering in a marital bond with Richard, she embarked on a new career via a college education, medical school, and the required specialized training to qualify her as psychiatrist. In between, she managed, with Richard's help, to bear and raise two fine children, Rachel and Julian. Despite all these responsibilities and pressures, she maintained and even enhanced her sweet and kind disposition growing each year into an ever more rounded and mature human being, a person of compassion and kindness.

Our visit to their Clayton home, a charming enclave in greater St. Louis, was an experience of love and appreciation. In a series of events, from Shabbat observance at home and in temple to Succoth observance in the backyard Succa (thanksgiving booth) to visiting the outstanding botanical garden to an excursion ride on the Mis-

The gardener and the peony, 1996.

souri River, we spent a few days of joy and quality time with each other. However, Richard's piano recital in a beautiful nearby chapel was the emotional highlight of our visit. His great love for music, his considerable talent, and his unflinching dedication were present in every note of his performance. Richard has magically combined a successful career (medical director, SSM Rehabilitation Institute, St. Louis) in medicine with a precious avocation as a most talented musician. With all this, he always remained a sweet and caring human being. We felt privileged to have been there.

As Bea's 70th birthday approached, I was again reminded of Dobson's poetic lines, "Time goes, you say, ah no, alas, time stays, we go!" As we passed through time during some precious days, we celebrated my dear wife's special anniversary in a most fitting way. In accordance with her fervent wish, the entire family spent a week in August on New Jersey's Long Beach Island. Our three children with their families and the Katz-Smiths, who are like children to us, had, together with us, a marvelous time in sand and sun, on water and land, night and day, in love and in joy. It was a celebration of life, of Bea's life and of those so dear to her.

On the big day, the 13th of September, our East Coast family, including Eunice, gathered in our home to congratulate and to celebrate, to be followed by a dinner in Bea's favorite restaurant, Librettis. On the following day, we marked the occasion together with relatives and friends, about 40 in all, with a wonderful garden party at 15 Orchard Lane. With Leslie's indispensable choreography and the help of an excellent caterer and others, it was an occasion that did justice to my dear wife. We were blessed with marvelous weather, a prime ingredient for any outdoor affair. Our "in-house" gardener had labored diligently to show off our grounds in the best possible light, and from all comments the setting was appreciated by all. As is my usual custom, I do not let such special occasions pass without a poetic attempt. To fit Bea's years, it was rather lengthy, so here is just an excerpt:

> What did you do during those three score and ten?
> What prose did you write with your human pen?
> What path did you choose at those forks in the road?
> What did you accomplish which is now of note?
>
> Your name is aptly Bea, for each flower you touch
> Helps both humankind and the blossom as such.
> Sharing with hummingbirds the nectar of life
> While with labor and love you continue to strive.
>
> God of time and of space, you Supreme Author of life,
> We thank you for our mother, our Nama, my wife.
> Shehechiyanu, for you Dear, your reaching this day,
> For health, joy, and Shalom we now pause to pray.

It was a day to remember!

Later that fall of 1996, Bea and I sensed that Danny was struggling with a significant problem that he did not discuss with us at that time. Bea was concerned that either Abby or Danny were stricken with a physical illness of consequence, and I guessed that Abby's emotional state was at the root of the problem. Over the years, I had observed considerable swings in her mood, and while I surmised that Danny's preoccupation might be due to his wife's problems, I simultaneously resorted to the human habit of dismissing such a possibility as unlikely.

Immediately after we returned in early February 1997 from a winter vacation in St. Lucia, Danny made a formal appointment to talk to us. In a highly emotional state and in painful whispers, he informed us that Abby had requested a divorce. When, in the fall of 1996, Abby initially spoke to Danny about her unhappiness, he had suggested they seek the guidance of a counselor. Though Abby explored their problems in this manner for three or four months and both Danny and she saw a marriage professional, the effort was to no avail. Abby was firm in her determination to end the marriage.

By February, Abby was intent on seeking a divorce, and Danny was utterly devastated. For two or three weeks, Abby agreed to join Danny in a weekly session with a different marriage professional, but without success. Abby quickly ended this attempt at reconciliation.

We were, of course, all shocked and upset, and with this "we" I mean not only Bea and I but also our other children and spouses, our family-friends Richard and Stacey Katz-Smith, and our circle of friends and acquaintances. It was difficult to comprehend how a dedicated and loving family man such as Danny could be in such a horrendous situation. When Bea met Abby's mother sometime after the initial shock, this nice lady burst into tears while embracing Bea. We understand that many members of Abby's family were also upset over this sad turn of events.

Bea and I shared Danny's primary concern, the welfare of Joanna and Jeremy, who at the age of six and four were going to be subjected to painful emotional events of potentially long-lasting consequences. We pray that Joanna and Jeremy will continue to love each of their parents and that the current darkness will give way to a brighter future.

RETURN TO GERMANY

In 1996, 50 years after my tour as a soldier in Patton's Third Army, I returned to Germany. Before this trip, Bea had visited Konstanz, the town of her birth; I had gone with her at the time, but because Konstanz was so contiguous to the Swiss side, I was able to rationalize my return. Otherwise, since our emigration to escape the horrors of the Shoah, I had consciously and deliberately avoided any excursion into the German heartland. Now, accompanied by Bea, Leslie, Dick, and the Wiehns, I returned of my own free will to central Germany, to the town of Suhl, where I was born.

Roy Wiehn had been involved in Holocaust research for many years and was responsible, as catalyst, author, and editor, for about 50 books on the subject. It was in response to his request that I initially issued, in German, the story of my experiences as a Jewish boy in Hitler's Germany. Wiehn had also sponsored the publication of another book, entitled *Juden in Suhl* (*Jews in Suhl*), by Hans Nothnagel and Ewald Daehn, local historians. As a result of the foreword I contributed to their book, Suhl rediscovered my existence and, for my 70th birthday, invited me to visit. Though newspaper headlines and letters from their youthful mayor, Dr. Martin Kummer, former classmates, author Nothnagel, and others all conveyed simultaneous messages of congratulations and invitations to visit, I initially declined to return. I agreed only when I realized that there exists, even in former East Germany, a nucleus of people who are attempting to confront the Nazi period with honesty and contrition.

I decided at that juncture of my life to visit this town of my youth so as to give encouragement to those descendants of the Nazi generation who are intent on examining the Holocaust by the light of day. I decided that to turn my back to the possibility of a better tomorrow, theirs and ours, would not be consonant with our prayers. If I were to leave the field to apathetic onlookers, apologists, revisionists, and skinheads, if I and others like me were to remain silent by our neglect or absence and thus would not bear witness, then the future of tomorrow's generations would be gloomy indeed.

The Suhl preparations for our visit were thorough. In our few days there, I had the opportunity to participate actively in a number of official events, including the opening ceremonies of the exhibit "Time witnesses of Suhl 1933–45, Jews in Thuringia." In addition, the mayor asked me to address the students of the Gymnasium and engage in a question and answer session with them; to read from my biography in the Buchhaus Suhl; and to exchange thoughts and reflections with a group of townspeople that included the mayor, his assistants, teachers and principals of public schools, members of my former high school class, and ordinary citizens.

The opening ceremonies of the "Time Witness" exhibit had a particularly emotional impact, providing many in attendance with an opportunity to unburden themselves of feelings of guilt about the Nazi era. Naturally, this was a self-selected group, about 200 people who made it their priority to attend this ceremony on a weekday morning. For them, I represented the first Jewish survivor of Suhl to whom they could indicate – with gestures of welcome, gifts, flowers, and tears – the pain they were feeling. Following the opening ceremonies, I visited the Gymnasium to address the students of the senior grades. After a most cordial welcome by the principal, Rektor Dr. Kiehle, I spoke at length to the students, who gave me their full attention. I tried to enhance their knowledge of Holocaust studies, now a mandatory subject in their school, with a description (in German) of my personal experiences during the Nazi years in Suhl. Some of their questions appeared to indicate that I struck a responsive chord. Germany's future will tell whether such exposure will help to ensure a compassionate, tolerant, and democratic society.

During the evening of the first day of our Suhl visit, I did a reading of portions of my German language autobiography at the bookstore. As we arrived at the store in the mayor's limousine, the car stopped at the loading platform, where we waited for an attendant to admit us through the back door. I realized then that the two-story store was filled to the rafters and the front door had to be locked temporarily to keep out the overflow crowd while temporary chairs (some of which collapsed during the program) were assembled. Hans Nothnagel and I were both on the program; I read selected portions of my biography, then greeted well wishers, who lined up to ask me to sign their copies of my book. I was, to say the least, gratified.

As the first Jew to visit the town officially in over half a century, I was somewhat of an attraction, a curiosity. But I sensed a sincere interest on the part of those few hundred whom I met personally not only to see me but to listen to my message, to welcome us with kindness and sensitivity. Because the media in both Suhl and the Thuringian area gave our visit considerable coverage, a much larger audience heard my story and my message.

Between now and the time I had left Suhl half a century earlier, the town had changed significantly in appearance. With the threefold increase in population, whole new sections were added and entire old historical sections were razed, to be replaced by modern structures. I remember thinking immediately that these changes were not all for the better. For me, the ugly highrise buildings constructed during the more than four decades of the postwar Communist East German regime, possibly in an effort to imitate western metropolitan areas, stood out as a symbol of destructive modernization, contributing nothing to the aesthetics of the town. Still, some portion of the center of Suhl, so familiar to me, was preserved. The old main street, the Steinweg, on which the Nazis used to march, was now a charming pedestrian mall framed by old rococo houses such as that of the Sanders, with garden memories, and that of the Goldmanns, with whom we lived in 1939.

On the adjoining Rimbachstrasse, I recognized house number four, our apartment residence until the end of 1938. The facade had recently been restored and each of the windows carried childhood memories; I saw the one I had opened on Kristallnacht, when the flames of our synagogue lit the sky. The inside of the building was transformed into commercial space and bore no relationship to our former apartment. It was strange to visit there, a link to my youth and my growing years, but also a reminder of a horrible past.

Further up on the Rimbachstrasse, I showed Bea, Leslie, Dick, and the Wiehns the Mittelschule where I attended classes from 1934–38. Leslie was particularly interested in having me identify specific locations that related to my experiences during the Nazi period. Thus, in the schoolyard of the Mittleschule, I pointed out to her the spot where my teacher had stood when he announced the Hindenburg disaster and blamed New York Jews. We also stopped at the Hohelohschule, now Herder Gymnasium, my elementary school from 1930–34. Most of the building's appearance matched my memory, except for the top floor, where the skylight now illuminated impressive scientific laboratories.

I knew I would need to see once again the Brylewski villa, the designated Jew house where my mother, sister, and I spent the difficult and dangerous last months prior to emigrating in November 1939. When it came into view, I was drawn to it as if by a magnetic force. My daughter was particularly affected by this site; she hung on to every word of my explanations: "Yes, we lived in the tower room while Mr. Brylewski was brutally beaten by the German stormtroopers in the garden." I heard the agony of his screams again and recalled that of the 13 residents, only those of our family, including uncle Max, escaped in time. The others – including the Brylewskis' two grandsons Hans-Gunther and Ernst-Jochem, respectively about nine and four when we emigrated in 1939, were murdered after being deported to the East.

There were other nostalgic and difficult moments as well. We briefly paused with words of memory at the memorial of the synagogue, which had been destroyed 58 years before. I recalled that I could not bring myself at that time to view the ruins, and when, a year later, I finally had to pass by there on the way to the train station and to America, I felt that I had sinned against God to have looked at the remains. Hans Nothnagel , the co-author of *Jews in Suhl*, composed a poem, "Symptoms of Flames," about that now-distant event, which I reproduce here in translation:

> The town's ornament turns to ashes
> And, alas, so many are silent. . . .
> That is the prologue for a horrible grave –
> But not for Jews alone.

Most of today's German population, and in particular the younger generation, has been sensitized to empathize with the enormity and tragedy of the Holocaust. This was not always the case during the post World War II period. In East Germany under the DDR, the Holocaust was depicted as a secular tragedy of human beings, a consequence of the class struggle that distorted the Communist minds. Thus, together with a tasteful replica of the building and a star of David, the inscription on the memorial stone for the destroyed synagogue reflects the wording of hundreds of such monuments: "On this spot stood the synagogue of the Jewish congregation. It was dedicated in 1906. During the pogrom night of November 9th, 1938, it was destroyed by arson by the fascists."

It is left to the reader of this inscription to determine the identity of these mysterious "fascists": Were they intruders from another country? Were they extremists or terrorists who were violating the law of the land? Or were they German citizens clad in brown or black uniforms who, like thousands of others, were acting in accord with the Nazi Germany government seated in Berlin? I really do appreciate that such a memorial for my synagogue, where I observed my Bar Mitzvah in 1937, exists in the first place. But I would prefer a more forthright inscription in order not to mislead future generations.

During the morning of our second day in Suhl, in a dreary and rainy atmosphere, I conducted a memorial service in the Jewish cemetery. This I had prepared just for us, and it was therefore in Hebrew and English. But to my surprise, about 20 local people were waiting at the entrance to join us when we arrived. I recalled those whom I had known in my youth and were buried there and those from the congregation who had made the ultimate sacrifice while fighting for Germany during the First World War. Twelve thousand German Jews, including my uncle in whose memory I am named, died then for their so-called fatherland. And finally, I recited the long list of names of those men, women, and children who in 1942 were deported from this town of my birth to the extermination camps of the east. Even with all the preparations for this visit and particularly this service, both programmatic and emotional, I had considerable difficulty reading this list, for the names had faces and souls and memories. Fortunately, my dear Bea stood at my side and we completed this memorial in the rain. Among those present from the local population was Holger Uske, a deputy of the mayor. His poem, "Andacht" ("Reverence"), which he dedicated to me in response to this memorial service, is most touching, and I attempted not to lose its sensitivity in the following translation:

> Rain falls on your prayer
> Mist from nearby hills
> Drops give off the sound
> On the dark moist ground.
>
> Names are carried on air
> Which, long ago, the wind dispersed

So it held still, listened
To words now so estranged.

The rain falls heavier, heavier
Increasing with each of the dead
As if beating drums without us
The never quiescent lament.

Behind our brows there grew
This hour' admonition:
Do not depend upon the mist
Let your voice be the rain.

The Kaddish we said there was repeated by us four more times in other cemeteries at the graves of grandparents and great-grandparents of the distant past, ancestors who did not know of the great evil that lurked down the road. The Kaddish prayer does not once mention death but instead honors our departed by praising God and transforming our grief into sanctifying our Creator.

On this journey, we also stopped in Muhlfeld, a neat little village and the birthplace of my great-great-grandfather Josef, and the nearby Jewish cemetery in the village of Bauerbach. When Josef married Rosel Baer in 1793, they established their home in Bauerbach and in the prolific custom of the times had eight children. To the best of my knowledge, all Jews with the Muhlfelder name are the descendants of that union. In Muhlfeld, we were most cordially received by the town's speaker and former mayor Gerhard Schneider and a Heinrich Stuetzel, a seventh-generation citizen of the place. They had never before met a "Muhlfelder" in their village. During our subsequent visit in the Bauerbach cemetery, it became obvious that numerous Muhlfelders had spent their entire lifetime, from cradle to grave, in this little town. This was the birthplace of my paternal grandfather Jonas and great-grandfather Moses. Leslie was able to identify the final resting place of the latter, and it was a poignant moment as we gathered there in prayer. We had followed this most meaningful custom during a previous stop at the graves of my father's parents in nearby Meiningen.

Prior to my emigration at the age of 15, I had never entered a cemetery because according to our religious tradition it was thought to be improper to do so while one's parents were still living. There are some who still to this day do not participate in memorial services or the recitation of the Kaddish as long as their parents are living. For me, the tragedy of the Holocaust has made this practice of denial an archaic relic and no longer acceptable. In our synagogue, we have made it a practice to add one name of the one-and-one-half-million Jewish children killed in the Holocaust to our weekly Jahrzeit list; at this rate, it would take nearly 30,000 years to complete the roll of our young Jewish dead. Besides our own loved ones, our six million martyrs are also deserving of every one's Kaddish.

On our way back to Konstanz, we made two more stops of memory. The first was in the charming hamlet of Unteraltertheim, literally untouched by the outside except for the TV antennae, where Bea's father was born well over a century ago. Mr. and Mrs. Thoma, the couple who by prearrangement welcomed us, remembered from their childhood how the "Juden" were being rounded up and taken away. They showed us a page in a book that listed the names of all the local Jews, together with dates and possessions. There were many Bravmanns among these victims. The Thomases spoke with warmth about their childhood memories, probably as told in part by their parents. The Juden observed the Shabbes, and therefore the population had to buy their meat early on Friday; the only butcher in town was Jewish. And when the Jews would frequent the coffee shop on Saturday afternoons, they could not pay because they were not permitted to carry money on the Sabbath and thus returned on the next day to pay their debts. After such reminiscences, the Thomases escorted us to the Jewish cemetery, which was a few miles away and well-maintained. We entered deep, beautiful woods where the silence of nature enveloped the graves and we subconsciously talked very softly. There we found the grave of Bea's grandfather, surrounded by many other Bravmanns. No burials appeared to have taken place there since 1941. The local couple explained that each spring they walk, instead of drive, the several miles to the cemetery to clean it from winter's damage, and that they remembered that the Jews had also followed such an annual custom; therefore, they have continued that practice up to the current time. Before departing, they also led us to the synagogue, now used for agricultural storage, which, though desecrated, survived Kristallnacht because it was too close to other buildings.

Our last stopover was in the small town of Neidenstein, the birthplace of Bea's mother. It, too, was a beautifully maintained and quaint community and relatively untouched by incompatible modern construction. The mayor, a young man of 37, dressed in a starched white shirt, was waiting for our arrival in the square outside the townhall. Soon a small crowd gathered, and some women were busy trying to identify Bea's relatives from pictures she had brought along. Led by the mayor and the owner of the town's inn, we were shown where Bea's mother had lived with her family, the house of the kosher butcher, the first residence of her parents after they married and where her brother Bert was born, and the synagogue that was desecrated in Nazi times but not torched because of its proximity to neighboring buildings. My father-in-law conducted services there when officiating in his first cantorial position before World War I. Since 1938, it has been used for storage. We could still see the outlines of the bricked-in large arched windows on the side of the building. After the local innkeeper, who was in mourning for her father, opened her restaurant just for us to serve lunch, the mayor showed us the way to the Jewish cemetery, where Leslie was able to locate the grave of Bea's maternal grandmother. Typically, it was again a quiet woody setting, and the site was in good order. We had touched our families' past, and now it was time to return to Konstanz and then back to America, to the present time.

Once home, I received correspondence from residents of Suhl, including a letter from one of my Mittleschule classmates, who could not understand why I refer to Suhl as the town of my birth rather than as my "Heimat" or hometown. I tried to explain why I considered Livingston, New Jersey, U.S.A. – a place that has welcomed me and my family, where I have lived for over 40 wonderful years, where our children grew up – as my semantic and emotional hometown. A letter also arrived from a cultured, well-educated woman whom I met briefly after the exhibit dedication ceremony. A confessed Christian and knowledgeable theologian, she asked me a number of questions about the Jews' perception of themselves as a chosen people, wondering whether that sense of being specially loved by God may have contributed to others' hatred. I explained the historical significance of the term – at the time of Sinai, there were no alternative monotheistic religions – and the Jews' sense of wanting, therefore, to be a light to all nations. And I added my belief that the defamation and persecution of Jews was primarily caused by the upbringing of descendants, noting that in the well known American operetta *South*

Pacific, there is a song that expresses this with clarity: "You have to be taught to hate, you have to be carefully taught."

This lady also postulated, that a quarrel between two individuals can only be reconciled by forgetting and forgiving. Furthermore, for a Jew to repeatedly holding up a mirror in front of other eyes would result in the other one to question the Jew's own reflection. If the postulated analogy was intended to represent the Jewish and German people, then one can only expect a reconciliation generations after the Nazi period. In fact, the concept of a "quarrel" in this case of perpetrator and victim seems inapplicable. Today's Jews as well as today's humanity have no right to forgive for the murder of millions of victims and these martyrs are forever silent.Furthermore,the Nazi crimes cannot be shifted into the shoes of the progeny of the German perpetrators. These succeeding generations have no responsibility for the mass murder, although it is of utmost importance to learn from this horrendous history and confront the past with honesty. To forget in order to achieve reconciliation would be unconscionable. The memory gap of the world has unfortunately resulted in repetition of mistakes, wars, and atrocities. We do not need to hold up that mirror for each other; it is only required to examine the reflection of the past, of the history of humanity which is a mirror for all of us.

As a direct result of our trip, and particularly to the town of my birth, I have established a number of valuable contacts with people who instill confidence for the future, the progeny of the perpetrators who, as beings of conscience, have their own burden to bear. Hopefully, people such as these will succeed to develop future generations who are dedicated to human decency and justice for all.

STILL IN THE SECOND MILLENNIUM

When I was a young man, I once did some mental gymnastics trying to visualize my possible life experiences for each decade of the twentieth century. Without too much difficulty, I could postulate various milestones along the projected way such as those identified by family and career events. However, when I attempted to think of the final decade of the second millennium, my imagination blanked because I would be "too old".

Bea frequently explains human reactions with: "if it isn't logical, it's psychological". How mistaken I was not to continue this mental exercise. But it is easier to look back than to project ahead.

Reunion

Soon after our return from Germany, I gave a lecture on my Holocaust experiences at Lafayette College and encountered someone from my past. Just before I was to begin my talk in the school's chapel, an older man approached me: "You were a member of the 288th Field Artillery Observation Battalion Battery A, and so was I. I remember you." Not being able to reciprocate the recognition, I begged off to start the lecture. For more than half a century, I had not been in touch with any of my wartime buddies. Here, out of the blue, contact had been reestablished. I spoke with Mel Friedman after the program. He had recognized my name from the flyer advertising the talk and informed me of the existence of a small alumni of my wartime outfit. It did not take long for mail to arrive from several individuals, all urging my participation at the next reunion. At first, I was hesitant to consider seriously such an excursion in addition to all my other activities. What finally convinced me to say yes for a fall 1997 gathering at the Ozark Folk Center in Arkansas was an invitation to participate in the program: "Now this is where you come in if you come and are agreeable to it. You could give us a talk on the Holocaust in the conference center room. So, old buddy, how about it?"

In the fall of 1997, after stopping in Nashville, Tennessee, to spend a few quality days as guests of our old friends Peter and Marion Katz, we traveled to the picturesque area of Mountainview, north of Little Rock, Arkansas. There we spent a few precious days in the Ozark Folk Center with the remnants of my World War II outfit, the 288th Field Artillery Observation Battalion (primarily Battery A). These men and their spouses had previously met biennially in other locations. Bea and I did not know what to expect, but we were delighted by the experience. The place and its surroundings were rustic and charming. The state-managed Folk Center is a well run facility dedicated to preserving the heritage and way of life of the Ozark Mountain people. We were entertained with mountain music and met those who still actively pursue various pioneering skills and crafts.

Surrounded by the lovely Ozark National Forest, we were in an ideal setting for our reunion. I was the only member of my former sound survey section to participate. Although I was not able to recognize most faces nor recall most names of the eight old buddies who attended, I was bound to them by the common memories of U.S. military life and combat duty with Patton's Third Army. The jovial and the sad, the challenging and the dangerous, the miserable and the surviving were all intertwined in our seemingly endless recollections. Nostalgia and gratitude permeated our every conversations. Bea observed that it was fascinating to hear about various wartime events from other people's mouths that only I had related to her during the past 50 years. During one of the evenings, I spoke to the group at some length about my Holocaust experiences. I certainly had their full attention and appreciated their questions and sensitivity. We made some new friends during these few days and found ourselves looking forward to the opportunity of meeting again in two years.

Visitors from Germany

That summer, we were pleased to host in our Livingston home the Holger Uske family from Suhl. Holger, who holds a key position in Suhl's city government, is a talented and sensitive poet, and his wife and two teenaged sons were a pleasure to get to know. While in America, the Uskes visited our nation's Capitol and spent a few hours in the Holocaust Memorial Museum. There, while pausing in one of those typical railroad cars used for the mass deportation of Jews, Holger experienced the most poignant moment of his journey. With his permission, I offer a translation of the poem he wrote in response:

> Inside the cattle car
> With its weathered wood
> The traces of deportation
> The stagnant air
> yet still. And intense
> This scent
> Of German machine oil. . .

Both in Suhl and in the aftermath of the visit, I was aware of how important it is to talk with one another across borders, oceans, and generations, and to continue to build bridges between us.

My Operation

Shortly after returning from the Arkansas reunion, I was troubled by some pains on the right side of my back. These seemed to be aggravated when I attempted to take deep breaths. Thus, I "explained" to Dr. Gillette, my dedicated general practitioner, that I must be afflicted with a lung problem. He quickly determined that my medical conclusion was mistaken and instead informed me that my heart was misbehaving with mitral fibrillations. Since my youth in Germany, I had a damaged heart valve, a defect that was most likely caused by scarlet fever.

After getting further information from a battery of tests and confirmation from two cardiologists, we made arrangements for a mitral valve operation at the New York University Medical Center. Inaction on my part, i.e. ignoring the threatening heart condition, would have resulted in my incapacitation within a year. A prominent heart surgeon confirmed the diagnosis of Dr. Arthur Fox, the Center's senior cardiologist: that the valve could be repaired by him rather than replaced. This represented the more favorable procedure in terms of mortality statistics.

Dr. Colvin , the chief of cardiothoracic surgery at NYU Medical Center, is one of the leaders in the development of minimum invasive cardiac surgery and is widely recognized for his work in mitral valve

reconstruction. Instead of resorting to standard heart surgery technique which requires exposure of the heart and its vessels through
median sternotomy, one of the most invasive and traumatic aspects
of open chest surgery, a minimum invasive approach is now utilized
by Dr. Colvin and some other surgeons. This involves the repair or replacement of the mitral valve via a single, small incision between the
ribs on the right side of the chest, also known as port-access procedure. Using specially designed instruments, this minimum invasive
approach provides access to and direct visualization of all vascular
zones and the pertinent internal anatomy. After cardiopulmonary
bypass, the most critical phase of the operation, in my case the mitral
valve repair, is conducted on a protected, briefly motionless heart.

Because of his prominence, Dr. Colvin is sought after by many patients. Therefore, he restricts his clinic appointments to Tuesdays
during the late afternoon and evening hours. We waited with some
impatience from 5 to 9 o'clock, and watched with amazement as the
room became more and more overcrowded and spilled its humanity
of all ages into the adjoining corridor. Repairing pediatric congenital
heart abnormalities is a part of Dr. Colvin's practice; therefore his patients also include babies younger than one year. While awaiting our
turn, more experienced patients told us that these weekly clinic
hours begin, whenever the doctor completes his Tuesday operating
duties and often end well after midnight. When we finally saw him,
he was most cordial. But it soon became obvious that he is a driven
man, working to the maximum on the repair of his fellow human beings. When scanning my completed questionnaire, he was intrigued
by my involvement in the aerospace profession. He was well acquainted with the Geo Positioning System (GPS), which uses satellites to very accurately determine any location on the earth's surface.
Since I had worked on the design and development of satellites for
this navigation system, the enthusiastic doctor sidetracked the conversation to this area until I diplomatically brought us back to the
main topic: my impending operation. Some weeks later, I sent Dr.
Colvin brief descriptions of some of the patents issued to me during
my career. He was very reassuring that my heart would be successfully repaired via the relatively new "minimum invasive" technique,
and was not concerned about any risks during the six week wait until
surgery, a delay imposed by his crowded schedule. I had little or no
anxiety during that hiatus, and looked forward to the operation with
considerable confidence and curiosity.

Preceding the operation by one day, on February 3, 1998, I underwent a coronary arteriography, also known as an angiogram catherization, an invasive procedure which also had been conducted ten years prior for exploratory purposes. Dr. Colvin's medical report indicated, that "this very nice 73 year old gentleman" had severe mitral (valve) insufficiency, a very large atrium(chamber), atrial fibrillation, a large circumflex vessel, an enlarged heart, and a small abdominal aneurysm. Most of our immediate family had gathered to give me their support with their presence and love. It was reassuring to see our three children, our son in law Dick, and our good friend Richard Katz. Bea had made arrangements for room accommodations in an NYU facility directly across the street from the medical center

When I was being wheeled into the operating room, I realized that only a brief window of time would be available before the anesthetist would terminate my sightseeing opportunity. So I was busy peeking! This large room was filled with sophisticated equipment, which covered every square inch of ceiling and wall space as well as most of the floor. The entire facility looked more like a complex laboratory than an operating room. But I, as the patient, was lying there center stage, thus providing the medical imprint. With the words of the anesthesiologist: " Are you ready? I'll put you now out of our way so that we can get to work", my conscious presence disappeared and the team of ten labored for the next eight hours.

When I regained consciousness, I learned that the operation had succeeded. This was not the first instance that modern medicine and science had restored my health and saved my life. In spite of the lingering effects of the anesthesia, my thoughts were immediately filled with feelings of profound gratitude.

The last third of my three and a half week hospital confinement was dedicated to a most beneficial rehabilitation program. Bea remained near me during during almost my entire stay. On a few occasions, I was transported by wheelchair to the hospital's greenhouse, where I not only admired the well cared for plants but also engaged some hands on horticulture. Especially in my my case that represented excellent therapy. Finally, I was released to complete my recuperation at home. I expected that only a couple of weeks would be required for full recovery and thus was surprised and somewhat disappointed that this process stretched out into a twelve week obstacle course. Side effects such as insomnia, lack of appetite, and breathing difficulties because of substantial fluid accumulation around the lung all made life a little trying. My three physicians, the general practitioner, the cardiologist and the surgeon diligently monitored my condition and attempted to independently alleviate my post operative problems and side effects with various medications. Eventually, this recuperative care was coordinated by Dr Gillette in order to preclude confusion. Everyone agreed, that my repaired heart is now in excellent shape, a fortunate result which really overshadows all the other, mostly temporary, problems. No day passes without expressing gratitude for my survival to our Maker.

Our Miracle Baby

Two years had passed since we celebrated Leslie's wedding to Dick. While the biological clock was ticking towards the end of Leslie's fourth decade, we still harbored hope for an offspring of that union. In November 1997, our daughter cautiously mentioned that she just might be pregnant; this hope was based on the most meager evidence. A short time later, standard tests were positive and, together with the expecting parents, our family was elated beyond words. While sensing and enjoying the growth of new life within her body, Leslie continued with her professional duties till the ninth month of her pregnancy. Considering the age of the parents as well as Leslie's medical history, which included the removal of an ovary and several surgical interventions to correct her kidney function, the idea of a miracle baby from the expectant mother was certainly in place.

Our grandchildren Joanna and Jeremy observed the physical changes of their aunt and future cousin-to-be with great curiosity and thus received an undistorted biology lesson. I recalled how two generations ago my mother prepared me for my sister's arrival with the traditional fabrication of the stork delivery. I was even induced to place sugar on the window sill to attract the bird to our home. Fortunately, we have made progress in explaining the beginning of life to our youngsters. Shortly before the predicted delivery date, I attended two baby showers, my first experience with that secular practice.

While spending a weekend at their recently purchased summer home at the New Jersey shore, Leslie and Dick had to rush back to the hospital for the birth process was at hand. Douglas was born on the first day of summer and received the middle name Bravmann in honor of Bea's family. Our practice of passing on the paternal family

Our five grandchildren with Leslie's dog Cassidy in spring 1999, L. to R.: Joshua, Jeremy, Mira (on chair), Joanna, and Douglas.

name might make pragmatic sense but it is an insensitive tradition for the mother, who gives birth to new life, to swallow. Thus we were very pleased with the choice of Douglas' parents. I was honored and elated when Leslie asked me to conduct the religious naming ceremony, which is usually performed by a rabbi as part of a Synagogue service. Various family members participated in this initial milestone of our newest grandchild in the midst of joyful relatives and friends who had gathered in Douglas' beautiful home. Bea and I were particularly grateful for this latest family addition, because now each one of our children was blessed with his or her own progeny. Each now had the opportunity to pass our values and traditions from generation to generation, l'dor vador. This is indeed a great privilege and responsibility, and I am so glad that Leslie can have this wonderful experience.

During his first few months, Douglas thrived physically under the diligent nursing care of his mother. I have a lot of confidence that his emotional and intellectual growth will be similarly successful, since he is blessed with such caring and thoughtful parents. Most likely, the normal progression of life will not permit me to personally convey to him his maternal background and the history of our people. Leslie will undoubtedly see to that with sensitivity and wisdom. Hopefully, these writings will also reinforce the bridge to his past.

RETROSPECTION AND REFLECTION

This biography would be incomplete if I neglected to take a retrospective view of my life and some of the events and concepts that had particular impact on my being.

With Gratitude

As I look back on about 75 years that I have walked the path of life, I am filled with deep gratitude. I have survived while traveling near the valley of death, through the uncertainties and earthquakes of humanity, in the presence of the suffering and the murder of millions. Blessed with good fortune on my way, I have been privileged to experience so much of the beauty and the challenge of this journey.

The words of the Hashkiveinu prayer that we recite on Friday evenings, the beginning of the Sabbath, have very profound meaning for me: "Grant, O Eternal God, that we may lie down in peace, and raise us up, O Sovereign, to life renewed. Spread over us the shelter of Your peace; guide us with Your good counsel; and for Your name's sake, be our help. O guard our coming and going, that now and always we have life and peace." Let us never take life and peace for granted.

Chronologically, I think first of my youth and my family, whose love, guidance, and care helped so much to ease my path during the trying period of the thirties. Even under such difficult circumstances, my parents succeeded in creating and maintaining a warm and religious home. Like many of their Jewish contemporaries, my parents did not initially recognize the great danger posed by Nazi Germany, an ominous period when undue delay could have led to almost certain death for each one of us. And yet, once fully alerted to the grave danger, they did their utmost within the limits of possibilities to protect their children and rescue the family. They were little heroes in a huge and tumultuous world, and I will be forever thankful to them for their love and care.

The flight from Nazi Germany to the safety of America's shores was one of the highpoints of my life. Almost as if torn from the grave, I regained my freedom and my future. The significance of this event was more than obvious to me already as a 15-year-old boy, and the appreciation of this fortuitous rescue has been in my conscience throughout my days.

After only a few short years, I was in the U.S. Armed Forces, participating in the monumental struggle to defeat the greatest evil of that time and the history of humankind. My participation in the Second World War gave me considerable satisfaction, for it was not only my obvious duty as a U.S. citizen and my expression of gratitude for giving refuge to my family, but it also resonated with a personal and religious desire to help rescue the remnants of European Jewry. That I was able to survive the dangers of the Second World War, and at that even without sustaining any bodily injury, is included with fervent thanks in my daily prayers.

I learned then that, at best, war is a necessary evil, although heroic and self-sacrificing deeds were performed at times in World War II for the sake of preserving and furthering the humaneness of humanity. War represents a carnage of body and soul. It should never be glorified with the poetry of nationalism and patriotism, it should never be glamorized by the desire for adventurism; it may only be considered as an option if all else fails.

The U.S.A. is deservedly known as the land of opportunity, so dramatically demonstrated millions of times by the success of its immigrants. The prerequisite to progress is primarily the willingness and motivation to labor with mind and body. Although prejudice still exists to this day and family background tilts the playing field, the American experience has demonstrated again and again that one can rise from obscurity and poverty to a successful and fulfilling life. In this sense, I have no doubt that I would have carried out my postwar studies even if the generous GI Bill of Rights provisions for veterans would not have been in place. Together with many others, I would have opted to pursue my college education for eight or more years at night while supporting myself with a daytime job. My uncle Max Frank followed such a course in the twenties, so why couldn't I emulate his good example? I was fortunate to be blessed with good

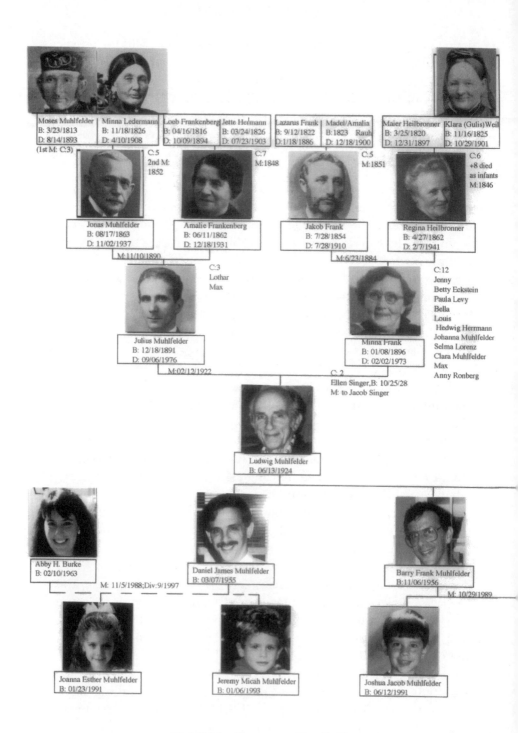

Muhlfelder-Bravmann Family Tree

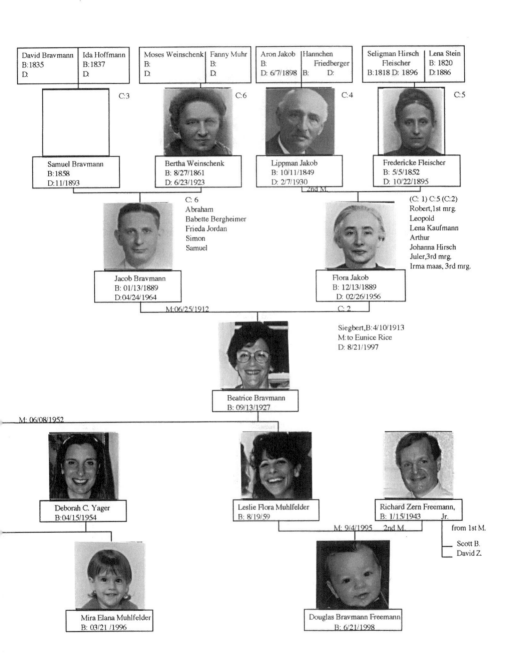

| David Bravmann B:1835 D: | Ida Hoffmann B:1837 D: | | Moses Weinschenk B: D: | Fanny Muhr B: D: | | Aron Jakob B: D: 6/7/1898 | Hannchen Friedberger B: D: | | Seligman Hirsch Fleischer B:1818 D: 1896 | Lena Stein B: 1820 D:1886 |

C:3

C:6

C:4

C:5

Samuel Bravmann
B:1858
D:11/1893

Bertha Weinschenk
B: 8/27/1861
D: 6/23/1923

Lippman Jakob
B: 10/11/1849
D: 2/7/1930
2nd M.

Fredericke Fleischer
B: 5/5/1852
D: 10/22/1895

C: 6
Abraham
Babette Bergheimer
Frieda Jordan
Simon
Samuel

(C: 1) C:5 (C:2)
Robert,1st mrg.
Leopold
Lena Kaufmann
Arthur
Johanna Hirsch
Juler,3rd mrg.
Irma maas, 3rd mrg.

Jacob Bravmann
B: 01/13/1889
D:04/24/1964

Flora Jakob
B: 12/13/1889
D: 02/26/1956

M:06/25/1912

C: 2

Siegbert,B:4/10/1913
M:to Eunice Rice
D: 8/21/1997

Beatrice Bravmann
B: 09/13/1927

M: 06/08/1952

Deborah C. Yager
B:04/15/1954

Leslie Flora Muhlfelder
B: 8/19/59

Richard Zern Freemann,
B: 1/15/1943   Jr.

M: 9/4/1995   2nd M.

from 1st M.

Scott B.
David Z.

Mira Elana Muhlfelder
B: 03/21 /1996

Douglas Bravmann Freemann
B: 6/21/1998

health and to have chosen a career that satisfied and challenged me for so many years. I was privileged to participate in the development of the modern space age, a fascinating and demanding field, and even in my early seventies still enjoyed being active as a part-time consultant. The material reward for one's labors, although important, is insufficient for leading a meaningful and satisfying life. In spite of the normal obstacles and disappointments, my work also provided me with a sense of accomplishment and satisfaction.

My Bea, My Family, My People

For special occasions such as milestone birthdays and anniversaries, I have been moved to express my feelings in a poetic way. When we observed Bea's 50th, the following stanza was included in my presentation:

> So much accomplished in these years
> So many Simchas and some tears
> Your spirit, looks and heart are young
> You're precious, Dear, just number One.

Even with all the rewards of my professional career, my life would have been empty, lonely, and unfulfilled without walking this path with my Bea, my dear wife, the dedicated and loving mother of our children, my best friend and sacred partner. It might be wrong and ungrateful to apply relative measures to the components of life, and this is particularly so for a survivor of the Holocaust, but I cannot visualize the goals, the content, and the very core of my existence without Bea. As long as I breathe, think, and feel, I thank my God for the love of this so very special woman, the heart and soul of our family and of our Jewish home.

From this union came three wonderful and loving children, beings with good hearts and unshakable determination, who mark their years with character, responsibility, and ambition. They are aware, both from their own experience and that of our family's history, how precious and fragile our lives are. Thus, they measure their days and years while living in their own homes and walking on their own paths together with their families. Their precious children are our link to the future, theirs and ours.

During the passage of my decades, I was generally blessed with good health. There were a few exceptions when I was struck by serious illness, but with God's help and the miracles of medical science I fully recuperated from each interlude. The medical field has made tremendous strides in my lifetime, and for this reason alone I consider it ludicrous to yearn for "the good old times." Nostalgia cannot be permitted to distort the truth that I would not have survived the diseases that invaded my body, that I would not be able after more than three score and 10 years to write of my experiences and impressions.

Particularly during the last 35 years, I have had many opportunities to contribute to the functioning and leadership of my congregation and the Reform Jewish community. This participation was only possible because of the help and empathy of my dear wife. Thus I was not only able to serve our Temple Emanu-El as president and in many other capacities, but I could also devote my efforts in support of liberal Judaism, the Union of American Hebrew Congregations, both on a regional and national basis. As a survivor of the Shoah, there is for me no alternative, a principle expressed so eloquently by Hillel ages ago: "If I am not for myself, who will be for me? But if I am only for myself, what am I? And if not now, when?"

The Struggle For Justice

Following the termination of the World War II, much effort was expended in our country and a good part of the Western world on the expansion and the enhancement of human rights. In particular, the civil and economic rights of minorities and of women have received considerable attention. The progress attained in those areas did not just derive from the goodness of the human heart but had to be fought for and sometimes even died for in a multitude of struggles during the last half century. Considerable advancement has been achieved in the struggle for justice and equality, especially for the descendants of America's African slaves. Much of the initial impetuous for these direly-required repairs to our democratic fabric are directly traceable to an inspiring black minister, the great Dr. Martin Luther King. His struggle to alleviate the disadvantage and discrimination of Afro-Americans was carried out within the confines of peaceful protests and with the power of eloquent words. Many others, including the churches and synagogues of America, helped to further these objectives, but this inspired man was the pinnacle. As the result of that effort, our government became more responsive, our population became more sensitive, and various other minorities became co-beneficiaries. The struggle for justice, the fight for decency and equality was and still is essential to the enhancement and survival of the American soul. Wherever injustice exists, wherever might attempts to squelch right, we cannot and should not be silent onlookers.

The equal treatment of women in the areas of commerce, education, and government has also made significant headway. Not only has the opening of doors and opportunities benefited the well-being of our country, but the bell of democracy has now attained a truer sound. Much has been accomplished, but much remains to be done. Our country and this world are still plagued by the curses of prejudice, discrimination, injustice, and xenophobia. There is no dearth of forces that desire to turn back the clock. We have to be ever-vigilant and determined, and that "we" is here particularly addressed to future generations. Unfortunately, many of the disadvantaged of our country still do not choose to participate in the elective process, thus abrogating their rights and leaving decisions to those who might have other priorities. Further educational efforts will, I hope, alleviate this problem and thereby strengthen our democratic structure.

Modern Technology

One of the most striking spheres of progress identified with this century is the phenomenal development of modern technology. The evolution and revolution in such fields as communication, computers, biological and nuclear science, automation and transportation have left us breathless and bequeathed to the world a precious legacy as well as a multitude of new problems. Our political and social insights and resolves have frequently not kept pace with our scientific leaps. I was fortunate and privileged to participate in the astrospace component of these fantastic developments. Many aspects of this technical revolution led to greater efficiency and relief of human toil, an improved standard of living and quality of life, healthier bodies and greater longevity, and last but not least, vastly enhanced educational tools. These notable accomplishments, primarily identified with the past 50 years, are a dramatic demonstration of the benefits derived from the peaceful striving of humanity. I say this in spite of the military impetus underlying some of these developments. Hopefully we, as God's partners, will continue to strive to improve and heal the world and thereby remove the sicknesses of body and soul that still threaten and plague us at the end of the 20th century.

Materialism

The striving for the improvement of one's earthly comfort is a natural and beneficial desire. As in all other areas of the human endeavor, excesses tend to be destructive, and more often than not self-destructive. It seems that with the decline of organized religion of the western world, the gods of materialism have become ever more popular and powerful. Humankind demands immediate satisfaction and compensation, and the inflation of this desire appears to have no sensible bounds. This chase for the ever more, this insatiable hunger for the attainment of excessive materialistic goals so often leads to greed, dishonesty, and criminality in the realm of human affairs. Consequently, our descendants will have to pay in their tomorrows for our excesses of today. This includes the abuse of planet earth, the rape and destruction of our environment. The ever-escalating excesses of materialism lead to a distorted view of the purpose of our very being. The human family of the 20th century and probably beyond are witnessing not only the deterioration of our ethical striving but also the corruption of our governments, even sports, the morality of honest work, and possibly the ideals espoused by religion itself. Materialistic success has become for too many their idol, relegating religion and God to secondary if not trivial importance. We have created our modern "Golden Calf."

A tremendous danger, directly traceable to these excesses, is the abusive use of narcotics, including the nicotine of cigarettes, and even more so the utterly destructive hard drugs. The growth, manufacture, and distribution of these harmful substances has a direct link to greed. Thus, unbridled materialism destroys not only the basic decency of human interaction but also millions of human lives. To reduce if not eliminate this tragic madness requires not only major educational initiatives but also the pro-active cooperation of all countries of this little globe. The nations of the world truly have to unite in order to eliminate the international criminality that greedily furthers this curse.

Greed appears also to be at the root the continually increasing divergence between the haves and the have-nots. Throughout the ages of human history, there were always those who were endowed with considerable material comfort and those who struggled to barely stay alive. The twentieth century with its scientific innovations has opened up the possibility not only to provide adequate food and shelter for all human beings, but also health and education for all of God's children. However, many of those who live in the darkness of despotism, ignorance and filth have yet to reap the potential benefits of our modern society. Their "living" continues to become ever more removed from those known as the well-to-do. This divergence is an unhealthy phenomena and could, with the passage of time, become a danger to all. The economic playing field does not have to be completely level, but if it becomes ever more inclined, it could have dire consequences for our world.

While considering the topic of materialistic excesses, I am also reminded of the deterioration of our large cities. Unfortunately, the ever-mushrooming urban sprawl tends to lead to the dehumanization and degeneration of the indigenous population. There is no easy or simple solution for the geometric population explosion of the world and the problems that derive therefrom. Intense education of modern birth control methods would and does help, but even so growth continues, albeit at a somewhat reduced rate. A utopian notion to raise our younger generation primarily in smaller towns is incompatible with the need of the masses to reach their place of employment with affordable transportation, a feature provided only within our large cities. Thus, particularly those on the lowest rung of the economic ladder are relegated to live in marginal and over-crowded urban environments that are often infested with hopelessness, narcotics and crime. Notwithstanding repeated notable efforts of recent decades to improve their lot, generation after generation is submerged in the same squalor. The priorities of our government and our commerce are mostly directed elsewhere, and the country as a whole is the poorer for it. To substantially alleviate this ingrained situation requires leadership with character, resoluteness, and creativity; it requires people in and out of government who selflessly give a damn for the sake of a better future.

The above remarks on the dire consequences of the broad area of materialistic excesses should not leave us with a sense of despair and depression. Rather, if we recognize our shortcomings as individuals and as a society, there will always be an opportunity and a challenge to mend our ways and repair our world. This age-old concept, known to Jews as Tikkun Olam, should be the mission of our entire human family.

In a D'var Torah, a commentary on the week's Torah portion, in this case "Ki Tissa" from the book of Exodus, the story of the golden calf, I closed with these words when addressing the UAHC Regional Board in January of 1994:

The golden calf is all around us, and we find it difficult to prevent being contaminated by its presence. And yet, *we* who are the descendants of those who gathered at Mount Horeb, *we* who are to be a light to the nations, *we* who are espousing ethical Judaism as liberal and enlightened Jews, *we* must resist the materialistic excesses of our time and adhere to the basics of our Torah. We will not receive a third set of Tablets. The future is in our hands.

Our Social Fabric

One of the saddest post World War II phenomena is the destabilization of the family structure. Children need a sound and fertile soil for growth and development, otherwise the succession of generations will follow a downhill path. Without question, marriage, morals, and responsibilities have to be taken much more seriously. If not, then we and certainly our descendants will have to pay a dear price, an ever-diminishing quality of life and moral fiber.

Our children and grandchildren grow into a world that seems to know no limits of decency and behavior, a world that is intoxicated with possessions, violence, and sex. We are being overwhelmed by a hedonistic atmosphere which threatens to choke off the basic moral quest of our society and is an affront to the fundamental guidelines of all religions. Our children and children's children are at great risk to become the victims of this world without limits and without direction. I have always maintained that we cannot expect to receive our moral guidelines from Washington or Moscow, from the politics of nations or the board rooms of corporations. People of decency and good will have to cut through all this confusion and permissiveness and work within their families, communities and religious bodies to counteract the destructive excesses of our time. We have to approach this with tact, with patience, and with determination, for should we fail then our progeny will suffer severe damage in body and soul and sink ever deeper into the hedonistic abyss.

The development of the two-income family has had both beneficial and detrimental by-products. Inability to keep up with basic needs or ever greater desire for materialistic attainments was and still is a driving impetus for this trend. Greater equality for women and their consequential participation in the workforce certainly represents a positive factor here. However, such benefits do not come without a price. When both parents are fully employed, the caring and sheltering home, which is so desirable if not essential for the development of our children, is significantly diminished and stressed. Surrogates are not a complete and optimum substitute for parenting, and older children are often left to their own devices during after-school hours, with detrimental results. I was always most appreciative that Bea was able to devote herself completely to the care and upbringing of our children, a task that she accomplished with great love and dedication. We were able to manage on just one salary, an arrangement no longer feasible for many current families of modest income. For many middle-class families, however, there is a choice to be made between greater family income and greater care for the children, especially the younger ones. Nothing comes without a price, and in this case the youngest generation is frequently penalized by the diminished quality of the home environment. At times, work is even utilized as a substitute for home. I recall when, already in my Curtiss-Wright days in the fifties, some colleagues habitually worked long hours, including many weekends, at the expense of their family time. I commented repeatedly to Bea that such priorities must have detrimental effects at home. One's occupation should provide satisfaction, and mine certainly did, but the essential home environment should not be sacrificed to upside-down priorities. Throughout my professional career, my guideline was that I work to live, not live to work. Of course, there were occasional exceptions due to emergencies, proposal deadlines, and satellite launches, but I never permitted these exceptions to become a habit.

The pervasive breakdown and breakup of families, the apparently ever-increasing divorce rate, is a sad barometer of our social fabric. One cannot expect all marriages to succeed. But if, as has been the case in more recent decades, approximately half of these unions end in divorce, then the traditional approach tends to become anachronistic, with either the informal "living together" or the complexities of second marriages taking its place as time moves on. Marriage, which often has its beginning in an intoxicating romantic climate, has to be given a chance to mature as we pass through our life span. Bea and I view our union as a 60:40 proposition: 60% for my spouse, 40% for me. There has to be an overlap of feeling and giving; otherwise, the initial bond, enhanced by romance, will not stand the test of time. Again, Hillel's admonition comes to mind: "If I am only for myself." From my perspective, the rewards of such a lifelong bond, walking hand-in-hand through sunshine and rain, is worth all the effort and reciprocity one can muster.

The Shoah, Israel, and God

"Shoah" is a Hebrew word that stands for a severe storm, a cyclone of destruction. It has been applied to the murder of the six million Jews by Nazi Germany and its European cohorts during World War II. "Holocaust," the commonly utilized word for this cataclysmic period, derives from the Greek and, despite a lack of accuracy, has been widely accepted to connote this event and the Nazi years that led up to it. I experienced only the rise of Nazism in the thirties and the defeat of this evil by my participation in World War II. Thus, my reactions and reflections to these tragic times are based not exclusively on personal experience but also on historical evidence and the testimonies of survivors, perpetrators, and rescuers.

Thus, in the spirit of the 19th century Danish philosopher Kierkegaard, who stated that "Life must be lived forward, but can only be understood backward," let me reflect on the night of horror, the Shoah. In the entrance hall of the "Bet Hatefutsoth," the Diaspora museum in Tel Aviv, I saw the following inscription when I visited there in the seventies:

> In the year one thousand nine hundred and thirty-three of the Christian era, Adolf Hitler came to power in Germany. In his time the Germans and their accomplices murdered six million Jews, among them one-and-a-half million Jewish Children. Imprisoned in the ghettos, the victims fought desperately for their lives while the world stood by in silence.

Thus, we are confronted here by the relentless persecution and murder of a people, my people, and the action or rather the inaction of the onlookers.

So as not to be misunderstood, we are all aware of and appalled that five million civilian non-Jews were also murdered by the Nazi perpetrators during this time. Amongst these were the Gypsies, the mentally or physically handicapped, and the Communists. In addition, there was a multitude of non-Jewish victims who chose, primarily in Nazi occupied lands, to resist or disobey Germany's brutal laws and measures. These valiant and courageous human beings put their lives on the line in defense of humanity. Had they opted to be passive, they would most likely have survived.

Jews, on the other hand, had no choice. All of them were targeted to die because they were born of Jewish parents. Here, I quote the eminent Holocaust author, scholar, and Nobel Peace prize laureate Elie Wiesel: "It is true that not all victims were Jews, but all Jews were victims." On one hand, the Holocaust was a genocide like a number of others, a moral depravity that resulted in the mass murder of human beings. On the other hand, it differed from other such tragedies because here the Nazi murderers aimed to wipe out a group, in this case a religious group, in its entirety. All Jews, independent of age, nationality, or background, were identified in the Nazi ideology as racially evil and part of the irrational concept of "International Jewry," a group that had to be eliminated like vermin. There was no territory to be captured, no armed adversary to be defeated; there was an exclusive ideological objective to annihilate all men, women, and children of a specific religious group in a premeditated program of degradation, isolation, and death. Just as any other sensitive human being, I harbor great compassion for all genocide victims, but the Shoah, the murder of two-thirds of European Jewry, is a nightmare that will not pass, a wound that will not heal, a mourning that will not stop. For me, it stands alone and separate in the annals of man's cruelty towards man.

I have asked myself these unanswerable questions so many times: Why was I so fortunate to see the Statue of Liberty in New York harbor? Why did six million of my brothers and sisters perish and I survived? Why do I still live today and they lie in unmarked graves or have no final resting place at all? Why were people such as Bea and I granted the privilege to live, a chance denied those millions of innocent victims?

The perpetrators of the Holocaust can never be forgiven. We have no right to speak for the victims, and those who were slaughtered remain mute. Our task is Zachor, to remember, and Lo Tishtach, never to forget; for to do otherwise would represent killing our dead a second time. After being murdered and incinerated by the Nazis, we would be guilty of eradicating the memory of these millions of innocent lives. That is why Yom Hashoah is such an important day in the modern Jewish calendar. Our congregants are annually given the opportunity to light a yellow candle in memory of all those souls cut short during the Shoah, for the millions of "candles" whose lives were extinguished prematurely. Such a recalling and reminder should not just be exclusively a matter of Jewish concern, for the lessons to be learned and the past to be confronted are at least as pertinent, if not more so, to non-Jews as they are to the remnants of the "children of Israel." In fact, some Yom Hashoah observances have been conducted in recent years by churches and secular organizations in addition to those by the nation of Israel and the Jewish Diaspora.

Beyond this memory, it is essential to prevent the ever-present obscene attempts of evil or sick minds to revise the history of this cataclysmic event. That is one of the reasons why I, as a survivor, write these memoirs. That is why the work of Steven Spielberg's Shoah Foundation and similar, though more modest efforts dedicated to videotaping the testimony of thousands of witnesses, including my own, are such essential missions. That is why the efforts of my friend Roy Wiehn and others like him, the authors and editors and catalysts of Holocaust literature, deserve our special and sincere gratitude.

While the Holocaust is primarily a Jewish memory, it represents a non-Jewish problem. The Nazi German perpetrators were not Jewish, and the world that stood by in silence was not Jewish either. How should such a problem be confronted? Which approach would be of greatest benefit to humanity? Whatever has been said or done since 1945, whatever will take place in the future with respect to facing the Holocaust history, the fundamental and underlying principle should always be one of honest confrontation to derive maximum benefit from lessons learned. Thus, today's generations of Germans, the descendants of the perpetrators, cannot be held responsible for the gruesome deeds of the Nazi period. What I expect, however, from today's Germans and Austrians is to look at the history of their parents' and grandparents' generation with an unshakable desire for the truth, where neither blurred vision nor distorted rationalizations get in the way, to learn from the past so as to build a better future. They, more than anyone else, must fervently wish that such a tragedy will never soil the human soul again.

Much publicity has been given to the 85 billion mark restitution paid by (West) Germany during the past 50 years. Individual survivors and the State of Israel have benefited from this humane gesture. Even Bea and I received many years ago a payment of $2,000 each, in this case for our interrupted education. Obviously, no one has the ability to compensate materially for the destruction of families and communities, for expropriations, for incarcerations, for untold suffering, and certainly not for the murder of six million Jews. But the gesture was made in good faith although the past cannot be erased. More important than the monetary restitution is the sincere attempt of today's Germany to educate its children to become fair minded citizens of the world, seeking peace and justice for all human beings. It is significant that there are currently only two nations on our globe that have mandated the teaching of Holocaust history in their schools: one is Israel, the descendants of the victims, and the other is Germany, the descendants of the perpetrators. I have no illusions that the Germany and Austria of today have essentially shed the curse of racism, prejudice, hate, and xenophobia, but neither have so many other countries.

The post-Holocaust Nuremberg trials, which were conducted by an international tribunal from 1945 to 1949 of about 220 of the most prominent Nazis and resulted in the execution or imprisonment of most of that elite group, were certainly a necessary act of justice for the human family. But what happened to the hundreds of thousands of perpetrators who operated below this top leadership at intermediate and lower levels? The history of the so-called de-Nazification program is a sorry chapter, a shamefully lenient chapter. Only a very small percentage of these murderers and tormentors of millions of innocent people were tried and found guilty. Of the more than ninety thousand perpetrators who were investigated by the West German justice ministry, about ninety percent were not convicted, and only about seven percent were found guilty, most of whom received rather light prison terms. In West Germany, justice had to give way to Cold War expediencies, to the decades of the struggle between the free (western) world led by the United States of America and the totalitarian (eastern) block led by the Soviet Union. The Nazis of the Hitler era became to a large extent the capitalists and democrats of the Federal Republic and thus managed to escape well-deserved punishment for crimes committed against humanity.

The elite of the German scientific community, and in particular those dedicated to the development of the "delivery system" commonly known as rocketry, were welcomed by the United States to play their part on our side in the Cold War. Shortly after the end of the European war, I briefly acted as interpreter in the process to convince a prominent German scientist (whose name I cannot recall) to relocate from Bavaria to the U.S.A. No questions were asked with regard to his past in the Nazi era. Wernher von Braun, the foremost German rocket engineer, who was in charge of developing the rocket-propelled V-2 guided missile, was invited with his technical team to come to the United States shortly after the war's end. Starting in 1944, these V-2 rockets were most effective in devastating British cities. After transferring to the United States, von Braun became the director of the George C. Marshall Space Flight Center at Huntsville, Alabama, and contributed immeasurably to the success of the U.S. rocket and space programs. Under the Hitler regime in Germany, he was a member of the Nazi party and an officer in the notorious SS. Apparently, it was expedient for our authorities to overlook his background in view of his scientific expertise.

The Communist regime of East Germany, known by the misnomer "German Democratic Republic," was not as expedient as the west and displayed somewhat more determination in its pursuit and punishment of the Nazi criminals. Even so, many of the "eastern" Holocaust perpetrators became part of the totalitarian power structure; "good" Nazis of yesterday converted into "good" Communists of the postwar era.

In 1985, German Chancellor Helmut Kohl and American President Ronald Reagan chose to visit Bitburg, where members of the notorious Waffen SS (elite storm troopers) are buried. Visiting that place and thereby honoring those who were the epitome of terror and murder during Nazi times was a conscious act to bury the Holocaust symbolically, to sweep it under the carpet. I say "conscious" with deliberate care because of the uproar prior to that visit by many sensitive and responsible people, including this direct appeal by Elie Wiesel to the President, but to no avail: "That place, Mr. President, is not your place; your place is with the victims of the SS." Such a historical revision, or even just the crude attempt in that direction, was not only a gross injustice towards the millions of victims but was also very damaging to the striving of all decent people who yearn to attain a peaceful, a just, and a humane future.

Much has been researched and written and said somehow to explain this tragedy. What was the motivation for the Nazis to murder a multitude of innocent men, women, and children? How could cultured and enlightened countries like Germany and Austria, the countries of Bach, Beethoven, and Schubert, of Goethe and Schiller, descend to such depth of depravity? What happened to the fundamental Christian ethic of love that was espoused by these populations for centuries? What happened to the Judaic roots on which this Christian faith is based? How could a nation like "Greater Germany" have made mass murder its national mission? These are questions with which many human beings of conscience have struggled for decades.

How to understand the incomprehensible, how to explain the utterly inhuman and still preserve a thread of human hopes and dreams? A recent book by a young Harvard professor comes closest, in my judgment, to addressing some of these fundamental questions. Daniel Jonas Goldhagen traces in his milestone work, *Hitler's Willing Executioners, Ordinary Germans and the Holocaust*, the development and penetration of anti-Semitism into the minds and sinews of the German masses, a process that reaches back for centuries. For example, Martin Luther, the prominent German religious revolutionary and Protestant reformer of the 16th century, stated:

"Besides all this you still have the Jews, who do great evil in the land. If they could kill us all, they would gladly do so, aye, and often do it, especially those who profess to be physicians. . . . I say to you lastly, as a countryman, if the Jews refuse to be converted, we ought not to suffer them or bear with them any longer. . . . What shall we Christians do with this rejected and condemned people, the Jews? . . . I shall give you my advice. First, set afire their synagogues or schools. Second, their houses should also be razed and destroyed. Third, all their prayer books and talmudic writings should be taken from them. Fourth, their rabbis should be forbidden to teach. Fifth, safe-conduct on the highways should be abolished completely for Jews." (from his treatise: "On the Jews and their lies")

In the nineteenth century, the prominent and revered German composer Richard Wagner stated with conviction:

The Jew is the graphic demon of the decay of humanity (A. Rosenberg, *Die Protokolle der Weisen von Zion*, 1933) and

Only one thing can redeem you from the burden of your curse - annihilation.

In subsequent centuries, the church aimed not to kill the Jews but to convert them to Christianity by bribery of social acceptance or by threats and intimidation. Pervasive prejudice convinced a not insignificant number of Jews, especially those of larger cities, to become acculturated into their western environment, thus opening doors to success in their careers and social standing. These Jews did usually not convert because of religious conviction but because of pragmatic convenience, thus soiling the faith they left and the faith they entered. They sold their souls for the sake of secular salvation.

Although promulgated and catalyzed by the age-old deicide charge of the collective Jewish guilt for Jesus' death, an accusation finally repudiated in the post-Holocaust period by the Second Vatican Council in its famous "Nostra Aetate" proclamation, anti-Semitism evolved into other self-serving forms. Thus, Jews were accused of being responsible for a multitude of problems and calamities that plagued either humanity in general or Germans in particular, such as the communist threat, capitalistic exploitation, economic downfalls and unemployment, international intrigue, the loss of World War I, and the curse of criminality. Jews as a group, with their diligence and work ethic, with their thirst for education and resulting intellect, were seen as undesirable introducers within the social, economic, industrial, and academic spheres of the nation. Thus, discrimination served the dual purpose of 1) relegating them to less desirable occupations and an isolated section of society, and 2) depicting them as evil for their deep-seated religious belief in one indivisible God. In *South Pacific*, there are lyrics that aptly capture this centuries-old poisoning of the masses: "You've got to be taught to hate and fear. You've got to be taught from year to year. You've got to be taught before it's too late, before you are six or seven or eight, to hate all the people your relatives hate. You've got to be carefully taught."

Much more could be or has been said on this subject, but there is adequate evidence that anti-Semitism was well ingrained into the masses long before the rise of Nazism. The observation has been made that antipathy towards the Jewish people was widespread throughout Christian Europe, so why did it assume such monstrous expression by Nazi Germany? Goldhagen demonstrates that the Teutonic land was particularly fertile ground, not because of inherent genetic, ethnic, or national characteristics but because the German minds were poisoned generation after generation with anti-Semitic venom. Finally, in the early years of the fourth decade of the 20th century, the German nation, under a Weimar Republic weakened by political and economic turmoil, elected into leadership a gang of totalitarian degenerates who promised them not only "Arbeit und Brot" ("work and bread") but also world domination and elimination of the Jewish people. In the last free election, 44% of the vote was cast for the Hitler's Nazi party and an additional 8% for the sympathetic Nationalists; the remaining parties were badly splintered, with the Social Democrats obtaining the second largest plurality of 18%. The German people made a choice by killing democracy at the polls. Hitler's book, *Mein Kampf*, already widely available in 1925, and his basic objectives as spread by the media were no secret to the masses. Let me say here with emphasis that not all German citizens were intoxicated with the Nazis' racial and national superiority complex and the savagery to follow, but a large majority of the German population, later joined enthusiastically by that of Austria, gave full endorsement to the objectives and the subsequent actions of their installed Nazi government.

The Holocaust was not merely or exclusively carried out by Adolf Hitler and his elite, not only by the SS guards and brown-shirted stormtroopers, but also by hundreds of thousands of ordinary Germans. To murder six million men, women and children required a major effort of organization, preparation, cooperation, communication, falsification, transportation, and dehumanization. Professor Goldhagen clearly demonstrated in his milestone book that there were no shortages, no lack of willing participants in the annihilation of European Jewry by Nazi Germany. No doubt there were also some brave Germans who did not participate and might even have protested or saved some lives, but these were far too few to make any difference to the final outcome, or in Nazi terminology the "final solution."

Besides these many perpetrators, there was also the world of silent onlookers. Just before the Reverend Martin Luther King delivered his famous "I have a dream" speech at the March on Washington in 1963, Rabbi Joachim Prinz addressed the assembled multitude, including these words: "When I was a rabbi of the Jewish community in Berlin under the Hitler regime, I learned many things. The most important thing that I learned under these tragic circumstances was that bigotry and hatred are not the most urgent problem. The most urgent, the most disgraceful, the most shameful and the most tragic problem is silence."

Who were these onlookers who constituted 'the world that stood by in silence'? Certainly the millions of Germans and Austrians who witnessed the discrimination and persecution of the Jews in their own towns and cities, on their streets and public places, in their media and schools, in their academia and commerce, in the houses next door and those in which they lived. They witnessed boycotts and disenfranchisement, bloodthirsty parades and public meetings, book burnings and synagogue burnings, degradations and brutality, humiliations and arrests, expropriations and deportations. They witnessed all this and remained silent in the face of hate and brutality. Although many became fully aware of the mass murder of the Jewish people only towards the end of the war, anyone living in Germany during the thirties would have had to have been both deaf and blind or an ostrich with the proverbial head in the sand to be unaware of the mushrooming evil rapidly enveloping the country, leading finally to the ominous deportation of all the Jews for "resettlement" without their belongings. With very rare exceptions, their silence over the years was deafening, and their leadership interpreted this silence as consent.

The Holocaust was promulgated not by a few but by the many; it was not the product of a pagan society but that of a Christian society. But how could such a society, based on faith and love, permit the evolution of such a tragedy? What actions did the church take in face of the ever escalating barbarity towards the people of the Old Testament? Without doubt, there were numerous Christian heroes of conscience who swam against the stream and risked their lives to save lives. Many of these have been recognized by Israel's Yad Vashem as the "Righteous Among the Nations." However, these courageous deeds do not exonerate the passivity of the organized church bodies. If silence does not mean consent, then it stood at least for the tolerance of ultimate evil. German churches collaborated with the Nazi regime, and the Vatican signed a concordant with Hitler's government "to consolidate and enhance the existing friendly relations." This agreement was negotiated by Cardinal Eugenio Pacelli as Secretary of State to the Holy See and the future Pope Pius XII. The Vatican's policy of strict neutrality calls to mind the observation by Elie Wiesel: "Neutrality always helps the killer, not the victim." Pope Pius XI's (reign 1922-39) single encyclical "Mit brennender Sorge" ("With burning anxiety"), issued in 1937, was the only official response of the Holy See during the 12 years of ever-escalating Nazi terror. Pope Pius XII's (reign 1939-58) silence about the Shoah represents a sad and disturbing message for the post-Holocaust era, not just for Jews but even more so for today's church and the millions of believing adherents of the Catholic faith. The revisionist justifications being promulgated to this very day for the silence of Pope Pius XII during these tragic years cannot erase the Vatican's moral failure. We are being told, that discretion and silence were ostensibly necessary because of Jews being hidden within the Vatican's walls, because of potential revenge of the Nazi government toward the European Jewish people, or because of the Vatican's utter dependency on the fascist Italian government as an ally of Germany. The equivalency between silence and consent may be applicable here, especially if one considers that this well informed Pope, who had previously served as nuncio under Pope Pius XI in Berlin, did not raise his voice in protest while one and one half million Jewish children were being murdered in Continental Europe.

In fact, based on evidence collected by the Simon Wiesenthal Center in Los Angeles, the Vatican, under the direction of Bishop Alois Hudal, provided shelter and false travel documents, including those from the International Red Cross, to prominent Nazi criminals fleeing near the end of World War II via Spain, Portugal, and Italy to sympathetic Argentina, Brazil, Chile, and other South American hideouts as well as to Canada and Australia. The Vatican has maintained that Bishop Hudal and his superior, Msgr. Montini, Undersecretary of State and future Pope Paul VI, acted out of Christian charity. When Hudal threatened to become a public embarrassment, the inner circle of the Vatican replaced him with Father Draganovic, a Croat with strong Ustashi connections, as a more discreet and more effective escape coordinator for Nazi fugitives (Aarons and Loftus, *Unholy Trinity*, 1991). The apparent motivation of fighting the Soviet threat rings hollow, since these infamous war criminals were already residing, often incognito, in the West and were wanted fugitives from western democratic justice. Apparently the Vatican did not actively assist Nazi Germany, but its silence during and even for some years after the Holocaust was deafening and its aid to war criminals most disturbing.

During the Nazi era, no German Protestant or Catholic bishop ever made a public statement deploring the Nazi mistreatment of Jews. To the contrary, quite a few German churchmen openly supported the government's anti-Semitic outrages. Even the well-known anti-Nazi Pastor Martin Niemoeller held the Jews eternally guilty of deicide. In the state of Thuringia where I was born, the Protestant Bishop Martin Sasse called attention to Martin Luther's anti-Semitic venom to justify the Nazis' Kristallnacht actions. For a pertinent example at the local level, I refer to the Reverend Siedersleben of Suhl. This Protestant parson of the Hauptkirche, the oldest and main church of the town of my birth, distinguished himself as one of the more dedicated supporters of the Hitler regime (*Juden in Suhl*, Nothnagel and Daehn). Whether in utter silence or by verbalized consent and support, the actions of the Christian churches during the Holocaust were not in consonance with the teachings of Jesus.

The failure of religious bodies under such dire circumstances is particularly disconcerting and might easily lead to a pessimistic and cynical expectation of the future of humanity. Fortunately, at the end of the 20th century, we have the advantage of a retrospective view. The issuance of "Nostra Aetate," "In Our Time," by the Second Vatican Council, called into session by Pope John XXIII, was a monumental and uplifting event. This revolutionary document of the bishops assembled in Rome repudiated in 1965 the collective Jewish guilt for Jesus' death and not only affirmed Christianity's Jewish roots but also validated the ancient covenant of Sinai between God and the Jewish people. No doubt, the postwar Vatican was horrified by the Shoah and saw a dire need to alter its relationship with the people of the Old Testament. This radical Catholic step served as a catalyst for other Christian movements to follow suit in eliminating the destructive component of negative theology from their teachings. Thus, for example, about three decades after Vatican II, the Lutheran Church in America repudiated its (German) founder's anti-Semitism and began to teach the lessons and the consequences of destructive prejudice instead. Much work still remains to eradicate the impact of nearly two millennia of prejudicial church-sponsored dogma, but it is gratifying to note the results achieved so far in the post-Holocaust world. There is reason for hope rather than despair. However, the time is yet to come when

the Vatican will publicly acknowledge its passivity or even tolerance in the face of irrefutable German Nazi cruelty and criminality,
when the Vatican in good conscience will finally make its assessment and declaration on its role in the Holocaust.

What about the world beyond the German lands, the Europe under Nazi domination, the twilight countries of the neutrals and the
world of the Allies? There are some revisionists of history who in-
credulously claimed that the Holocaust was a "European" phenome-
non. This misconception or deliberate distortion might derive from
the fact that the elimination of the Jewish people was carried out in
many European countries. Yes, after Germany had captured most of
Europe, it recruited brutal anti-Semitic cohorts across the continent
to participate in the Shoah. But let us remember who was in charge!
Nothing, but nothing occurred in the German-occupied lands without Nazi initiative and consent. Yet there were vast differences in
behavior among the various nations under the Nazi yoke.

On one end of the spectrum were the Danish people, whose heroic actions, with Swedish sanctuary, resulted in the rescue and
survival of more than 99% of their Jews. Notable also is the fact
that about 83% of Italy's Jews survived, indicating that behind the
scenes this predominantly Catholic land and the Vatican succeeded
in saving Jewish lives. But sadly, on the opposite end of this spectrum, there were the countries of Lithuania, Latvia, and Poland,
where about 90% of their Jewish population was exterminated. A
group that distinguished itself as one of the most diligent murderers was the Croatian Fascists, the Ustashes led by Ante Pavelic,
who became the notorious epitome of the cruelty and terror that
characterized the Shoah. The right-wing Iron Guard of Rumania
distinguished itself by matching or even outdoing the Nazi Germans in the mass slaughter of Jews. Granted that other factors
such as geography and variations in Nazi policies had some influence; there is nevertheless little doubt that the attitude, the degree
of courage and basic decency of the indigenous populations of the
various European countries made a telling difference to Jewish survival. Most if not all countries had their individual "Righteous
Among the Nations" who, at great personal risk, hid and thus saved
Jewish lives. But the large variation in national extermination ra-
tios tell a tale of unmistakable difference and utmost significance,
which so often translated into either life or death for those persecuted. It is most fitting here to recall the words attributed to the 17th

century British statesman Edmund Burke: "The only thing necessary for the triumph of evil is for good men to do nothing." Some countries maintained their neutrality during the great conflagration known as World War II. But the influence of Nazi might cast its shadow over all of Europe and at times tainted their political neutrality with actions of expediency and accommodation. Switzerland, Sweden, Spain, Portugal, and even distant Argentina supported the German war machine with self-serving economic ties, and some if not all were the recipients of Nazi loot, including that from the Holocaust victims. About 80% of Europe's ball-bearing production was in Swedish hands, and until 1943 this country found dealing with Nazi Germany a profitable proposition. Although Switzerland was not the only neutral nation to enrich itself surreptitiously by these unseemly means, it was certainly the most flagrant. The now camouflaged collaboration of Vichy France with Nazi Germany is an embarrassing and degrading chapter for this nation that cannot be counterbalanced by the actions of the French resistance movement. For these countries, in varying degrees the hunger for economic benefits spilled over into moral degeneracy. Survival of the not-so-neutrals was often their highest priority.

Jews fleeing from Germany and Austria across the Swiss border were frequently not only apprehended but returned to the Nazis by the Swiss authorities. While about 1,000 Jews did manage to overcome highly restrictive immigration obstacles and legally enter Switzerland between 1931 and 1942 (Bower, *Nazi Gold*), it appears incomprehensible that people fleeing for their lives were returned into the arms of murderous perpetrators. Swiss survival did not depend on such despicable complicity, and no amount of distorted rationalization of the post-Holocaust world can cover up this appalling chapter. In the latter years of the war, Switzerland did announce its willingness to give shelter temporarily to 50,000 refugee children from France provided that no Jewish ones were included. This I became aware of when listening to a Swiss TV documentary during a 1994 visit in Davos. Switzerland's "eternal neutrality" is convenient and necessary for institutional capitalist trade; a moral rationalization is not possible. Much has been made of Switzerland's duplicity and obstinacy in the attempt to enrich itself with the stored gold, including that of dental origin, or the dormant bank accounts of Jewish victims. Deplorable as this may be, such materialistic greed pales in comparison to the refusal to grant refuge to desperate and doomed human beings. Leviticus 19:16 of the Torah (Old Testament) teaches: "Do not profit by the blood of your neighbor," which traditionally is explained as: Do not stand by idly while your neighbor's blood is shed, do not abandon him while he is in danger. The behavior of these countries during the distant past should, however, not be used to condemn the current generation. Nevertheless, it is up to today's governments and populations of these "neutral" nations to confront their past honestly, then to react appropriately and finally to learn from this chapter of moral expediency. Let us sincerely hope so.

The world of the Allies was primarily concerned with the winning of the war, a tremendous task that required superhuman effort and much sacrifice. But there was another "war" that was pursued by the Nazis with at least equal intensity: the "war" against the Jews. In fact, "war" is a misnomer in this case, because it involved the annihilation of a selected and defenseless group of human beings, but I use the word here to connote the hugeness of its scope and the major effort by Germany to carry it out. The Allies were not ignorant of the ever-escalating anti-Semitic events inside Germany and Nazi-occupied Europe. Great Britain was unsympathetic if not cruel in its policy to minimize the flow of doomed European Jews who attempted to reach Palestine. The need for its oil from the Arab world, a world led by the spiritual leader of the Palestinian Arabs, the Grand Mufti of Jerusalem Hajji Amin al-Husayni, who was most sympathetic with the Nazi cause, was the basis of this deplorable British action.

During this time, our northern neighbor, the vast country of Canada, carried out a relentless anti-immigration policy against Jewish European refugees, (*None Is Too Many*, Abella and Troper). While the slaughter of the Shoah was taking place, the Canadian government, with rigidity and determination, kept its doors essentially shut to human beings whose lives were threatened because they were born as Jews. No pleas of their non-Jewish allies mattered, no entreaties from Canadian Jewry had any impact. Fully supported by public anti-Semitsm, which permeated its civic culture, Canada, a country blessed with huge natural resources while being highly underpopulated, remained adamant in its rejection of Jewish refugees during the Holocaust and even shorty thereafter. After having read the well annotated Abella/Troper book, I understood why the family Spangenthal of four, with whom we briefly lived in Germany in 1939, were never admitted to Canada in spite of valiant efforts to immigrate there; instead they, including their two little boys, became a statistic of the Six Million.

And what about France, which sees itself as the fountain of liberty, fraternity and equality? After about four years of dutiful collaboration with the Nazi authorities, this country tried to reinvent its past (1940-44) under the patriotic mantle of Charles de Gaulle and his famous and courageous Free French fighting contingent. Although there were those of the underground as well as other noteworthy French individuals who performed heroic deeds to save the lives of Jews hunted in France, the French Vichy government record of embracing the German occupiers and capturing Jews for deportation stands loud and clear. It cannot be hidden under the mantle of de Gaulle or erased by ex post facto fairy tales. The promulgation of anti-Jewish stereotypes by French Catholicism over the centuries evolved into a natural and virulent anti-Semitism in Vichy-sponsored policies and actions and spilled over into the German-occupied part of France. Contrary to postwar protestations by a number of prominent French leaders, Vichy was not some "foreign" entity; Vichy was France. Silence was the rule of the day and only a few uttered sentiments for the hunted Jews. While about 76,000 French Jews were being deported (destination Auschwitz) from the Drancy internment camp near Paris, Cardinal Baudrillart, the rector of the Catholic Institute in that city, defined the Nazis' mission as a noble one.

Starting in 1941, Great Britain and the United States were receiving reliable evidence through various channels about Germany's plans and initial actions to exterminate the European Jews under its control. But in spite of appeals from eminent individuals such as Rabbi Stephen S. Wise as president of the World Jewish Congress, Eleanor Roosevelt, Henry Morgenthau as Secretary of the Treasury as well as numerous organizations, little if any action was taken during the following three years to attempt at least the partial rescue of the defenseless Jews or the destruction of the extermination apparatus. After having maintained a highly restrictive immigration policy, which was carried out by a U.S. State Department with disturbing anti-Semitic overtones and pursued with vigor by Undersecretary of State Breckenridge Long, President Roosevelt was reluctant to divert any effort from the war or to confuse its ultimate objective with that of Jewish rescue. A relatively feeble attempt in the form of a War Refugee Board was finally initiated in 1944. Late as it was, this action still was instrumental in saving about 200,000 lives.

I am not the only one to wonder how many more of the Six Million could have been retained among the living by more prompt, sympathetic, and resolute actions of the U.S. and its Allies. Who knows how many hundreds of thousands were exterminated while desperately waiting their turn to squeeze through the barely-open entry doors of the free world? In retrospect, the U.S. and its Allies were heroic in the war to fight and defeat the Nazis, but during the slaughter of the defenseless Jews they stood by in silence, apathy, egoism, and inaction far too long. Franklin Roosevelt was a great and heroic President: in times of peace, he extricated the U.S. from a devastating depression while preserving our democratic heritage; in times of war, he gave his all to lead the Allies to victory over Nazi Germany. But in the time of mass murder, the Shoah, he failed to act with courage and conviction to try the rescue of millions of threatened lives or at least to slow the extermination process. When, during a White House press conference five days after Kristallnacht, on November 15, 1938, FDR was asked if he would urge amending the restrictive immigration laws in light of the recent events in Germany, his answer was "No."

Even after WWII started, it was not too late to rescue threatened European Jewry. From the outbreak of September 1, 1939 to the U.S. entry into the conflict, December 7, 1941, twenty seven months of precious time passed by during which we could have opened our doors and transformed Emma Lazarus' words on the Statue of Liberty into the reality of letting " huddled masses yearning to breathe free " find refuge on our shores. Even while the war raged in Europe, there were opportunities to impede the German factory-like mass murder and emulate Raoul Wallenberg and other courageous individuals. Instead, the doors remained barely ajar and rescue was considered to be of low priority. Today's revisionists dismiss this sorry chapter of the free world by sinking to the lowest level of morality: by blaming the victims. False and despicable as this is, it is also shrewd, for most victims cannot bear witness- they have been silenced a long time ago.

Thus the Allies, including the U.S., stood by in passive complicity, and even to this day there are those who attempt to justify the free world's failure to act while a great wrong was being committed during a 12-year period of terror. The myths promulgated by mean-spirited revisionists cannot erase the realities of the past. Hindsight might be 20:20, but the free world knew too much for it to come up with any plausible reason why it did so little and so late. Contorted ex post facto rationalizations cannot explain away this complicity of silence and inaction.

It is painful for me to make this statement. Had it not been for the U.S. visa, which I obtained on my third attempt after waiting well over two years for the U.S. immigration consent, I would have become just another Holocaust victim. For this opportunity to live, I will always be grateful to my country of refuge.

During recent decades, the world has witnessed a number of genocides, this in spite of the lessons of the Holocaust. Chinese communists massacred Buddhist Tibetans, Stalin's Bolsheviks killed countless Soviet citizens, Africans murdered Africans in tribal warfare, Muslims slaughtered Muslims in Syria, Afghanistan, Iraq, and Iran, Muslims tried to eradicate Christians in Lebanon, Pot Pol executioners ravaged Cambodians, and Christian Serbs massacred the Muslims of Bosnia and called it ethnic cleansing. These horrible, perverse events were religious or ethnic or civil wars for territory and national identity. They all differed fundamentally from the Shoah during which all Jews widely scattered throughout Europe, independent of age or sex, were ideologically targeted by Nazi Germany for murder in a colossal genocide. They were annihilated because they were born as Jews. It was not a war, it was a Holocaust.

The Holocaust was unique, but its lessons are universal. Morally, one cannot make a distinction between mass murder and mass murder. Consequently, the passive onlookers to all of these events, the nations with selective visions and convenient memories, have not yet learned the basic lesson of the Holocaust. In 1995, when the full impact of the Bosnian atrocities reached its peak, I sent a message to the *Metro West Jewish News*, a widely-read weekly paper of the metropolitan area. The Jewish community was in the midst of observing the annual anniversary of Kristallnacht, with the newspaper deploring this turning point, which made "physical violence as accepted state policy . . . knowing the world would not get involved. All were bystanders, none came to the aid of the Jews." For me, the parallels were too pertinent for silence, and I commented to that effect in my letter:

"Thus, it is particularly painful to witness the world's callous disregard and convenient impotency during the atrocities of recent years in the former Yugoslavia. Without in any way comparing this sorry chapter of humankind to the Shoah, which stands alone in state-sponsored criminality in the annals of history, the lessons derived from the Holocaust are applicable today and forever. With the notable exception of the U.S. Holocaust Memorial Museum, little if any cognizance has been given, even by the Jewish community, to the slaughter of defenseless men, women, and children. Most stand by silently or dismiss this tragedy as just a civil war, whereas in fact much of the carnage in Bosnia is unadulterated murder. What will they say about us 50 years from now?"

And yet, there is hope for the future in spite of some occasional setbacks. This is not just an empty wish of mine but is based on a conviction that the widespread dissemination via modern communication means of yesteryear's often tragic history and today's still too frequent resort towards violence will teach the human family a lesson that will not go unnoticed, that cannot and will not be ignored. I cannot believe that humanity will continue to tolerate the resort to violence and atrocities that still plague so many parts of our globe. Whether these actions are conducted in the name of nationalism, fundamentalism, or tribalism, humanity must and eventually will come to its senses by recognizing the futility of violent deeds. These senseless and brutal actions are often committed against innocent and defenseless people in the maddening delusion to resolve disputes and conflicting interests. Education, communication, and self-interest will win the day in the end.

After these comments on my views of the Holocaust, my thoughts quite naturally turn to the State of Israel. Its founding after two thousand years of dispersion was a direct consequence of the Shoah. Although Theodor Herzl's Zionist vision had rejuvenated the Jewish resolve for its own national identity long before Hitler came to power, the secular world became more inclined to assist in the attainment of this goal in the post Holocaust period. This sympathy was not a restitution for the Shoah, for that would be incongruous, but it was a sensitive action in view of a horrible past.

As a survivor of the Holocaust, I am particularly proud of the tremendous progress that is so evident in the rebuilding of the state. Here is a small country with a population of not even five million that has absorbed just during the past decade nearly a million refugees from the former Soviet Union and Ethiopia. It is, as intended in its founding, to be a haven of refuge for any Jew who is in need of a home, in need of sanctuary, in need of a future. I am proud of the courage, the determination, and the confidence of the Israeli people who since the founding were forced to defend themselves several times against an invading multitude of Arab armies. These assaults were intended to wipe out Israel's existence, to throw the Jews into the sea. It is ironic that a good part of these heroic Israeli defenders were survivors of the Holocaust. Trying to rebuild their shattered lives, they were forced once again to fight for their being, and many made the ultimate sacrifice in this mission. And still we can say "Am Yisrael Chai!", the people of Israel live!

Pride is not the only sentiment that I harbor for the state and the people of Israel. I am increasingly concerned about the growing influence of the rigid right, the ultra-Orthodox population, which to a considerable extent does not recognize the State and corrupts its existence. Most of the adherents of this fundamentalist group do not even serve in the military, thus refusing to defend the land. Maybe world Jewry has to stand by and thus tolerate this revolting inaction, but the State of Israel can ill afford to have such irresponsibility if not betrayal in its midst. Why should one part of a population fight, suffer, and even die while the ultra-Orthodox use the freedom thus preserved to criticize the State and even question its right to exist? The simultaneous and ever-escalating attempts by the ultra-Orthodox wing to denigrate Conservative, Reconstructionist, and Reform Judaism, the more liberal and modern religious movements, not only undermines the unity of the Jewish people but is incompatible with the religious pluralism of a democratic state. By political intrigue and intimidation, these right-wing fundamentalists never rest in their attempt to hijack Herzl's dream and turn it into a nightmare of inequality, injustice, discrimination, and disenfranchisement. Such a path would lead Israel from strength to weakness, from democracy to theocracy, from the achieved reality of a Jewish homeland for this century and beyond to a return to the ghetto mentality of the middle ages. A country that rightfully grants religious freedom to Christians and Moslems cannot afford

to practice officially-sanctioned discrimination and de-legitimiza-
tion of the liberal arms of Judaism. I am convinced that the more
modern and rational constituency of the centrist Orthodox community shares this view of pluralistic democracy as well.

This fundamentally internal problem represents not the only
obstacle to the young Jewish state. From its beginning, in fact even
prior to that momentous event in 1948, Israel's 22 regional Arab
neighbors attempted to wipe it off the map. We have to remember
that the Grand Mufti of Jerusalem was an ally of Adolf Hitler. After
failing to eradicate the fledgling state, Arabs tried again and again
to accomplish their goal during the succeeding decades. The primary threat to Israel was always from without, although I am not certain if all Arabs living within the cease-fire borders established
after the 1967 conflict are loyal to the Jewish state. Israel finally negotiated its first peace treaty when it returned the entire Sinai peninsula in order to obtain Egypt's consent. As a result, its President
Anwar Sadat was assassinated by uncompromising Moslem ele-
ments, and since then the peace with Israel's Egyptian neighbor
has been a cold one indeed. In more recent years, considerable
progress has been made, with the help of the U.S. as intermediary,
to reach an accommodation with the Palestine Liberation Organization (PLO). As an encouraging by-product, a peace treaty with
Jordan has also been signed. Gaza and the West Bank seem to be
on their way to becoming an independent Arab entity, but I am
afraid that the PLO and its leader Yasir Arafat do not have the
backing and trust of a significant portion of the Arab population,
which is under the spell of fundamentalist Islamic movements such
as Hamas and derives its support from Iran. These fanatical ele-
ments of the Moslem world have never altered their objective to
eradicate Israel. In fact, even the current PLO manifesto still calls
for the destruction of the Jewish state.

The negotiations with Israel's Arab neighbors have been conducted under the banner "Land for Peace." I am not the only one
who hopes that this is possible while a secure and viable Israel
would remain and be acceptable to most Arabs. Somehow, the
words of Nablus mayor Al Shakkar always ring in my ears, when he
was asked in 1976 which part of the former British Mandate might
eventually be acceptable as a Jewish state: "Tel Aviv, maybe" was
his telling answer. Extrapolating this pronouncement to the current "Land for Peace" slogan, one could conclude that the only com-

plete peace would also require the complete disappearance of the Jewish State. Abba Eban said years ago that "National suicide is not an international obligation." In spite of Arab protests to the contrary, I am afraid that given half a chance by a naive lowering of the Israeli guard, most Arabs would seize the opportunity to eliminate the Jewish state.

Nevertheless, I am thankful to my government for acting repeatedly as a catalyst in the Mideast peace negotiations, although there is a certain irony in this well-intentioned U.S. involvement. About one century before the rebirth of Israel, the United States annexed half of Mexico's territory and converted this vast area into our six southwestern states. It seems that territorial sacrifice for the sake of tenuous peace is primarily reserved for the Israel of the latter part of the 20th century. Yet this appears to represent the best alternative.

How can those adhering to Islamic fundamentalism be convinced that the so-called hero's death for Allah is a most undesirable alternative to living in peace and decency alongside the Israeli people. Tremendous benefits could be derived for the family of humankind. How could one convince that powerful component of Mideast humanity, that it is far better to live in peace than to die in agony? When will Arafat cease to incite his people with a call for Jihad, the holy war? How much longer will he, as leader of the Palestine Authority, permit and even encourage fundamentalist terrorists to blow up innocent Israeli civilians while he deceitfully and simultaneously takes the high road of "peace"? Hopefully, with the passage of time, my pessimism for the realization of peace in the Middle East will be proven too negative; hopefully, the future for that area and all peoples residing therein will yet see the light of Shalom while "sitting under their vines and their fig trees, and none shall make them afraid."

The survival of the Jewish people has to be viewed both in context of both the State of Israel and the Diaspora. I cannot visualize an enduring Jewish existence without the continuation of the Jewish state. Thus, a peaceful solution for the Mideast problem is essential. After five major conflicts, Israel could possibly prevail in several additional conflicts, albeit at terrible sacrifice. But one lost battle could spell the end of the Jewish State. The argument could be made that the children of Israel survived through two millennia while dispersed in the Diaspora. True enough, but they prayed and lived for an eventual return to the land of their ancestors. Now that this dream has been realized subsequent to the inhuman Holocaust price, a hypothetical termination of the Jewish state would represent an insurmountable nightmare. The fate of Diaspora Jewry is inextricably linked with that of the state of Israel.

The clock cannot be turned back to the pre-Nazi period, for the Diaspora has been weakened not only by the murder of the Six Million and the consequent loss of irreplaceable communities and millions of descendants who were never born, but also by the toll of assimilation and neglect. The latter trend has been enabled and reinforced by the decline of anti-Semitic barriers in the western world, by societies that are more open and welcoming, by the very equality that democracies strive for. Furthermore, there has also been a general decline in the value placed on group coherence and affiliation, including the desirability of belonging to organized religious movements. One dramatic barometer of these effects is the intermarriage rate between Jews and non-Jews, a rate that has reached about 50%. This means that two out of three unions involving Jews are of the intermarriage type, since the "other" 50% marry each other.

Furthermore, about one half of all American Jews have no synagogue affiliation. For the continuity and viability of Diaspora Jewry, involvement with our synagogues is of utmost and singular importance. Regional federations and national organizations certainly can and do enhance our Jewish existence, but without a viable synagogue structure, Diaspora Jewry cannot survive.

Why is all this so significant? Because, aside from Israel, the U.S. contains the largest Jewish community of our globe. Rightwing Orthodoxy has repeatedly and publicly impugned the sincerity and integrity of non-Orthodox movements, claiming itself to be the sole authentic manifestation of Judaism. Aside from such a crude abrogation of democratic rights and the search of the human spirit, such gross intolerance ignores the essential function of liberal Judaism. For if it were not for the existence and dedication of the non-Orthodox movements, most of American and the rest of Diaspora Jewry would most likely have receded into the oblivion of assimilation during the past century. One may wonder about the consequences if over the relatively short time span of a few generations the Diaspora center of gravity would somehow shift to Orthodoxy or even ultra-Orthodoxy. An intolerable supposition from my point of view, for this would imply the marginal existence and disappearing identity of the vast majority of Jews outside Israel. Time moves forward and not back to the Middle Ages. As liberal Jews, and in a broad sense I include here those affiliated with the Reform, Conservative, and Reconstructionist movements, we have been charged with a duty and a mission that extends beyond artificial and untenable "Ghetto Walls". On the 50th anniversary of Kristallnacht in November of 1988, I included the following when addressing my Livingston congregation:

"So we meet here tonight, witnesses of Kristallnacht, survivors of the Holocaust--all of us are really survivors, no matter where we were born. We meet to commemorate the night of the broken glass, the night of the concentration camps, the night of broken hearts. But it was not the night of a crushed Jewish spirit, for that night will never come, as it did not in Egypt under the Pharaoh, as it did not in Spain under Tastamara, as it did not in Russia under the Czar, as it did not in the Warsaw Ghetto under the Nazi terror, as it did not in the Golan and Yad Mordachai and Yerushalayim under the threat of a hundred million Arabs!

Those of us who are among the remnants of European Jewry say to you: Israel lives and shall live! We shall live and labor and love and learn--privileges denied to six million of our people who suffered and died--Alkiddush Hashem. Ours is not the task of explaining Kristallnacht and the genocide that followed, but ours is the task of justifying our existence by providing continuity, by forging another link in that long chain of our people, by giving our children and children's children the ideas and ideals on which they can build their own lives.

Let us be God's partners by maintaining and enhancing our Jewish heritage, not just by synagogue affiliation of some but of all, not just by sending our children to religious school but by studying ourselves, not just by praying but by translating our prayers into deeds, not just by giving of our means but by giving of our time and our intellect, not just by calling the sanctuary our home but by making our homes into sanctuaries. This is the privilege we have--let us not defer nor neglect, let us do it now for we shall not pass this way again. Let us strive to be Jews today, and thus Judaism will live tomorrow.

Let us light candles not just on anniversaries but also in our daily lives, seeking truth and justice and compassion for all. Thus those that are enveloped by the darkness of ignorance, oppression, and depravation may yet see a great light. As inscribed on our Bima wall: "Or N'ta Ticha La Goyim" ("I will establish you as a light to the nations")."

In the fall of 1991, our Temple Emanu-El (God is with us), celebrated the 36th anniversary of its founding. Twice 18 is a significant number in Judaism, because the Hebrew Chai stands for both 18 and life. In a creative service, "Kiddushim: An Act of Recommitment," the congregation gathered in the sanctuary to observe this special moment. Rabbi Peter Kasdan had invited three members including me to join him in writing original liturgy for that night. One of the prayers that I contributed, "The Silent Prayer," is particularly meaningful in conveying my feelings of our Creator:

"Adonai, my God, in this moment of self-contemplation, in the stillness of this Sanctuary, in the privacy of my heart, let me thank You for the holiness of the Sabbath and all that it represents as Israel's festival of the spirit, as a symbol of the joy of creation. As a frail human being, I shall pass through this world but once. So, I pray, give me the fortitude, the sensitivity and inner strength to take advantage of my opportunities as a human being and to fulfill my obligations as a Jew. Let me not be timid for the sake of my comfort; let me not be callous in the presence of human suffering; let me not be silent in the face of injustice. May the words of my mouth and the meditations of my heart become the deeds of my hands, to help set the world right in partnership with You, my God."

When we were searching for an appropriate dedication plaque for our temple's Holocaust museum, Bea found the following inscription, which had been on the wall of a cellar in Germany where Jews were hidden:

> I believe in the sun even when it is not shining
> I believe in love when feeling it not
> I believe in God even when God is silent.

There are many in the human family, Jews and non-Jews, who have difficulty with a God concept after the ungodly Holocaust experience. They reason that God has either abandoned us by tolerating this ultimate evil and is thus also tainted with sin or that God's existence is altogether questionable. I can understand their doubts, but I cannot accept their conclusions. If the Jews hidden in that German cellar and the Jews of Theresienstadt praying with Rabbi Leo Baeck could reaffirm their belief in the Almighty, if the martyrs of yesteryears could perish with the Shema, the Hear O Israel, on their lips, then we as survivors should not and cannot use the killing of millions as a rationale to kill the God concept.

I believe that God is omniscient, omnipotent, and good, a God who created the universe in six very long evolutionary "days" and left its completion in the hands of time and humanity. Thus, we are God's partners in this great adventure, this awesome challenge. It might have taken many millions of years for our spirituality, for our souls to evolve, but that could not have taken place if the universe did not contain such a lofty characteristic in the first place. Thus, I am a traditional Jew for whom Reform is not a verb and who sees God in the miracle of creation and the continuing evolution of nature; however, I have no room in my soul and my being to hold God responsible for the blunders, the cruelties, the injustices, the degradation, and the waste of humanity.

How can we address God, as we often do, to help us come closer to the infinite heights of ultimate Goodness ("Godness"?) while we harbor doubts and thoughts that our Creator is at least partially sinful? Although we are created in the image of God, we have neither the vision nor the justification nor the fundamental right to transfer even one iota of responsibility for humanity's sins to Adonai, the Almighty. We dare not misinterpret the omnipotence of the Creator with the abrogation of the responsibility of the created. From the beginning, God's power may be seen as deliberately limited to provide for humanity the free choice between good and evil, thus permitting God's greatest creation to earn the privilege to be Adonai's partner. Permitting humans this latitude appears to be a voluntary concession on God's part. Unless those who doubt would also consider the creation itself as partially sinful, a supposition that is beyond belief, then the Jewish people and hopefully all humankind will have to follow the introspective path and consequently conduct themselves to be deserving of being God's partners.

Tikkun Olam, to repair the world, is our task and in spite of incomprehensible tragedies, we must take the opportunity of the temporal now to be worthy trustees for an immortal cause. God is the eternal Good, and it is humanity and only humanity that has to make amends.

I believe in God because of the miracle of evolutionary creation. I believe in a better tomorrow because I survived.

WORKS CITED

Aarons, Mark and John Loftus. *Unholy Trinity: How the Vatican's Nazi Networks Betrayed Western Intelligence to the Soviets.* New York: St. Martin's P, 1991.

Berenbaum, Michael. *The World Must Know: The History of the Holocaust as Told in the United States Holocaust Memorial Museum.* Boston: Little Brown, 1993.

Blumenson, Martin. *The Patton Papers, 1885-1940; 1940-1945.* New York: Houghton Mifflin, 1972, 1974.

Bower, Tom. *Nazi Gold: The Full Story of the Fifty-year Swiss-Nazi Conspiracy to Steal Billions from Europe's Jews and Holocaust Survivors.* New York: Harper Collins, 1997.

Goldhagen, Daniel Jonah. *Hitler's Willing Executioners: Ordinary Germans and the Holocaust.* New York: Alfred A. Knopf, 1996.

Muhlfelder, Ludwig. *Weil ich uebriggeblieben bin: Ein juedisches Ueberlebensschicksal aus Suhl in Thueringen und Amerika 1924-1994.* Ed. Erhard Roy Wiehn. Konstanz: Hartung-Gorre Verlag, 1995.

Abella, Irving & Troper, Harold. *None Is Too Many* Lester Publishing Limited, 1991.

Nothnagel, Hans and Ewald Daehn. *Juden in Suhl: Ein geschichtlicher Ueberblick.* Ed. by Erhard Roy Wiehn. Konstanz: Hartung-Gorre Verlag, 1995.

Wyman, David S. *The Abandonment of the Jews: A Memoir and the Holocaust, 1941-1945.* New York: Pantheon, 1984. (*Das unerwuenschte Volk*, 1989).